Those Legendary Piper Cubs

Those Legendary

Piper Cubs

Their Role in War and Peace

Carroll V. Glines

Schiffer Military History
Atglen, PA

Book Design by Ian Robertson.

Printed in China.
ISBN: 0-7643-2159-5

We are interested in hearing from authors with book ideas on related topics.

Published by Schiffer Publishing Ltd.
4880 Lower Valley Road
Atglen, PA 19310
Phone: (610) 593-1777
FAX: (610) 593-2002
E-mail: Info@schifferbooks.com.
Visit our web site at: www.schifferbooks.com
Please write for a free catalog.
This book may be purchased from the publisher.
Please include $3.95 postage.
Try your bookstore first.

In Europe, Schiffer books are distributed by:
Bushwood Books
6 Marksbury Avenue
Kew Gardens
Surrey TW9 4JF
England
Phone: 44 (0) 20 8392-8585
FAX: 44 (0) 20 8392-9876
E-mail: Info@bushwoodbooks.co.uk.
Free postage in the UK. Europe: air mail at cost.
Try your bookstore first.

Contents

Foreword

As I look back on my more than 90 years, I realize that I have devoted most of my energies as an employee, vice president, president, stock holder, and eyewitness to the company that my father made world famous. Our family name has been permanently linked to a small single-engine airplane we called the Cub. It was produced in larger numbers than we ever dreamed possible, and had an unprecedented beneficial effect on aviation in this country when light planes were needed to train pilots for the biggest war in history.

There is no doubt that the success of the company is due to my father, William T. Piper, Sr., who was an engineer by education, but a businessman at heart. He never drank alcoholic beverages or smoked because he felt that neither contributed to a person's longevity. He believed in individual responsibility and initiative. He took risks in his business dealings, but never without shrewdly calculating the potential outcome. My two brothers and I had a 24-hour-a-day role model who proved to us continually that work was honorable and rewarding.

It can be said that our father backed into the airplane manufacturing business because he felt an obligation as a stockholder to try to save the Taylor Brothers Aircraft Corporation, which was in serious financial straits. In the beginning days of the Depression, the company was turning out a high-wing, two-place monoplane called the "Chummy." It was being marketed at about $4,000, a sum that few could afford. Failure was inevitable when competing manufacturers were turning out better airplanes with a lower price tag. My father thought a very light plane could be produced and provided at a more affordable price for student instruction and airport flying services.

His concept of the low price, two-place light plane was sound, and Mr. C.G. Taylor, the company president, designed the first tandem Cub to meet this requirement. Unfortunately, Mr. Taylor and my father disagreed on the belief that a high volume of sales at a low price would be more profitable in the end than small numbers at a high price. Mr. Taylor departed and formed his own aircraft

manufacturing company. My father took over the reins, changed the company name, and encouraged design and production of advanced models of the original Cub. He believed in aggressive salesmanship, and his philosophy of no frills and hard work proved to be the secret of the company's accomplishments. He was always proud to say that four out of five American pilots in World War II got their original flight instruction in Piper Cubs.

As the reader will see in the following pages, the original Cubs and their "rag wing" successors were improved in many ways. Many thousands of Cubs and their derivatives have been built—more than any other type of plane in the world. They can be found around the globe doing all sorts of jobs that only light planes can do. If anyone thinks they are fading away to be seen only in aviation museums, they should attend the annual "Sentimental Journey" fly-ins at Lock Haven, where dozens of owners gather as if to prove that Cubs will fly forever. I hope they will.

William T. Piper, Jr.
Lock Haven, PA

The author (left) and William T. Piper, Jr., share a laugh at a meeting of Quiet Birdmen during the 2003 Sentimental Journey fly-in at Lock Haven. (Kevin K. Hudson photo)

Introduction

Now that the history of motorized, fixed-wing aircraft has completed its first century, it seems fitting to recall briefly what has happened since the two bicycle makers from Dayton, Ohio, proved that man could indeed fly heavier-than-air machines. After December 17, 1903, literally thousands of different models, sizes, and shapes of motorized aircraft have come and gone. They have been instruments of peace, as well as weapons of war. In the span of one century, the airplane has changed from flimsy combinations of wood, fabric, and wire to powerful aerial machines that can penetrate the atmosphere at ever-increasing altitudes and many times the speed of sound. As they have matured, airplanes have changed from symbols of dare-deviltry to those of national strength and character.

Of all the aircraft ever built, there are two that have contributed much to aviation progress, surpassing all others in longevity and faithful service. Both were born about the same time—during the years of the Great Depression in the United States. One of these was the Douglas DC-3 transport plane, which has flown the world's skies since 1935 after its progenitors, the DC-1 and DC-2, made their appearances two years before. The DC-3 was the first airliner to offer faithful service, dependability, and achievement to the flying public. It has been parked at the world's airports for over seven decades, and was the first to offer predictable comfort and safety to a skeptical world, as well as the first airliner that could make money just by hauling passengers. It was also used as a flying hospital, bomber, fighter, glider, officers' club, command post, airways electronic checker, amphibian, glider tow, spray plane, engine test vehicle, and fire fighter. Born during the days of wooden propellers, nearly a thousand are still flying as we continue our exploration into space. When they were permanently grounded, they have been given such unlikely roles as a restaurant, club house, wind direction indicator, and mobile home.

The other aircraft that has taken its rightful place beside the DC-3 in the history of aviation to be honored for its longevity and service is the Piper Cub J-3, a light plane also born in the early 1930s. It has the wing span of the original *Flyer* of the Wright brothers and is powered by a single engine not much more powerful than theirs. It has surpassed all others in service as a trainer of literally thousands of pilots the world over. It, too, has performed "impossible feats" not perceived by its original designers. It and its fabric-covered, high-winged successors have been asked to carry out tasks that included the roles of fighter, bomber, and patient transport. It was also used as a military observation plane to adjust artillery fire, find lost troop detachments, tow targets and gliders, and haul freight. Its civilian roles, even today, are to spot schools of fish, deliver newspapers and mail, rescue downed airmen, patrol pipe and power lines, run timber checks, make food drops to isolated communities, spray insecticides, hunt predators, string telephone lines, and round up cattle. It has had many modifications and improvements in subsequent spin-off models that have made it more useful, but without losing its appeal or its familiar profile.

Over its lifetime, the Piper J-3, like the DC-3, has been known by many names. It has been called the Grasshopper, Puddle-Jumper, Flea, Flivver, Flying Jeep, Flying Binoculars, Maytag Messerschmitt, and Minute Man of the Air.

The Piper Aircraft Corporation produced more than 40,000 planes that are truly eligible to be called Cubs, although the word "Cub" has long been a generic name for any single-engine light plane. This book is limited to the fabric-covered, high-winged, single-engine models from the original Taylor (later Piper) Cub to the Piper Colt. Hundreds are still on the register of the Federal Aviation Administration and are flying in most foreign countries.

During my teenage years, I bicycled regularly from my home in suburban Philadelphia, Pennsylvania, to the municipal airport to watch Ford Tri-motors, Boeing 247s, and military aircraft come and go. The Army Air Corps Reserve and National Guard pilots who flew from there on weekends would patiently answer my questions and let me look into the complex cockpits of their planes. I dreamed of flying them someday, but wondered if I could ever master such powerful machines.

The Author in 1940 with one of the Piper Cubs that he flew, NC19599.

I attended Drexel Institute of Technology in Philadelphia in 1938 and watched the autogiros take off from the nearby Post Office roof during their experimental flights, taking mail to and from the airport. The urge to become a pilot became stronger, but it still seemed far out of reach. The Great Depression was slowly receding, but I could not afford to continue in college. I went to work at General Electric Co. in Philadelphia in 1939 as a stock clerk and attended college night classes.

By chance, I learned from a fellow employee that an instructor pilot was looking for nine people to form a club and buy a used airplane called a Taylor Cub, which would cost $400. It was a two-place tandem plane powered by a 37-hp engine that was started by hand. It had no brakes and no tail wheel, only a metal tail skid that acted as a brake after landing. Taxiing required some advance planning, since it did not have the advantage of wheel brakes to make turns. The process of getting where you wanted to go on the ground was by the use of engine blast, stick, and rudder.

I saw flying it as the opportunity of a lifetime. I withdrew $40 from my very limited savings account and joined the club. The instructor recruited the other eight members needed, so each of us became a proud one-tenth owner of a real flying machine. We learned to fly with the agreement that the instructor would charge us $1.00 for each half hour of instruction. We began flying from a small pasture near Chester, Pennsylvania. The cost for each of us to fly the Cub solo was $1.15 an hour, which covered gas and oil, and also contributed to the rent of the renovated barn we used as a hangar. I took a night ground school course and was ready to fly.

The instructor never said much during a flight, nor did he conduct much follow-up instruction or comment about our performance after a flight. He demonstrated what you were to do in the air, then let you try. If it was not what he expected, he would shake the stick and demonstrate again.

Every pilot remembers his first solo flight—that happy day when the instructor gets out and indicates that he trusts you enough to let you go up alone. My solo date in the Cub was October 16, 1940. I shot three landings with the instructor, and when I came to a stop after the third one he got out, and without saying a word, motioned for me to go.

I took off, and the feeling of exhilaration was overwhelming. I was alone in the air for the first time and totally in charge of a flying machine! I suddenly realized that my personal safety depended solely on my own judgment and ability. I left the traffic pattern and flew briefly around the local area. I was so pleased with the freedom I had just been granted that I decided to see what my neighborhood looked like from the air. Below were the familiar landmarks I had known most of my life, but I was seeing them for the first time in the third dimension. I circled over our house, the high school, and the houses of friends, exuberant with my newly-found independence.

So ended my first day of triumph over gravity. I was accepted as a Flying Cadet by the U.S. Army Air Corps eight months and 60 Cub hours later, and began what turned out to be an accident-free military piloting career.

I will always have a warm place in my heart for the Cub because it allowed me to discover the pure joy of flying. Like the C-47 (the military version of the Douglas DC-3), the Piper Cub has a charm of its own. Although seemingly fragile compared to larger, more powerful planes, it is dependable and forgiving, and represents a kindly challenge for student pilots.

I did not realize when I soloed the Cub that it also signaled the beginning of a second career as an aviation author. I have often thought ever since about writing a book about the Piper Cub and its fabric-covered successors, but other book and magazine writing assignments intervened. One of those was *The Amazing Gooney Bird: The Saga of the Legendary DC-3/C-47*. The Piper Cub is just as well-known, and I wish to convey to the reader in the following pages why it is also a remarkable flying machine. But let no one think this is a eulogy for an airplane that no longer exists. There are thousands of Cubs and their more sophisticated descendants still flying today, and many have been copied, improved, modified, and customized in many ways to upgrade their capabilities for special work. I am sure there will be Cubs still flying long after all who read this book are gone.

Carroll V. Glines
Colonel, USAF (Ret)
Dallas, Texas

1

Birth of the Cubs

The name of Clarence Gilbert Taylor, referred to by his contemporaries as just "C.G." Taylor, is not well known today. However, the story of the legendary Piper Cubs cannot be told without reviewing the key role that he played in the development of the most outstanding light airplanes ever made.

Born in Rochester, New York, in 1898, C.G. Taylor was one of six children of Arthur Taylor, a skilled tool and die maker who had emigrated from England to the United States via Canada in 1885. The family settled in Rochester, New York, in 1889, where their father operated a metal and bicycle shop. Young CG was crippled by infantile paralysis when he was 18 months old and walked ever afterward with a limp. He demonstrated a natural mechanical aptitude and a spirit of determination to succeed, as well as a keen desire for perfection in everything he did. This longing to succeed also made him very impatient when he perceived ineptitude among those around him, and argumentative when others would not agree with his point of view. He has been variously labeled as an intuitive genius, aeronautical wizard, and an eccentric.

The year 1911 was a pivotal point in C.G.'s life. He reportedly saw Calbraith P. Rodgers fly overhead in the *Vin Fiz*, a modified Wright B type biplane. Rodgers was flying from Sheepshead Bay, Long Island, New York, to the West Coast in pursuit of a $50,000 prize offered by the Hearst newspaper chain for the first transcontinental flight. He did not win the prize because the rules specified the flight had to be completed in 30 days, and it took him 49 days of flying and nearly three months of elapsed time to complete the trip.

C.G. followed the many mishaps of the *Vin Fiz* in the newspapers and was hopelessly captivated by the thought of building and flying his own "aeroplane." He began to construct a machine in the attic of the family home modeled after the drawings and descriptions he found in newspapers and magazines. He made the fuselage and wings separately and lowered them to the yard for final assembly. He did not intend to make a glider first as the Wrights had done, and felt he needed an engine, but none was available. He

never was able to fly it, but it did not dampen his desire to make a flyable machine.

When World War I began in Europe, C.G.'s interest in airplanes was heightened as he read of the exploits of the aces on both sides. He made several trips to Buffalo, New York, in 1916 during his junior year in high school hoping to get a ride in a Curtiss JN-4 "Jenny," which was so much in the news then as a wartime pilot trainer. He finally persuaded a pilot to take him up, and this first flight convinced him that he was going to make a life for himself in aviation.

After graduation from high school in 1917, Taylor went to work first for the Anderson Gun Co. in Rochester operating a drill press, then was employed by the Northeast Electric Co. as an apprentice. These two jobs gave him valuable experience in the working world. As far as is known he had no formal college education in engineering, but he was an avid reader, which was probably encouraged by his parents as he recovered from polio.

C.G. and his younger brother, Gordon A. Taylor, joined their father, an expert machinist, in operating and managing the Tool,

C.G. Taylor, co-founder with his brother Gordon of Taylor Brothers Airplane Manufacturing Co. in Rochester, New York. The company moved to Bradford, Pennsylvania, and finally to Lock Haven. (Courtesy Matthew Simek)

The first aircraft built by Clarence and Gordon Taylor was this Arrow Wing Chummy A-2 completed in 1927. A side-by-side model, it was powered by a French Anzani 90-hp radial engine. (Peter M. Bowers Collection)

The second A-2 Chummy was shown at the Detroit Air Show in 1928. The engine was a German Ryan-Siemens engine. (Piper Aviation Museum)

Die, and Specialty Co. in Rochester after the war. Gordon got caught up in his brother's enthusiasm about aviation. Over the next five years C.G. studied everything he could find on aircraft manufacturing and design; meanwhile, Gordon proved adept at marketing the company's products.

The brothers bought a war-surplus Curtiss JN-4 Jenny for $750 from Jack Loomis, a local barnstormer, with the agreement that Loomis would teach them to fly. After a few hours of instruction, C.G. decided the performance of the Jenny could be improved by redesigning the landing gear assembly, placing the radiator in a different position, adding a third cockpit so two passengers could be carried, changing the stagger of the wings to compensate for the resultant shift in the center of gravity, and replacing the rudder bar with pedals. The plane, powered by an Anzani 10-cylinder 110-hp radial engine, was tested by Loomis in April 1926 and pronounced fit to fly.

Greatly encouraged by their success, C. G. and Gordon formed the North Star Aerial Service Corporation during the summer of 1927. They flew to surrounding New York towns to give rides, a practice that was still popular, although it was waning as the general public became concerned about safety in view of the many accidents in obsolete planes.

Jack Loomis was impressed with the work of the Taylors and asked them to design and construct a three- or four-place plane that he could use for passenger-carrying flights. They did, and the result was a strut-braced, high-winged, single-engine monoplane with an enclosed cabin that could seat two passengers side-by-side. A wide open cockpit for a pilot and possibly another very slim passenger was located behind the passenger cabin. The plane, labeled the "Loomis Special," measured 24 feet long with a 40-foot wing span and was powered by an Anzani 110-hp air-cooled radial engine. This design concept of side-by-seating became a hallmark of future designs of what would be known later as Taylorcraft planes.

Although C.G. left the family company briefly to work as a designer of machines to make paper boxes, his interest in aircraft designing was sharpened after Lindbergh completed his epic flight from New York to Paris in May 1927. Public interest in flying increased suddenly, and thousands of Americans decided they wanted to learn to fly. During 1928 over 17,000 young men and women applied for pilot licenses or student permits.

Public recognition and confidence in aviation seemed to come in an instant. Sensing that the time was right to build and sell small airplanes, C.G. and Gordon incorporated the Taylor Brothers Airplane Manufacturing Company with its headquarters in Rochester. C.G. did the designing and contributed the know-how, while Gordon handled the demonstrations and actively pursued potential buyers.

C.G. designed a two-place, side-by-side high-wing monoplane featuring wooden, fabric-covered wings and a welded steel tube fuselage. It was powered by a 90 hp Anzani and had a maximum gross weight of 1,500 pounds. The brothers called it the Arrow Wing Chummy because of the "chummy" side-by-side seating arrange-

The third Chummy model was the B-2, which was equipped with a Kinner K-2 radial engine certificated in 1929. (Peter M. Bowers Collection)

A special Chummy was a B-2 re-designated as the C-2. The wing was modified with a variable incidence controlled by the pilot. It was designed in an unsuccessful attempt to qualify for the Guggenheim Safe Aircraft Competition in 1929. (Peter M. Bowers Collection)

ment. They claimed it had a cruising speed of 100 mph and a landing speed of 38 mph. The announced price was around $4,000.

The brothers decided the time had come to manufacture planes like this in quantity, and in 1928 changed the name of the company to Taylor Brothers Aircraft Corporation and sold some stock for capitalization. They constructed a second plane, installed a Siemens-Halske 113-hp engine, and named it the Taylor A-2 Chummy. They took it on a barnstorming tour and introduced it at an aircraft show in Detroit in April 1928. While demonstrating the Chummy to a potential buyer, Gordon Taylor and his passenger were killed, reportedly because the passenger panicked and grabbed the controls during a landing approach. It was an extremely disheartening event

to C.G., and he withdrew from the business briefly to mourn and ponder his future.

Just as he overcame personal physical adversity during his childhood, C.G. eventually came to grips with his grief. He decided that his brother would have wanted him to continue what they had begun to make their life's work, and eventually resumed designing and manufacturing aircraft. Carefully considering the difficulties with using a foreign war-surplus engine built to metric measurements and lack of parts availability, he decided the A-2 Chuumy could be improved by installing a more reliable engine. He selected a Kinner K-5 (a 90-hp air-cooled radial engine) for the new plane and designated it the B-2 Chummy. It was slightly heavier than the

When sales of the Chummy were not encouraging, C. G. Taylor designed this inexpensive D-1 single-seat glider. It had tubular steel framework, tail skids, and elementary controls. It never flew. (Piper Aviation Museum)

The first successful aircraft designated as a Cub was this Taylor E-2 after the original engine, the Brownbach Tiger Kitten, was replaced with a French Salmson 40-hp engine. Shown is C.G. Taylor (left) with Rensselaer C. "Bud" Havens, company test pilot at that time. (Piper Aviation Museum)

A-2, and the company confidently claimed in its advertisements a maximum speed of 110 mph with a 90-mph hour cruising speed. It was formally approved by the Aeronautics Branch of the Department of Commerce in August 1929, and Taylor felt strongly that it should also be offered for sale at about $4,000.

C.G. Taylor's mind was now set on the future, and he designed a four-place monoplane that was fitted with floats. It was reportedly bought by a bootlegger who used it to fly liquor from Canada to the United States. It may have been too ambitious for the time, as only one was built and nothing more was heard about it. Meanwhile, Chummy production began in Rochester, and the planes, once

built, had to be disassembled and trucked to the nearest airport—about 10 miles away—where they were reassembled, tested, and turned over to customers.

1929 seemed likely to be a banner year for airplane sales, and C.G. was intent on producing the B-2 Chummy in quantity, but the facility at Rochester was too small. He did not have enough capital to finance a move, so he sent word to potential investors in Taylor stock that he was looking for a factory location near an airport and would entertain offers to finance the move to new facilities. In September 1929 representatives from the cities of Bradford, Pennsylvania, and Utica, New York, visited Taylor. Both groups found that,

First Taylor Brothers Aircraft Co. facility in Bradford, PA, after moving from Rochester, New York, in 1929. (Piper Aviation Museum)

Aerial view of Taylor factory in Bradford, PA, before the move to Lock Haven, PA, in 1937. (Piper Aviation Museum)

although the company showed promise, there was no money to finance the size building that Taylor required. Taylor decided that the airport at Utica was inadequate, while the Emery Airport at Bradford had great possibilities.

Bradford, located close to the border with New York, was then a small city of 17,000 that was sustained by a lumber industry and oil operations that had begun with discovery of oil there in 1881. Both businesses were playing out as demand shifted elsewhere. The city's politicians and bankers wanted another industry to bolster the local economy. In early October 1929, Bradford Chamber of

Commerce President and Spanish-American war veteran Andrew D. Burns persuaded his friends and associates to consider buying stock in the company. A committee went to work and decided that if Taylor would sell them stock, they would purchase $50,000 worth to encourage him to relocate and build a factory at the airport. A lumber company offered to barter lumber for stock shares; real estate brokers and bankers indicated increased interest when Taylor announced his intention to build at least 50 Chummys during the first year, then gradually increase production to as many as one per working day during the following years. This optimistic prediction

Taylor E-2 Cub with 37-hp Continental engine. (Piper Aviation Museum)

Taylor F-2 Cub with Lenape 50-hp engine. (Peter M. Bowers Collection)

encouraged local businessmen to agree to cooperate and approve the deal.

When about half of the stock had been sold and construction of the plant was underway, Taylor planned to move to Bradford in June 1929. However, construction took longer than expected and was not completed until September. A small work force then began to turn out the first Bradford Chummy. Taylor insisted that it be offered at the original price of $3,985.

Meanwhile, the nation's economy was suffering the first pangs of doubt about the future in the fall of 1929. Bankers became increasingly uneasy about making loans for new ventures. Stockholders of Taylor stock grew wary and wanted more promise of return on their investment when they learned there were no sales developing for the Chummy. C.G., impatient as always with anyone who disagreed with him, was adamant that the price was right, and tried to convince the nay-sayers that Americans would soon see that light airplanes could be used for business as well as pleasure.

One investor in Taylor stock was William Thomas Piper, son of a farmer who had located his family at Knapp's Creek, near

Bradford, in 1881. Born that same year, William worked in the Pennsylvania oil fields, and at age 17 enlisted in the Army and served in Puerto Rico during the Spanish-American War. Afterward, he graduated *cum laude* from Harvard University in 1903 with a B.S. degree in mechanical engineering. He joined a construction firm in New York City briefly, then returned to Bradford to enter the oil business.

Piper married in 1910 and fathered five children. The girls were Mary and Elizabeth; the three boys were William, Jr., Thomas Francis (nicknamed "Tony"), and Howard (nicknamed "Pug"). The boys were to follow their father into the aviation business, but none ever realized that their family name would eventually become known around the world.

Piper was commissioned a captain in the Army Corps of Engineers during World War I and served for two years, but the war ended before he could be assigned overseas. For about two years after the Armistice in 1918, the senior Piper devoted himself to developing his Bradford oil field holdings. "All I wanted was to produce enough oil through a partnership I had formed so that I

Taylor F-2 Cub with Aeromarine 40-hp engine. (Piper Aviation Museum)

Restored Taylor H-2 with Szekely 35-hp engine. (Piper Aviation Museum)

could look forward to a comfortable old age after the children had been raised," he wrote in a 1949 memoir titled *Private Flying: Today and Tomorrow.*

Piper's main interest was in the selling side of the oil business, but he could see that the oil was playing out in the area that had once been called the "Oil Capital of the World." He founded the Dallas Oil Company, which specialized in "secondary recovery" of oil, a process that was then being introduced in the Bradford area.

Piper heard about the move of the Taylor firm to Bradford, and a friend suggested he invest in some stock to help it get started, thus assisting the town's economy. Piper put down $600 to buy shares in an industry he admittedly knew nothing about. He had flown one time in an open cockpit Travel Air biplane and did not like it. He took calculated financial risks occasionally, although he wondered if he might be betting on a loser if he invested in a business he wasn't enthusiastic about. However, he was heartened by the rosy predictions of the stock brokers, and his $600 stock purchase, plus his business experience, led to an invitation to join the Taylor board of directors and become the company treasurer.

The Aircraft Yearbook, an annual chronicler of the business side of aviation published by the Aeronautical Chamber of Commerce of America, presented an up-beat, perhaps exaggerated, outlook for aviation for 1928. According to its analysts:

"...the number of privately owned airplanes operated by corporations on company business or by individuals for personal transport or pleasure in 1928 increased from hundreds to thousands. The number of persons licensed to become aviators increased from 1,572 and 2,573 others had applied for licenses."

Apparently, no one in the burgeoning aviation industry wanted to recognize, much less publicize, the developing economic storm clouds that the nation would suffer for most of the following decade.

By the end of 1929, after the stock market crash in October, the national economy was headed for the Great Depression as the "Coolidge-Hoover Prosperity Era" came to a close. Banks failed and unemployment mounted to unprecedented levels. The private aircraft industry suffered quickly, as the number of planes produced in 1929 fell from 1,700 to a record low of 550 two years later. A number of well-established aircraft manufacturers went bankrupt.

Only about two-thirds of the Taylor stock subscription had been sold by 1931, and the Taylor Brothers Aircraft Corporation joined the bankrupt list. At the Taylor factory in Bradford—a wood-and-tar paper building beside a 7-acre air strip—the first B-2 Chummy to be built there was under construction. There was no buyer for it, and the stockholders began to worry.

William Piper took a different stance. He obtained a bank loan of $1,000 to buy the land and the factory building, and agreed to allow Taylor to use the property rent-free to manufacture airplanes until the company's fortunes improved. With more of his own money

Rudder and vertical stabilizer of the Taylor E-2 before Walter Jamouneau rounded the plane's contour from the squared design shown here. The famous bear Cub logo had not yet been adopted. (Photo by the author)

Taylor F-2S with the 40-hp Aeromarine radial engine on EDO 990 floats. (Peter M. Bowers Collection)

at risk now, Piper thought if the company could be reorganized, continue making two versions of the Chummy—a Trainer and a Sport model—and offer them for sale at a much reduced price, it might be able to survive. He felt it his duty as treasurer and member of the board to tell Taylor he could not agree with his decision to market the two models of the Chummy at nearly $4,000 each. Taylor was adamant and vigorously defended the planes and their price tag.

Meanwhile, there had been developments in aviation that were to have far-reaching effects on the industry in the years ahead. Daniel F. Guggenheim, a wealthy philanthropist, had established the Guggenheim Fund for the Promotion of Aeronautics in 1926. Among the several projects to encourage new aircraft advances in the interest of improved safety was the Guggenheim International Safe Aircraft Competition. It was organized in 1929 to encourage aircraft manufacturers to find methods of reducing aircraft takeoff and landing speeds, and design ways to increase aircraft stability and control. One area of interest centered on fundamental changes in wing designs to incorporate a greater degree of "foolproof" safety in them. This focusing of attention of the aircraft industry on safety during 1929 had an important influence on future aircraft design. However, the emphasis was on solving aerodynamic, rather than structural problems.

A first prize of $100,000 was offered to the winner of the flight trials; five special $10,000 prizes for safety were to be given to the first five aircraft to meet the minimum flying requirements. The rules were very precise, and favored development of single-engine aircraft outfitted with special wing devices, such as slats, spoilers, and flaps to obtain greater efficiency and safer landing speed.

The rules stated that the structure of any candidate aircraft would have to be rugged and able to accommodate a pilot and one passen-

ger. All planes had to demonstrate they could achieve a number of minimum performance criteria. Among them was to show they could achieve a maximum speed of at least 110 miles per hour at sea level; attain a four hundred feet a minute climb rate at one thousand feet; maintain level and controlled flight at a speed no greater than 35 mph; perform a steady glide to a landing over a 35-foot high obstruction; and demonstrate a takeoff within a three hundred-foot run.

Taylor was anxious to enter the competition and designed a special Chummy during the summer of 1929 that he designated the C-2. It had a variable incidence wing that Taylor thought would help it meet the slow speed requirements, as well as assist in achieving the stability parameters at high speeds. Twenty-seven companies entered the trials that were held at Mitchel Field on Long Island, New York, that fall.

Taylor and Piper drove to Long Island to observe the required flights made by the Fund's three designated test pilots and were disappointed to find that the Chummy was eliminated early. It failed to attain the minimum high speed and could not maintain steady flight at low speed. The Chummy was returned to Bradford, and although Taylor thought he could solve its shortcomings with modifications, it was dismantled. The winner of the first prize as the "safest airplane" was the Curtiss Tanager. However, it proved to be too complicated and expensive to manufacture and was never put into production.

The failure to make a showing in the Guggenheim trials was disappointing, not only to Taylor, but especially to the stockholders and members of the Bradford Board of Commerce. There had been few sales of planes, and purchases of company stock had dwindled. Taylor addressed the board of directors and was followed by Piper, who tried to allay the members' fears. But the Taylor firm was not the only plane manufacturer in trouble. Others were also continuing to experience poor sales. Almost in desperation, Taylor quickly designed the D-1. The D-1 was an inexpensive single-seat training glider to sell for $300 that he hoped would encourage flying schools to consider as a vehicle to interest the public in getting into the air as cheaply as possible. Only one was built. Taylor then had a two-cycle engine installed that he said "barely got it off the ground."

W. T. Piper by this time knew that the company was on the verge of bankruptcy. Only six Chummy B-2s had been built by the end of August 1930, three of them at Bradford. The last one was sold to a buyer in West Virginia, and Tom Smith, the ferry pilot, reportedly had to bail out for unknown reasons during the flight en route to the buyer's town. He survived the parachute jump, but the company never heard from him again. This was the last straw; the Taylor Brothers Aircraft Corporation had reached rock bottom.

As the company's treasurer, Piper filed a voluntary bankruptcy petition with the local court in 1931, and the company's assets were put up for sale. The only bidder was Piper himself, and he became the owner with a bid of $761. The corporation was renamed the Taylor Aircraft Company, and Piper designated Taylor as the president and gave him one-half interest, while he remained as treasurer. His primary objective now was to restore the confidence of stockholders. The company was reorganized with the understanding that it would produce a smaller plane that could be sold and flown more economically than existing airplanes.

The assets included a light plane with a small engine that Taylor had designed in desperation as a possible alternative to the Chummy, but Piper thought it cost too much, although it had some potential if marketed to the right public at a more reasonable price. He thought it should be able to sell for about $1,500, rather than the advertised $3,985. He was not interested in personally demonstrating it to potential customers at this time, although he did get his private pilot's license in 1931.

Piper and Taylor had made a trip to Cincinnati in early 1930 to visit the facility of the new Aeronautical Corporation of America, makers of the Aeronca C-2, a light plane advertised at a very inexpensive $1,730, compared to other similar aircraft. It was a high wing monoplane with an open cockpit and was powered by a two-cylinder 30-hp engine manufactured by the company. It had quickly gained the nickname of the "Flying Bathtub" because of its dumpy, ungainly profile that looked as if its cockpit and nose were dragging the ground. However, it was simple to operate. It had no brakes, but could be effectively slowed and stopped by the pilot on landing by reaching one of the large wheels outside the cockpit with his gloved hand. Later that year a slightly larger and more graceful C-3 monoplane featuring side-by-side dual controls was introduced for training and sport flying. It was being offered at about $1,850.

Piper kept an eye on the success of the Aeronca and became convinced that an inexpensive aircraft that would be simple to maintain and operate could be built by the Taylor company and sold to flying schools, in addition to individual buyers, if the price were greatly reduced. He felt strongly that the Chummy could not possibly compete with Aeronca or any similar aircraft at a sales price of nearly $4,000.

William T. Piper, Sr., became company CEO and president after C.G. Taylor left the company because of disagreements, mainly about the sales price of the Cubs. The name was changed to Piper Aircraft Co. after Taylor started the Taylorcraft Co. (Fabian Backrach photo, History of Aviation Collection, University of Texas, Dallas)

"I thought if we could reorganize the company and get started making a little inexpensive plane it might be a pretty fair sale," Piper wrote in his memoir. "Although we had viewed the first Aeronca with tolerant amusement when it appeared, we had soon become so impressed by the way the public welcomed it that we had built this little plane of our own. In spite of our financial troubles, I had become a convert to flying and began to see wonderful possibilities in it.

"But the original stockholders apparently didn't. When none of them showed any interest in reorganizing the company, I got in touch with several of my more affluent friends and acquaintances and proposed that they each put up $5,000 along with me, and we would start turning out the little plane. They all said it was a most interesting proposal, but it so happened that their money was all tied up in other deals at the moment, although they certainly appreciated the invitation. Taylor and I soon realized that if anything was to be done we would have to do it ourselves.

"I had already spent a good deal of my own money trying to keep the original company alive, so that I didn't have too much loose cash lying around. Just about that time, however, I was fortunate enough to receive the sum of $2,000 for my share of an oil lease located in New York State which I had sold a year or so before. With this amount, plus whatever money I could take from my income as it was received, we reorganized the firm under the new name of the Taylor Aircraft Company. Taylor as president would furnish the engineering and manufacturing knowledge, while I as treasurer would furnish the capital and devote all the time I could spare to purchasing and sales.

"One of the first things we did was to engage an engineering firm to make the necessary stress analyses for the little plane so that we could get it approved by the Civil Aeronautics Authority as soon as possible. This engineering firm was headed by Howard Barlow, later Dean of the School of Aeronautics at Texas Agricultural and Mechanical College.

"In deciding to concentrate on a really light plane that could be flown more economically than existing ones, we had in mind the flying school operator, who at that time was finding it highly unprofitable to operate the heavier planes, which were usually powered with gasoline-consuming war-surplus OX-5 engines. They needed a small two-passenger light plane on which they could charge reasonable, depression-income fees for instruction and yet make a profit.

"This little plane on which we pinned all our hopes had already quite a history by the time we decided to go ahead with it. It was started on August 13, 1930, and on September 12, 1930, made its first flight and was designated the Taylor E-2. Taylor selected the type of airfoil or wing section to be used, and the fact that we used the same airfoil on later planes is a tribute to his engineering skill."

Taylor built a training glider based on his previous design and installed a small geared two-cylinder, 20-horsepower engine known as a Brownbach Tiger Kitten that was manufactured by the Light Manufacturing and Foundry Co. in Pottstown, PA. However, George Kirkendal, a pilot whose company owned the engine, was able to get the plane off the ground "only when it hit a bump" before having to cut the throttle, according to Taylor. Obviously a more powerful engine was needed, and Taylor beat the bushes to find other engine manufacturers who turned out small engines that might be suitable for light aircraft.

Although it wasn't successful, it was that Brownbach Tiger Kitten two-cycle engine that gave the name "Cub" to thousands of future aircraft. There is disagreement about who deserves credit for naming it, however. One writer has given recognition to Gilbert Hadrel, the company accountant, who reportedly said, "The first engine's name was Tiger Kitten. Why not name the plane the Cub?" According to C.G. Taylor, sales manager T. V. "Ted" Weld deserves the credit. Others who have been so attributed are Mose Hutchins, head of an advertising agency; Walter St. John, an employee; and J. Willard "Jake" Miller, operator of the Lock Haven Airport, who later helped persuade the company to move to Lock Haven, Pennsylvania.

Tail logo used on Taylor Cub J-2s built at the Bradford factory. (Photo by the author)

Whoever it was, from that time on the word "Cub" was not only the name for the original single-engine, fabric-covered, high-wing Taylor aircraft, but became the generic name that the general public uses, even today, for all similar light aircraft. The Cub logo on the tail surface of thousands of Cubs became famous around the world.

"We next tried a French-made Salmson engine, a foreign product that ran backwards, or clockwise, and had metric threads and dimensions," Piper recalled in a magazine article. "It was a 9-cylinder radial engine developing 40 to 45 horsepower and cost $1,300 to import. We got hold of a secondhand one for $350 and installed it on our new Cub. Powered with this smooth-running engine, the little plane was most satisfactory from the beginning. In the fall of 1930 we took the Cub on a demonstration flight over the Adirondacks to Canada and back to Bradford, where we hoped to interest a few backers if possible. Failing in this, however, we took the plane back to the factory. Before further steps could be taken, the bankruptcy intervened."

Meanwhile, in October 1930 test pilot Rensselaer C. "Bud" Havens had flown the Cub to several cities in Pennsylvania and New York to demonstrate its capabilities to potential buyers. He made over 150 "demo" flights and signed up the first Cub dealer in Warren, Pennsylvania. Three more dealerships were commissioned later, and an estimated 400 potential buyers were given trial flights.

It was soon found that the Salmson engine, although powerful enough, would not be acceptable for production of the aircraft in quantity. It was too expensive and was built to metric standards, which meant repair and maintenance would be difficult for mechanics. Besides, the propeller rotated opposite to American engines, which was inconvenient when a pilot tried to spin the propeller to start the engine alone while standing on the right side of the aircraft.

Taylor had ordered a new Salmson 40-hp radial engine from France, but it had not arrived in time for the first flight, which was why the Brownbach Tiger Kitten had been installed. Since the glider had been designated as the Model D, the plane was designated the Taylor E-2, with the "2" indicating that it had two seats. Advertising began immediately.

"Well, at least Taylor and I had proved to our own satisfaction that the little airplane was completely airworthy and lived up to our expectations," Piper wrote. "We realized, of course, that the high price of the Salmson engine ruled it out as the power plant for a low-priced plane."

It was a trip that Taylor and Piper made to Detroit to visit the Continental Aircraft Engine Company that proved the real turning point in the company's fortunes. Continental had produced the Model A-40 engine specifically for the small aircraft market because of the recognition of the growing need for a lightweight engine. What they came up with was a four-cylinder, horizontally opposed piston engine made of aluminum alloy. It was a significant departure from the radial, air-cooled engines that powered most planes of the day. Its flat profile promised to give a pilot better forward visibility over the aircraft's nose from the cockpit compared to the radials, and would enable the installation of more streamlined engine cowlings.

"The Continental Engine Company of Detroit had been promising us an engine for several months," Piper recalled, "but each time delivery was expected we would receive a letter stating that some new bug had developed, and that they hoped to have it licked in a couple of weeks. Finally, late in February 1931, the long-awaited Continental arrived. We couldn't wait to mount it on the airplane, but fastened it to a column and fixed up a temporary gas tank.

"It was a nice-looking little job, this model A-40. It developed 37 horsepower, started readily, and was surprisingly smooth in operation. But the manufacturer hadn't gotten all the bugs out by a long shot. To recount the number of things that went wrong with those early Continentals would take a whole chapter. Gaskets, carburetors, magnetos, cylinder heads, and crankshafts were all sources of trouble. At the Detroit Air Show in 1931, the Continental people had to keep a crew of mechanics on the field keeping our one demonstrator in running order. The engine makers were cooperative in the extreme, and together we worked out most of the troubles until the A-40 was a pretty reliable engine.

"Finally, in June 1931, the Taylor Cub, powered by a 37-horsepower Continental engine, was approved and licensed, ready for sale. From June until the end of the year we manufactured about one plane a week, or a total for the year of 24 Cubs. The first model, known as the E-2, was an open-cockpit plane. It was slow, short on power, and uncertain as to performance, and the airport operators took delight in making disparaging remarks about it. But we loved it as no parents ever loved their firstborn son. It was our baby, even if unkind critics called it an ugly duckling. We felt certain that the Cub would open a new era in the development of air transportation."

Taylor also recalled the acquisition of the Continental engine and was concerned about a propeller. However, that never presented a problem, he said:

"The Sensenich brothers, already established as reliable propeller manufacturers, drove up from their shop in Lititz, Pennsylvania, with their tools in their car and carved the first props on the spot."

The first production model of the E-2 was sold to a Joe Smith of an undisclosed location in New York State. The second was sold to Kenneth Tibbits, then the Taylor shop foreman, and the third went to a buyer in Canada. Slight improvements were made in the gas tank arrangement, and the windshield was installed at a steeper angle. It was reported that the gas gauges for the two 4-gallon tanks

The Piper Cub logo was first applied to late J-2 models after the company was officially named Piper Aircraft Corporation. It is one of the world's most famous aviation product symbols. (Piper Aviation Museum)

were adopted from the Model A Ford. The sale price was advertised at $1,325.00.

The future might have seemed favorable to C.G. Taylor by the end of 1931, as a total of 24 of the improved E-2 models were manufactured and advertised. But there were ominous signs which the Aeronautical Chamber of Commerce of America was duty-bound to report in its annual *Yearbook*:

"The aviation industry weathered two of the most critical years in its history in 1930 and 1931, and entered 1932 considerably stronger as a result of the achievements and readjustments of the preceding two-year period. Only lack of courage and foresight on the part of those in whose hands the national aviation program is entrusted can keep aviation from being a leader among industries in the slow but steady march toward general business recovery in 1932."

In a succeeding paragraph, the yearbook also noted tha:

"The general business depression cut sharply into the volume of private and industrial flying logged during 1931."

On the other hand, the organization did not want to spread gloom among its members. The editors stated:

"The United States led the world in private flying, and this market promised to offer a growing outlet for commercial planes of American manufacture."

The Taylor Aircraft Co., under its new management, may have found a little comfort in this prediction. In any event, a new aircraft had been born and named the Cub. It was to have an amazing and legendary future.

2

The Beginning of a Legend

Taylor could not agree on selling the E-2 Cub for such a low price as $1,325, but had grudgingly gone to work to design a plane to meet Piper's specifications. It had to be relatively easy to manufacture, effortless to operate, inexpensive to maintain, and safe for the general public to learn the elementary skills of flying. The result E-2 was a high-wing monoplane with a two-place tandem seating arrangement. The fuselage and horizontal and vertical stabilizers were of welded steel tubing; wing spars were made of Oregon spruce, and aluminum alloy ribs gave shape to the wing surface. Tubular struts were used to absorb landing shocks, instead of flexible cables as on the Aeronca. A metal tail skid was installed instead of a movable tail wheel, and there were no brakes.

For the wing design, Taylor had chosen the U.S. 35B air foil for its proven stability at low speeds, and because it gave the plane a more docile stall and somewhat better lift. The wing spanned 35 feet and had a total area of 186 square feet. While the cabin was open on stock models, an enclosure was added as an option and was later was made standard on models manufactured beginning in late 1932.

Despite the anticipated reliability of the A-40 engine, the first one delivered and fitted into the nose of an E-2 Cub failed to meet expectations. After Renssalear "Bud" Havens, the company test pilot, made the initial test flights, C.G. Taylor recalled "We had 26 forced landings in the first 30 days." One of the major causes was

that the carburetor had what Piper called a "built-in miss," which was disconcerting, but worse than that was the problem with crankshafts that broke in less than 100 hours of operation. Taylor added:

"It also kept blowing head gaskets, and the single magneto would sometimes fail. Despite the many internal failures, the deficiencies to refine the engine were eventually worked out and it turned out to be quite reliable."

In the meantime, the E-2 was being advertised as having a top speed of 83 miles per hour, which in reality was 75; cruising speed was touted to be 75 but was closer to 65. However, fuel consumption was an actual three gallons per hour, and its tank held nine gallons.

The gross weight limitation of the E-2 was 925 pounds, which included an allowance of 170 pounds each for two occupants; no luggage was figured since there was no compartment for it. The fly-away cost of $1,325 was more like the price that W.T. Piper thought might be acceptable and affordable for private flyers. He hoped it would provide a small profit on each one sold.

The E-2 was flown by a test pilot of the Aeronautics Branch of the Department of Commerce and an Approved Type Certificate was issued on July 11, 1931. This authorized the company to produce aircraft of "an exact similarity of type, structure, materials, assembly, and workmanship" as the test model.

C.G. Taylor's first advertisement after quitting at Bradford in December 1935 and starting a new company at Butler, PA, was this small ad in the February 1936 issue of several aviation magazines. (*Aero Digest*)

The Taylor (later Piper) J-2 was first advertised as the New Cub in aviation magazines in 1936. The ads featured the new streamlined profile designed by Walter Jamouneau. Buyers could fly one home for $490 cash, with the balance of $1,470 in monthly installments. This price was later reduced and made Cubs the least expensive light aircraft available in the mid-1930s. (*Aero Digest*)

Many J-2s had the wings and horizontal stabilizers painted orange, while the fuselage was black. Silver became popular, and was advertised as the New Silver Cub. Other colors were available upon request. (Photo by the author)

The E-2 proved to be easy to fly, although it had very little power reserve. Takeoff runs with a single pilot were generally about 200 feet; climb-out was satisfactory for about the first 1,000 feet, but tapered off rapidly after that. It was light on the controls and behaved well in all basic flight maneuvers. The interior was sparsely furnished but adequate for a training plane not intended to make long cross-country flights. Automobile fuel could be used.

Certification by the federal government added sales potential for the rejuvenated E-2. W.T. Piper refused to be discouraged by the initial lack of reliability of the Continental A-40, and his confidence increased when the Continental engineers made improvements. Piper felt sure there were still thousands of young people who wanted to learn to fly, and he saw special sales potential in the flight schools then being established across the country. He acquired loans to keep the company afloat financially with his oil leases as collateral.

It was apparent that Piper, now fifty years old, was getting heavily involved in a new business, but realized he did not know much about its product. He asked test pilot "Bud" Havens to teach him and his son Tony how to fly the Cub. Although Tony soloed quickly after just three hours of instruction, his father, continually engaged in company business, took longer, but eventually did obtain a private pilot license in 1931. At this time, he said he "rose from the rank of convert to evangelist." Years later at the age of 73, he checked out in a twin-engine Piper Apache.

The work force at Bradford remained small but enjoyed a unique fringe benefit unheard of during the Depression days. As a motivation for the workers, who were earning only about 20 cents an hour for nine-and-a-half hour days and five-and-a half day weeks, the company offered all employees flying lessons at a dollar an hour. After soloing, the opportunity for employees to fly Piper planes for only the cost of gas and oil became an additional benefit that continued for many years.

***

Taylor J-2 in 1937 with experimental one-bladed Everel propeller. Designed for engines of 40-hp, the manufacturer claimed less vibration, faster takeoff and climb, and greater fuel economy. It was never adopted by any light plane manufacturer. (Peter M. Bowers Collection)

Taylor F-2S on floats with an Aeromarine AR-340 engine. The F-2 did not sell well, and only about 33 were built. The fire at Bradford ended production of the F-2. (Piper Aviation Museum)

There were many would-be light plane competitors to the Cub in the late 1920s and early 1930s that produced only a prototype or an untested model, and were mentioned in the aviation magazines of that era. Their names are mostly forgotten now, and photographs of many of them are rare or nonexistent. Here are a few of them: Akerman Pusher JDA-8; Alexander Flyabout D-1; American Eaglet; American Sunbeam Pup; Buhl Bull Pup; Church Mid-Wing; Cycloplane Solo; Eyerly Coupe; Heath Parasol; Hunt Sport Chummy; Irwin Meteorplane FA-1; Lee Monoplane L-2; Lightplane Paraquet 5-M; Mattley Flivver; Peters Play Plane; Pietenpol B-4A; Prest Baby Pursuit; and Simplex Kite.

Bill Piper was not impressed or discouraged by this burgeoning list of rivals. He was confident that volume would make the difference and eventually prove profitable at the fly-away cost of

$1,325 for a Taylor Cub. The number of more viable competitors to the E-2, despite the Depression, was indicated by the advertisements found in *Aero Digest*, one of the leading aviation publications of the 1930s. Here are some examples of the manufacturers' offerings that survived past the prototype stage and announced the following prices in the 1933 issues: Aeronca - $1,730; Curtiss-Wright Monocoupe - $3,375; Davis K-5 - $2,295; Fairchild 22 - $2,775; Great Lakes Sport Trainer - $2,985; Hammond - $2,795; Kinner Monoplane - $2,490; Nicholas-Beazley NB-8 Trainer - $1,990; Rearwind Junior - $1,795; Stinson Model R - $4,595; Waco Model A - $3,585 to $4,895; and Warner Bird - $4,375.

The Aeronautical Corporation of America's Aeronca at the time was the most formidable competitor price-wise, as well as the most aggressive in its ads. The Taylor Cub ads were few and very small

Taylor J-2 after redesign of Taylor E-2 at the Bradford plant. Two controversial issues between C.G. Taylor and William Piper, Sr., were the Cub's profile changes and the selling price. (Peter M. Bowers Collection)

Above: Piper J-2S on EDO floats over Seattle. EDO floats were the most popular models for Cubs and their successors. The EDO Corporation has been making aluminum floats to convert landplanes for flight off water since 1925. (Piper Aviation Museum)

What the pilot sees upon arrival at the William T. Piper, Sr., Memorial Airport, known as "Cub Haven." It has a single concrete runway beside a grass strip. The Susquehanna River can be seen in the background, where seaplanes can tie up. (Piper Aviation Museum)

The factory at Lock Haven was formerly an abandoned silk mill, with 100,000 sq. ft. of space available for Cub production. It was ideally located, with easy access to a main interstate highway, the Pennsylvania Railroad, and an airfield with a wide river nearby. (Piper Aviation Museum)

at the time compared to the Aeronca ads, thus reflecting the difference between the financial conditions of the two companies during that period.

Problems were mounting daily, as dealers and buyers of Cubs continually complained about engine problems with the Continental A-40, especially the crankshaft. It was so unreliable that an automobile was dispatched sometimes to follow a plane on a delivery flight to make sure the pilot reached his destination. Taylor looked everywhere for a more reliable replacement engine. He tried an

Aeromarine AR3-40, a 40-hp three-cylinder air-cooled radial which changed the designation to Taylor F-2; although the plane was type-approved in February 1934, the engine continually ran rough and was unsatisfactory. Its fly-away price was $1,495, and only 33 were built.

Next, Taylor hurriedly designed a new experimental engine of 35-40 hp and attached it to an E-2 frame. He labeled it the T-50, which required the plane to have a new type designation as the Taylor G-2. No details of any structural changes are available, and it is rarely mentioned in company documents.

Piper J-3s being assembled at Lock Haven. Many women joined the Piper company when manpower was short as the United States prepared for World War II. Employees were offered flying lessons at $1 per hour as a fringe benefit. (Piper Aviation Museum)

The assembly of Cubs before adoption of assembly line production tech-niques were not efficient, as shown here. In the foreground is a Cub destined for a flying club during the late 1930s, when many youths were encouraged to learn to fly at the least expense. (Piper Aviation Museum)

Piper adopted many labor-saving devices to speed up production of Cubs just before and during World War II. Here wings are painted and then moved overhead automatically to dry before the next coat is applied. (Piper Aviation Museum)

The next version became the H-2, in which Taylor substituted a 35-hp Szekely, also a three-cylinder radial. It proved to be a bad choice, as the cylinders developed cracks and tended to separate from the body of the engine. The solution was to tie the three cylinders together with a cable that was tightened by a turnbuckle. It was type-approved in May 1935, but only four H-2s were built; all were conversions from E-2 or F-2 airframes. No list prices are found in the company's literature, and it is presumed that these airframes were reworked and became E-2s. However, there is one possible claim to fame for the H-2. In June 1937 Beverly Dodge, carrying a

passenger, reportedly flew an H-2 to 16,800 feet over Honolulu, Hawaii, to set an unofficial altitude record for women pilots in a light plane.

Meanwhile, Continental mechanical engineers focused on the crankshaft failures and improved the A-40 engine considerably, so that the subsequent models became standard on Cubs through 1938. Cub sales increased as a result, and grew from 20 Cubs in 1931 to 70 in 1934, including four that were sent to Sao Paulo, Brazil, the company's first export order to South America. As noted previously, one of the Cubs sold in 1931 was to a Canadian buyer, the

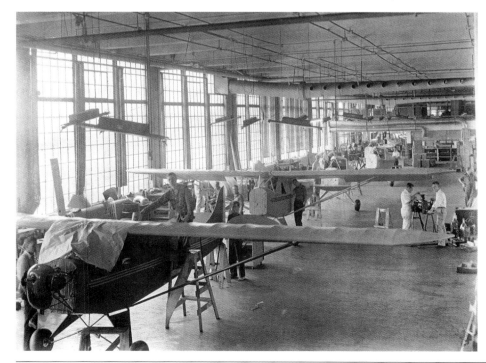

The concept of assembly line production, similar to that pioneered by the Ford Motor Co., increased the numbers of Cubs that could be turned out in a short time. Here J-2s are moving forward to the engine installation station after being painted. (Piper Aviation Museum)

Cub fuselages are welded by individual workers before being moved to an assembly area. (Piper Aviation Museum)

company's first sale across the northern border. By 1935 the Cub had become better known throughout the country because of its beneficial effect on flying school operations that had become more profitable. That year more than 200 Cubs were sold.

Advertisements in aviation magazines touted the Taylor E-2 as "the best plane in America today for the money." Anyone could learn to fly a Cub "with only a few hours' instruction and with a minimum of expense." Other ads boasted that:

"Pilots from Texas to Maine have thoroughly tested the Cub in a period of three months and all are enthusiastic over its remarkable flying qualities. It is so easy to fly that one who had not touched a stick since the War made a perfect landing on his first attempt."

Despite the Depression still haunting America, the Bradford factory was turning out E-2 Cubs in 1935 at about one each working day, and by summer was nearly doubling that number. By the

Assembled fuselages are ready to be hung on a monorail and moved to another department for fabric covering and installation of engines and landing gear. (Piper Aviation Museum)

Women employees proved especially adept at covering the Cub wings with fabric before painting. (Piper Aviation Museum)

end of the following year 541 had been sold, an unprecedented production record for any aircraft of that period. Meanwhile, one basic improvement had been made in the E-2: a cockpit enclosure that made the plane more comfortable for cold weather operations.

At first, all work had been done in one building at Bradford. As the demand for more production increased, additions were added to the original building in the form of long L-shaped add-ons, where

doping, fabric covering, and welding were conducted. By the middle of 1936 the floor area of the factory was 36,000 square feet.

While sales were encouraging, the relationship between Taylor and Piper was getting more contentious every day. Piper, pragmatic and rational to the core, and Taylor, obstinate and unwilling to compromise, began to argue continually about the sales price. But Piper saw a new market developing among the flying clubs

J-2 Cubs are nearing completion after the move from Bradford to Lock Haven in 1937. Each will be flight-tested before delivery. (Piper Aviation Museum)

that were forming around the country, especially among the colleges, and felt strongly they were logical buyers if the price were low enough. The National Intercollegiate Flying Club (NIFC) had been established, and flying contests were held among many member flying clubs that stimulated continuing press interest. Piper saw the sales potential in these clubs and insisted that the price had to remain low to encourage the concept of joint ownership by club members. Taylor argued that the firm could not make any money with such a low margin between manufacturing cost and sales price.

In the midst of the running dispute about money between the two principals, a young engineering graduate from Rutgers University in New Jersey appeared on the scene looking for a job. He had become interested in aviation and had earned a pilot license. His name was Walter Corey Jamouneau, a tall, bright young man with a forthright manner and engaging smile. His family was reasonably well off, but he had no job and could not stand being idle. He had applied unsuccessfully to the Kellett Autogiro and Pitcairn firms in the Philadelphia area, which were both making aircraft that could takeoff and land in small spaces. He drove to Bradford and asked if there was a possibility that the Taylor company might be interested in him. He was granted an interview with Piper and Taylor and told them about his background and his interest in aviation. They listened, but Taylor thought he would require too much salary because of his engineering degree. However Jamouneau added, just before he left, that salary was not important to him.

Both men had never heard any job seeker say anything like this before and were suddenly interested, but did not want to commit to an offer. No decision was made on the spot, so Jamouneau went back to his home in Irvington, New Jersey, to continue job-searching. Two weeks later, in January 1933, he received a letter from Mr. Piper that he was hired with the understanding that he would work without pay. Jamouneau, the only factory employee with a college degree, promptly began working at odd jobs and proved to be well-liked by the factory workers.

Piper observed how he fitted in with the other employees and did not seem to resent the fact that he wasn't being paid. Perhaps it became embarrassing to Piper, but after a few days he asked Jamouneau if he would like to be a salesman. The salary would be fifteen dollars a week, plus 25 dollars for expenses and the use of a Cub to cover his assigned territory.

Jamouneau agreed and flew the Cub on several sales calls. He noted where a few small internal changes would improve the Cubs with minimum additional manufacturing cost and obtained Taylor's grudging approval to inform the shop to make them, but was told not to make any changes that would alter the Cub's profile. Piper, on the other hand, after listening to the only really qualified engineer on their staff, told him to make all the changes he wanted. One of them was to add a partial enclosure for the open cockpit as an optional item that cost $45. This was an important improvement that Piper knew would make flying more comfortable, especially during cold weather operations and at higher altitudes. A horizontally split window on the right side was installed that could be pulled up and latched into place after the pilot and passenger were seated. This small addition was improved further as a drop-down door that became almost a Cub trademark and remained on subsequent models.

Although Taylor had forbidden Jamouneau to make any changes that would alter the plane's configuration, Piper told him he could design anything that would give the Cub a smoother contour. Jamouneau had never liked the right angle shapes of the wing and tail surfaces and rounded them off, giving the Cub a more modern, streamlined effect without altering the flying characteristics. Another change that Jamouneau suggested, and Piper quickly approved, was the addition of larger, lower pressure tires for softer landings

One of the first J-2 Cubs assembled at Lock Haven awaits delivery in 1937. (Piper Aviation Museum)

J-2 Cubs are being dismantled for shipment by rail to distant locations when ferry pilots were not available, or delivered to ports for overseas shipment. (Piper Aviation Museum)

on unprepared airfields, which Taylor objected to strenuously because of the slightly increased expense. These were only two of many other points of contention between the two men that had been slowly developing for many months.

Taylor became more quarrelsome almost daily, and even stopped speaking with Piper, choosing to communicate only with terse notes. He had not been well and was stricken with appendicitis in 1935. The operation and recovery restricted his energy so much that he could not go to work every day, and was not always aware of what was happening in the shops, even though he lived in a two story building close to the factory.

Piper approved all of the changes Jamouneau was suggesting in the interest of salability and told him to continue making alterations when Taylor wasn't around to check on the production line. Sales did increase, and 1936 looked as if it might mark a major turning point in the financial history of the company.

In addition to rounded wingtips and a new tail profile, with Piper's continuing encouragement, Jamouneau designed an improved cockpit, and a shaped and faired turtle deck aft of the wing. Other changes included a wider track landing gear, a three-piece windshield, and stronger window frames that created a closed cabin; however, the side windows could be easily removed, if desired. The length and height were increased slightly, and the new design led to an allowance for 20 pounds of baggage behind the rear seat. There was no change in the center of gravity, so pilots flying solo still had to occupy the rear seat, and the stabilizer was adjustable from either seat. Thus, the Cub had been somewhat glamorized, and after the last of the E models rolled out of the Bradford factory in February 1936, civil aircraft regulations required that the internal and external changes required the Cub to have a new model designation.

Instead of becoming the Taylor I-2 after the H-2, the resultant model label skipped a letter, and the designation officially became the Taylor J-2. Although many Piper historians attribute this as honoring Jamouneau, it is disputed by others who say that the letter "I" was skipped to avoid it being mistaken for the figure "1." Besides, Jamouneau was certainly not high on Taylor's list of people to be so honored.

Full-page advertisements in the aviation magazines showed a new aggressive promotion style by Piper to accompany the new image. J-2 Cubs could be flown home from Bradford for only $490, with the balance in easy monthly payments. Cities in 26 states and the District of Columbia were listed as "immediate delivery" points for "America's SAFE airplane, the sturdy New Cub which is Easy to Buy, Easy to Fly."

Equipped with a Continental A-40-3 engine that had incorporated improvements and a Sensenich propeller, the J-2 was awarded an airworthiness certificate on February 14, 1936. The initial price was $1,470, but as production increased, it was lowered to $1,270 and was featured in advertisements as the "New Cub." Sales for 1936 totaled 541, and the publication of this increased number injected new energy into the company.

The official specifications and performances for the New Cub were as follows:

Wing span	35 feet, 3 inches
Overall length	22 feet, 5 inches
Overall height.	6 feet, 8 inches
Wing area	178.5 square feet
Wing loading	44 lbs./sq.ft.
Power Loading	25.5 lbs. per h.p.
Fuel Capacity	9 gallons
Oil capacity	1 gallon
Empty weightÖ	563 lbs.
Useful loadÖ	407 lbs.
PayloadÖ	175 lbs.
Gross weight	970 lbs.
Maximum speed (sea level)	87 mph.
Cruising speed	70 mph.
Landing speed	30 mph.
Rate of climb	450 ft./min.
Cruising range	210 miles

Taylor was not impressed with the increased production rate because, in his opinion, it still produced an unacceptable, much-too-modest profit. He had wanted to design a side-by-side plane, which was in opposition to Piper's desire to continue to improve the tandem-seat model as Jamouneau was suggesting. Taylor was

Opposite: Piper advertisements in the 1930s featured the low price of the Cubs that "cost no more than a medium-priced car." They could be purchased in 1937 on an easy payment plan with only $425 down. (Aero Digest)

furious at the many physical changes that had been made without his knowledge and, in a fit of rage, fired Jamouneau and two of his helpers. The next day, after an argument with Taylor, Piper immediately rehired them. It was probably the last straw in their relationship as far as both men were concerned.

All had not been peaceful between the two top executives for far too long. Taylor found that even Piper himself was making production and engineering decisions he thought that he, as company president, should be making, and his frustration had been growing for too long a time. Piper, too, was fed up with the unpleasant daily hassle and told Taylor that he would be willing either to sell his interest to Taylor or buy him out. He offered to pay Taylor $250 a month salary for three years and take care of any life insurance premiums that Taylor had to pay for that same period. Piper felt secure in making such an offer because he knew that by this time he could get credit for these expenditures from the local Bradford bank in view of his other oil and real estate holdings. Taylor may have had no funds to buy Piper's interest anyhow, or may not have wanted to because he had other plans. He accepted Piper's offer and walked out in December 1935.

Piper immediately took total control of the Taylor Aircraft Co. and, in addition to being chairman of the board, became president and remained as treasurer. He now was in total charge of the company's recovery, if there were to be one, and began making decisions that focused on producing a low-cost plane that would put it within the range of public acceptance and affordability. When asked about the split between them years later, Piper would only comment that Taylor was an unusually talented engineer, but "he just had a hard time getting along with people."

Taylor described the parting arrangements differently in a 1982 interview with Chet Peek, author of *The Taylorcraft Story*:

"Piper didn't hold a gun to my head, but he might as well have," he said. "He offered me $5,000 for my half of the company, paid at the rate of $40 per week. He said that if I didn't accept the offer he would bankrupt the company and 'then where will you be?' I agreed to those terms."

The Taylor Aircraft Co. had struggled desperately between 1931 and 1936, showing little or no profit. Between 1931 and 1933, the years the Great Depression reached its lowest point, only 57 Cubs had been sold; in 1934, 70 Cubs had been bought but, according to William Piper, Sr., in his memoir, "We were still operating on half a shoestring." Production did improve in 1935 to 210 Cubs, and the following year leaped to 551. Taylor Aircraft Co. was now producing more than one-third of all private planes made in the United States.

"I took no salary during those years," Piper said. "Instead, I kept putting in more and more of my own money, watching with grim fascination as it disappeared in the mounting overhead and purchasing costs. Our credit was wearing pretty thin, and many a time we couldn't pay for an engine until somebody made a down payment on a plane. The company payroll wasn't always met on payday. I once had to take my personal note to a wholesale grocer and arrange for him to supply our employees with their weekly groceries on credit. Prosperity, however, was just around the corner."

This is the proper way to start a Cub when alone. Early Cubs had no electrical system, no brakes, no tail wheel, no radio, and few instruments. (Air Line Pilots Association)

Meanwhile, C.G. Taylor did not just fade away. He quickly surfaced as a viable competitor, first in Butler, Pennsylvania, and then in Alliance, Ohio, as head of the Taylorcraft Company. In an interview conducted by *Air Progress* magazine in 1975, Taylor stated that he had been "squeezed out of the company" and blamed William T. Piper, Jr., for "disrupting the production line," not the senior Piper or Jamouneau for his innovations on the Cub. By the time of the change of top management, Bill Piper, Jr., oldest of the three sons, had graduated from college and was appointed secretary and assistant treasurer but, although he agreed with the changes on the Cubs, had nothing to do with any disagreements between his father and Taylor.

It was quickly obvious that Taylor had already quietly laid the groundwork for his new company before he left Bradford. What was actually the first public revelation of what he had been doing was an advertisement that appeared in the February 1936 issues of several aviation magazines, only two months after he walked out at Bradford. In one-inch ads, a few terse words simply announced: "Taylorcraft by C.G. Taylor, Pittsburgh-Butler Airport, Butler, Pa. A New Light Plane that is Stable, Economical, Fast and Low-priced." There was no further description of the plane or explanation of the start-up of the new company. Later ads showed inaccurate side views of the plane, and then in July 1936, the first photos of the Taylorcraft prototype appeared after its first successful test flight the previous April.

Taylor was offered an old factory next to an airfield with hangar facilities at Alliance, Ohio, rent-free in order to encourage this new industry, and he moved there quickly from Butler in July 1936. He was able to line up $50,000 in commitments from local industries, businessmen, and banks, and owned all of the stock. He appointed himself president and treasurer and persuaded a few of his former employees to move from Bradford, including his father, Arthur Taylor, who made the transfer with his own machine tools and equipment. The Alliance Chamber of Commerce helped to finance the relocation.

The March 1936 edition of aviation magazines carried an ad larger than one used the month before. It stated: "Mr. Taylor was formerly president of Taylor Aircraft Co. This enterprise has no connection with that company." In bold letters, the ad announced that "A new production design for early delivery that combines the most asked-for features plus automobile comfort in Lightcraft, Sportcraft and Trainercraft" was available. No prices were stated.

That "new production design" turned out to be the Taylorcraft Model A, a light plane powered by the same Continental A-40 as the Cub. It had a side-by-side seating arrangement that became a hallmark for many of the Taylorcraft models that were to follow. It was advertised at a fly-away cost of $1,495.

In 1937, Taylor formed a partnership with W.C. Young, and the company was listed in the Alliance city records as the Taylor-Young Co. A few of the first aircraft were briefly labeled the Taylor-Young Model A.

"I'd been trying to get Piper to improve the design of the Cub for some time, so it was not a new idea to me," Taylor recalled years later. "We had even built a set of wings for the Cub using the new airfoil (NACA 23012), but after trying them out, Piper decided we didn't need them; they were stacked back in the hangar and finally scrapped. The 'tear drop' shape of the Taylorcraft actually was the result of observing the Cub in flight. I noticed the fuselage fabric would actually bulge out at certain places near the front. This led me to believe, correctly, that a side-by-side configuration would have less drag than the square tandem arrangement of the Cub."

Under Taylor's leadership, production began to increase, and the output reached eight planes a day by the end of 1938. Taylorcrafts were to prove formidable competitors for Mr. Piper's Cubs for the next few years.

3

How the Cub Became a Household Name

As soon as Taylor had left the premises, William T. Piper, Sr., set about building up sales of the J-2, which had been officially certificated on February 14, 1936. The improved Continental A-40-3 and -4 engines were now the models of choice, and the color of the planes was standardized as silver, with accents of various colors, although other colors were available. They were advertised at $1,470 at the factory or $1,035 without the engine and propeller if a customer had others in mind.

Full page ads were inserted in several aviation magazines touting "The Sturdy New 'Cub' is Easy to Buy, Easy to Fly" and could be flown away with a $490 cash payment and comfortable monthly installments. A few months later, the price dipped to $1,270 and required a down payment of only $425. A seaplane version, designated the J-2S, was produced with EDO floats and sold for $1,895; it was licensed to hold a useful load of 416 pounds. Walter Jamouneau flew the first one to the west coast for the buyer, V. R. McNulty of Wilmington, California.

There were now Taylor Cub distributors in 28 states and the District of Columbia. A traveling sales force, based in Bradford, was increased and took to the air around the country to show would-be Cub buyers that, according to the ads, "...when you take off, you quickly discover she's faster, smoother, easier to handle and much more comfortable."

Several universities established flying clubs as an extracurricular activity, and the National Intercollegiate Flying Club (NIFC) was created to foster interest in light plane flying. It was exactly what W. T. Piper had encouraged whenever he had the chance. One of the members who came to the company's attention was William D. Strohmeier, founder and president of the NIFC club at Amherst College in Amherst, Massachusetts. He had taken his first aircraft

flight as a young teenager while sightseeing in Washington, D.C., in April 1928, and made scale model airplanes which he sold to his classmates. "So," he says, "I was one of the first to be able to say that I made money in aviation in those days." He felt from then on that he was destined to be associated with aviation in some way in

Right: Mike Murphy waves to the crowd before taking off in a Cub from a moving automobile during the 1936 Miami Air Races. This has been repeated many times by other pilots, but Murphy is said to be the first to do it. (William D. Strohmeier Collection) Opposite: This Piper advertisement appeared in aviation magazines in June 1938. The purchase of a Cub included free instruction. (*Aero Digest*)

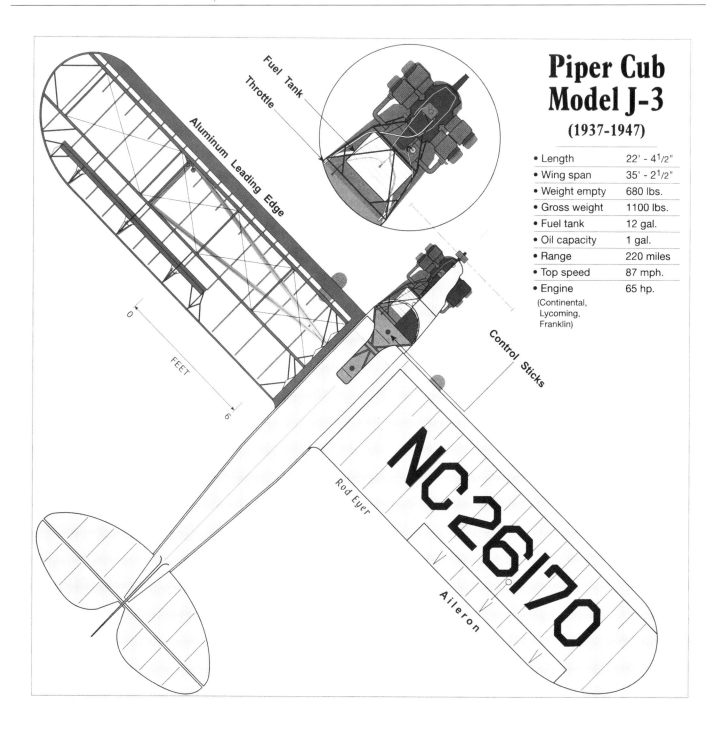

Piper Cub Model J-3

(1937-1947)

• Length	22' - 4$^{1}/_{2}$"
• Wing span	35' - 2$^{1}/_{2}$"
• Weight empty	680 lbs.
• Gross weight	1100 lbs.
• Fuel tank	12 gal.
• Oil capacity	1 gal.
• Range	220 miles
• Top speed	87 mph.
• Engine	65 hp.

(Continental, Lycoming, Franklin)

Fuel Tank

Throttle

Aluminum Leading Edge

0

FEET

6

Control Sticks

Rod Eyer

NC26170

Aileron

Above and following; Courtesy Rod Eyer.

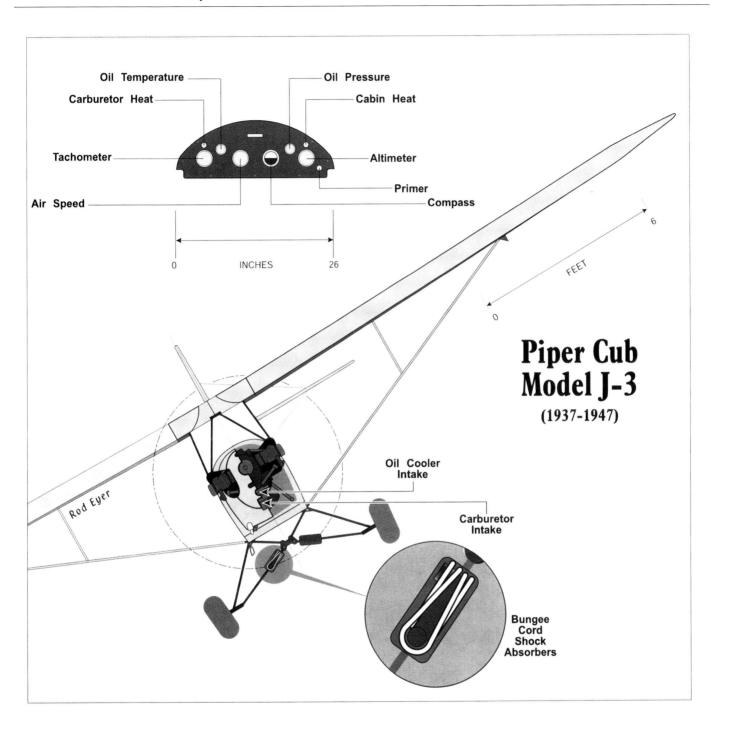

Oil Temperature

Oil Pressure

Carburetor Heat

Cabin Heat

Tachometer

Altimeter

Air Speed

Primer

Compass

0   INCHES   26

6

FEET

0

Piper Cub
Model J-3
(1937-1947)

Oil Cooler Intake

Rod Eyer

Carburetor Intake

Bungee Cord Shock Absorbers

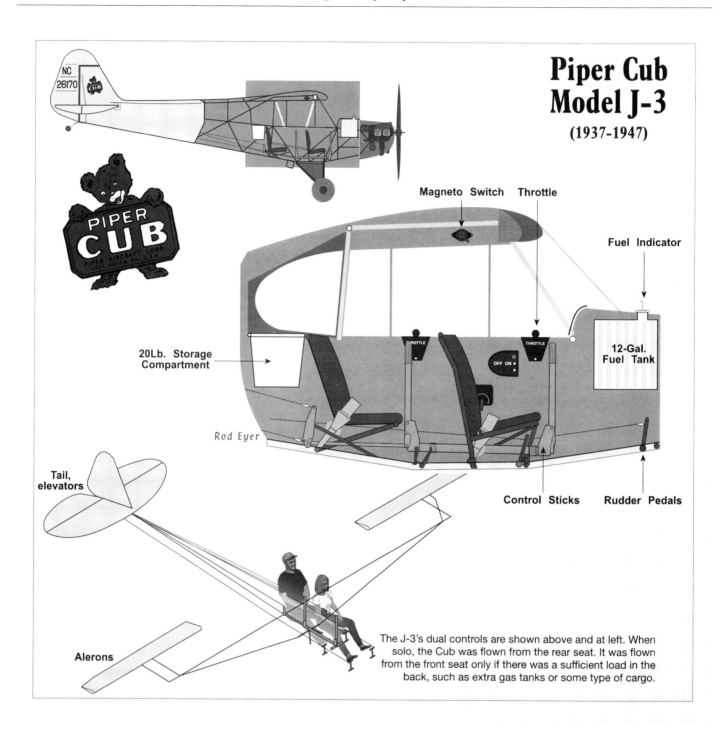

Piper Cub Model J-3
(1937-1947)

PIPER CUB
PIPER AIRCRAFT CORP.
LOCK HAVEN, PA., U.S.A.

Magneto Switch   Throttle

Fuel Indicator

20Lb. Storage
Compartment

12-Gal.
Fuel Tank

Rod Eyer

Tail,
elevators

Control Sticks   Rudder Pedals

Alerons

The J-3's dual controls are shown above and at left. When solo, the Cub was flown from the rear seat. It was flown from the front seat only if there was a sufficient load in the back, such as extra gas tanks or some type of cargo.

Takeoff from a moving automobile was relatively easy for a Cub when the car reached takeoff speed. Landing was more difficult, and was accomplished by placing one wheel firmly in one chock first, then the other. (Peter M. Bowers Collection)

the future. He eventually soloed in an E-2 in 1935 after less than three hours of dual instruction.

In his role as the college flying club president, Strohmeier complained several times by letter to Ted Weld, Taylor sales manager, that the E-2 Cub they had bought second-hand for $500 (the seventeenth one built) was grounded too frequently for engine repairs, mainly a split crankshaft. Since he had soloed in it so quickly he was convinced that it was a plane that anyone could and should fly, but the engine problem was distressing and did not give students a feeling of confidence.

When Strohmeier graduated from Amherst in June 1936 jobs were hard to find, but he knew he wanted to be associated with the stimulating new light plane industry in some way. He applied to

Piper for a job that July under Ted Weld as one of the Piper sales representatives. Weld liked his enthusiasm, and he was hired and promptly assigned a Cub for demonstration purposes. Weld approved of him having BILL STROHMEIER - FACTORY REPRESENTATIVE boldly painted on its sides in large letters and sent him out to sell the world on flying and buying Taylor Cubs.

On his first day away from the factory, Strohmeier decided to land in a pasture near a diner along a highway, buy a hot dog, and be as nonchalant as possible when people gaped at the strange sight. The idea might have been a good one, except that as he lined up for the approach to the field he failed to notice some power lines along the edge of the pasture until the last second. He pulled back on the stick without adding any power and stalled into the ground. The

A stunt man was picked up from an automobile and is hoisted aboard a Cub at an air show in Texas. (Jay Miller Collection)

Mike Murphy startled the crowds at the National Air Races in 1938 with this rebuilt E-2 Cub. He took off and landed inverted from the bottom cockpit. Murphy said it was the most difficult flying he had ever done, because every maneuver was opposite to what was normal. (John Wegg Collection)

landing gear spread out from the hard landing and the plane sat on its belly. Fortunately, the propeller stopped horizontally when he had cut the switch just before the crash and it was not damaged. As he later recalled, "So ended my first day on the road selling the common man he should buy his own Taylor Cub." Although he thought he might be fired when he telephoned the company, Weld asked only if he were hurt, and when Strohmeirer said he was not, Weld sent landing gear parts that arrived three days later. The young novice salesman attached them to the Cub and hopped off for his next planned stop.

Strohmeirer toured small airports in nearby states looking for likely buyers. He would buzz an area and land on grass airfields or pastures wherever he thought he could stimulate some interest in flying and, hopefully, sell a Cub. He would land in fields near gas filling stations to buy automobile gas, then costing 18 to 25 cents a gallon, and persuade potential customers to go for a ride. Strohmeier made his first sale to the owner of an itinerant crop duster company in Caribou, Maine, who also taught students on the side:

Beverly "Bevo" Howard, international aerobatic champion, is shown making an inverted ribbon cut as part of his act. It required a long straight-in approach in an inverted position. His act included slow rolls after takeoff, inverted 360-degree turns, inverted 4-point rolls, inverted snap rolls, and an outside loop. (Peter M. Bowers Collection)

"Bevo" Howard disliked the term "stunt flying" and always flew with white shirt and tie to indicate the casualness of performing aerobatics in a light plane. He was a keen supporter of Piper Cubs, and was the only pilot ever to persuade Piper to make him a short wing version of a J-3 to improve its aerobatic performance. (Beverly E. Howard, Jr. Collection)

"It took several weeks of hanging around before they finally saw the light and decided that a Cub was what they needed for flight instruction," he recalled.

"I never did get any formal sales training," Strohmeier said. "Closest thing to it was a little booklet which Ted Weld gave me that preached neatness in appearance. The sales routine consisted mainly of getting a prospect to fly the airplane, and this led to an occasional 'hairy' situation when a prospect you thought could fly couldn't and put you and your airplane in a perilous situation.

"My salary was $15 a week, and I had an expense allowance of $30 a week for fuel, food, lodging, taxis, and maybe a beer," he said. "I sometimes ran out of money, so on Tuesdays I would send a telegram to Bradford telling where to send the checks for me to get them on Friday. Often the checks and I never got together on Friday. I had to barnstorm and sell rides to make a few bucks so I could eat, and often had to bargain with cab drivers for a ride from a boarding house to the airport in trade for an airplane ride."

There was another way to make a few dollars. To encourage the Cub salesmen to keep moving, they received an extra dollar a night for every different town where they remained overnight. If they decided to stay in a town more than one night, they lost any further bonus for that locality. If they were able to sell a plane at a location, they received an extra $25.00. If a buyer wanted to buy the demonstration airplane, he had to pay an extra $10.00 for the magnetic compass; otherwise, the salesman removed it and brought it back to the plant:

"Ted Weld told me to remove the compass before you made a sale," Strohmeier recalled, "because after you make the deal, you wouldn't be able to say the compass was extra. Well, I ran into a hot prospect in Waterville, Maine, and made a deal on the spot before I could remove the compass that probably cost the factory four bucks. When I got back to Bradford, Ted said my new demonstrator was ready, and the boys were waiting to install my compass. When I

"Bevo" Howard was head of several flying training schools during World War II. He performed frequently for graduating classes to show that the Cub could do much more than just fly straight and level. (Beverly E. Howard, Jr. Collection)

Proof that a modified Cub could be flown safely by an experienced pilot upside down is demonstrated by Beverly "Bevo" Howard's famous low altitude inverted fly-by. (Beverly E. Howard, Jr., Collection)

Al Bennett was one of several pilots who proved that a Cub on floats could be landed safely on grass landing fields. The plane slid along to a normal and gentle stop. It could also take off from landing fields, but required more power and takeoff distance than if on wheels. (EDO Aircraft Corporation)

sheepishly told Ted my story, all he said was, 'too bad.' They also were short of altimeters at the time, so I spent the fall of 1936 trying to sell airplanes around Virginia and the Carolinas without a compass and an altimeter.

"Almost everywhere I went I found deep disdain among airport operators for the Cub. They did their training in OX-5-powered, open cockpit Wacos or similar biplanes, which were expensive to operate; they usually also had a Stinson or Waco cabin plane for charter work. A Cub, to them, was just a powered glider. It was tough trying to sell them on the benefits of teaching students in an enclosed cockpit and of the economy of operation."

The Cub's salesmen benefited from much favorable publicity generated by air shows and record-setting. Strohmeier met a barnstorming pilot named Mike Murphy who performed stunts in light planes at air shows. At the Miami Air Maneuvers in 1936, Murphy asked if he could borrow the demonstrator Cub for an act he was planning. He wanted to see if he could land the Cub on a scaffold

mounted on top of a Dodge coupe while speeding down the runway. It sounded like a hair-brained idea to Strohmeier, and he felt the company would take a dim view of it, but Murphy persisted and Strohmeier finally gave in. He was successful, and a photo of the Cub climbing away from the car made the front page of the

New York Daily News and was copied by many newspapers across the country. His stunt was duplicated later by many other performers with variations. When Weld asked how he had managed such a great publicity coup, Strohmeier just grinned.

Murphy had taken possession of an abandoned airport at Kokomo, Indiana, in 1930 and formed an aerobatic group known as the Linco Aces. One of the acts included aerobatics in a Ford Tri-motor with neon lighting. In an effort to attract customers willing to pay for rides, Murphy perfected original aerobatic stunts in Cubs that gained him national acclaim and an international following. In addition to being the first to take off and land on a moving automobile, he was the first to take off and land a standard pontoon seaplane on land without damage.

One way to slow a Cub down on landing is to use a drag 'chute. This technique was later used on certain military aircraft and the Space Shuttle. (Beverly E. Howard, Jr., Collection)

Pilots Danny Fowlie and Don Berent used two Cubs, one mounted on top of the other, for their act during pre-World War II air shows. They would take off, perform aerobatics, and land separately. Both are designated as Experimental by their registration numbers. (Jim Marshall, Jr., Collection)

Strohmeier later visited Murphy's home town in Kokomo in 1938 and saw Murphy perform what he termed "the most superhuman feats any pilot had ever done." Murphy had an upside down airplane built from Cub and Taylorcraft parts. It had two cockpits and two landing gears, one real and the other for show. Mike strapped himself in the lower, upside-down cockpit, while his friend Bill Moose got into the upper cockpit as a safety pilot. Mike's act was to take off while hanging upside down, then do some rolls and half rolls, then land upside down again. This meant every control movement was opposite to what was normal. When Mike finished the first test hop he admitted it was the most difficult flying he had ever done. His first solo flight without a safety pilot in the upper plane was at the Cleveland Air Races in 1939 and, according to Strohmeier, it looked so easy and routine that the crowd hardly applauded.

Strohmeier spent much time getting to know the air show performers in his territory and persuading them to use Cubs in their acts. Dick Granere, a famous Canadian World War I ace, used a Cub for a hilarious drunken flying act. Pilots Danny Fowlie and Don Berent used two Cubs, one mounted upright on top of the other. They would take off together and do acrobatics, then would break

Attempting to "prop" a Cub engine in flight is not recommended as this pilot is doing. It is not known if this was a stunt, or if the engine actually had a malfunction. (James Sara Collection)

A J-3 Cub with a Super Cub rudder makes a one-float take off from the Salton Sea. Flying Cubs on floats requires special techniques, and pilots are advised to take a special course from experienced instructors. (Don Downie Collection)

away and perform individual acts before hooking up again and landing.

Mr. Piper appreciated the publicity value in showing the Cubs off to the public in other ways. He conceived the idea of sending out trios of Cubs on barnstorming trips. His son Tony led one group:

"They would buzz a town, put on some razzle-dazzle aerobatics, then land at a nearby field and sell passenger rides," Strohmeier said. "This was supposed to make the whole operation self-supporting."

Strohmeier developed an act of his own at air shows. He would put a dozen rolls of toilet tissue in his lap, climb to 1,500 feet and throw them out one by one. He then turned back to clip the descending streamers in two. Later he found it was more dramatic if he threw the rolls out at the top of a loop and chased them down as he completed the loop.

One unusual stunt by air show performers was hand-propping a Cub's stopped engine while in flight. The pilot credited with starting it was featured in Ripley's "*Believe It or Not*" series in national newspapers. He was Roland Maheux of Lewiston, Maine. The stunt reportedly began when Maheux was flying with a student when the engine quit. He had the student hold the brakes while he got out, held on to the window frame, placed his right foot on the wheel and flipped the prop to start the engine. He did this stunt many times afterwards solo at air shows at a very low altitude so the public could see that the engine was not operating until he propped it as he flew by.

***

A Cub with experimental pneumatic floats was tested for landings on ice, as shown here. However, they would expand at altitude, and some of the air would bleed off. Wooden floats were tried, but were also unsuccessful. Amphibious floats provided the solution for water and airport landings. (Peter M. Bowers Collection)

NOTICE
BEVEL
2 Point Black line
no white line between Picture
and line at top and bottom.
only

Endurance flying often required in-flight engine maintenance. *Miss Dairylea's* windshield was modified to allow pilot Merrill Phoenix to check the engine during a record-setting 106-hour flight in September 1938. (Russell Phelinger Collection)

As the sales force beat the bushes for sales, Walter Jamouneau was appointed chief engineer in late 1936 on a salaried basis. The workforce was then on two shifts, and the output rose to 18 planes a week. Advertising increased, and it looked like 1937 was going to top the previous year in sales. But 1937 was to be a memorable year in the history of the Cub for another reason.

The original building where the Cubs were assembled had to have additions constructed as production increased, but the entire ramshackle, make-do complex was a fire hazard. However, W.T. Piper, Sr., and Jr. felt the premiums for industrial fire insurance were excessive for the shops and buildings valued at about $200,000. They decided not to pay an annual premium more than $14,000 to cover the plant and the growing inventory of planes being assembled indoors. There was no sprinkler system, the town water hydrants did not reach to the factory, the airport had a run-down fire engine manned by a volunteer crew, and the Bradford fire station was many blocks away from the airport. The paint shop was particularly vulnerable, with barrels of flammable cellulose nitrate dope on hand that was used on the planes' fabric. There were a few hand fire extinguishers hanging on wall racks and a fire hose or two, but that was about the extent of the fire protection that was available.

On the night of March 16, 1937, at 10:30 PM, several explosions were heard by Bradford residents. Two stories about what happened have been told. One is that two members of the 20-man night crew were using an electric drill on the firewall of a Cub. A spark from the drill spun off as it hit a piece of metal and landed in some nitrate-soaked rags on the floor. There was an instant ignition, and flames engulfed the plane and spread quickly to nearby wood spars, lacquer thinner, and gasoline.

Endurance flights using Cubs during the 1930s were refueled and re-supplied by pickups from a moving automobile. Here Tom Smith and Clyde Schleiper receive a food package at Lancaster, California, in *The Little Bear* during their record-setting flight of 218 hrs., 23 min. October 23-November 2, 1938. (Piper Aviation Museum)

Clyde Schleiper and Wes Carroll in September-October 1939 set what is believed to be the current endurance record in a Cub: 726 hours. They estimated they flew 55,000 miles and made 1,547 pickups of gas and 75 gallons of oil. (Russell Phelinger Collection)

One-wheel landings were favorite end-of-show finales for famous Cub aerobatic pilots like Beverly "Bevo" Howard (shown here), Mike Murphy, and Dick Schram. (Piper Aviation Museum)

The other story is that a furnace located near the paint shop overheated and the heat had interacted with the nitrate fumes and flashed into an uncontrollable fire. Whatever the reason, the closely parked planes under construction caught on fire as the flammable materials on hand instantly leaped into a huge blaze and spread throughout the wood sections of the main building. The flames were enhanced by a brisk wind blowing across the landing strip when the main doors were opened by escaping workers. Explosions occurred when the flames reached a stack of five gallon cans of nitrate dope and spread the fire further throughout the plant. Employees quickly moved about 15 nearly-completed planes not yet on

fire outside to the snow-covered parking area, but could not save any more. In less than two hours, despite the help of firemen from the Bradford Central Fire Station, most of the factory was completely destroyed. Fortunately, everyone inside had escaped unhurt.

Most of the management team was out of town. W.T. Piper, Sr., was in Los Angeles attending the Pacific Aircraft Show when he got the bad news from Ted Weld, then general manager. He had to spend nearly four days driving to get back to Bradford. Bill Piper, Jr., was at home in Bradford, but did not know about the fire until the next morning. Tony Piper, who had recently joined the firm, was in Georgia on a sales trip. Walter Jamouneau had just returned

One air show feature is this daring stunt by a man who has been picked up from a car by a Cub Super Cruiser and then is pulled through a pile of burning wood before climbing inside the cockpit. (Peter M. Bowers Collection)

This J-3 Cub's owner, for reasons not explained, elected to re-cover his aircraft with a transparent plastic material. Note that the wings have been shortened and the tips squared off. (Peter M. Bowers Collection)

from Ottawa negotiating for a Canadian certificate of airworthiness and establishing a sales organization there. Bill Strohmeirer was in Key West, Florida, and did not learn about the fire for three days. He received a telegram in Miami saying that the future was uncertain and that he may not have a job. He was instructed to sell the demonstrator or fly home with it. Meanwhile, other sales and management personnel hurried to the scene to assess the damage, which was estimated at about $200,000. The factory was a total loss.

Piper said the insurance they had been able to buy at extremely high rates amounted to only ten thousand dollars, or about one-twentieth of the value of the planes and equipment. He thought at first it meant the end of the Taylor Aircraft Corporation:

Crop dusting became one of the Cub's many useful agricultural tasks. Different cockpit and other modifications have been made to spray chemicals as well. Here one swoops low over fruit trees to kill larvae. (Piper Aviation Museum)

"Things were not absolutely hopeless, however," he wrote in his memoir. "Some jigs and tools were salvaged. New materials were promptly forthcoming from our suppliers. An old foundry building and a few abandoned garages were rented in Bradford, and in these makeshift workshops our boys managed to build a Cub within one week of the fire. The courage and determination these men showed undoubtedly made it easier for me to raise funds for a new factory."

Employees, not knowing if they would be paid, nevertheless had gone to work to see what they could salvage to complete the planes that were saved. There were some manufacturing items like fuselage and metal-bending jigs, hand tools, and metal parts that could be recovered from the ruins of the factory, and assembly slowly resumed in a borrowed hangar on the airport to fill more than 75 orders that were on hand. When Jamoumeau found that all the drawings and blueprints had been lost, he called the Civil Aeronautics Authority headquarters at the Department of Commerce in Washington and requested copies of the J-2 drawings that were on file. Slowly, Cubs began to be assembled again in parts of the factory that had been reconstructed, as well as in an empty building in town; when assembly was completed, the latter were trucked to the airport to be test flown and ferried to buyers.

The fire could not have come at a worse time. It seemed that the corner to profitability had just been turned, and the orders had been increasing daily. But the pragmatic elder Piper, an optimist at heart, had returned from Los Angeles with a financial plan in mind to save the company. With the help of friends, he was able to obtain a promise of credit for a reported $100,000 from a New York banker. With that assurance he was determined to resume production, but there were many decisions to be made. He authorized the transfer of some parts from Bradford to a plant operated by Aircraft Associates, Inc. in Long Beach, California, a Cub distributor that had obtained approval for assembly. These became known as the "West-

Many duster operators modified their Cubs to satisfy local crop requirements. This owner chose to customize the fuselage and square off the wing tips. (Jay Miller Collection)

ern Cubs" and filled orders from West Coast distributors and buyers. A week after Piper's return from Los Angeles, the first Cub built of salvaged parts at Bradford was in the air.

On the fire site, after the debris was cleared away, several small wooden buildings were hurriedly constructed or repaired and new patterns and jigs were reproduced by using completed planes as a guide. Space for management offices was obtained at the airport's administrative building; hangar space on the airport was loaned by a local owner, and production resumed in a hodge-podge of locations, including an iron foundry.

It was quickly obvious that the company could not continue to function long under these hectic conditions. Should the factory be rebuilt, or should the whole operation move to another location?

"It became apparent by November 1937 that reorganization was necessary," Piper recalled, "not only production-wise, but financially as well. I found myself holding all of the company's stock, which wasn't very practical from a number of standpoints. Consequently, I sold it all back to the company in return for common stock."

By the end of 1937 future sales prospects seemed exceptionally bright, and Piper needed additional financing to expand. He went on a money-search, but found that investors were wary about the company that still bore the founder's name. Taylor was now manufacturing his own planes as Taylorcraft, and his small magazine advertisements implied that he was succeeding in garnering increasing orders for his own design. Potential buyers, salesmen, and distributors of Cubs encountered this resistance in their sales efforts and the latter, especially, wanted a company name change.

This criticism had merit, and Piper agreed to change the company name to Piper Aircraft Corporation in November 1937. In March 1938 the company went public with a stock offering totaling $250,000.

There seemed to be an undercurrent of antipathy for the company in Bradford after the fire. Its wages were low compared to what the oilfield workers were drawing. It was still an oil town at heart, and airplanes did not fascinate the local populace as much as

they did before the fire. Relocation offers were received from more than two dozen city fathers, bankers, and politicians in Oklahoma, Texas, Illinois, Indiana, and California who were looking for new industries to broaden their tax base and provide jobs in areas still suffering from the Depression. William Piper, Sr., talked it over with his oldest son, and they agreed that they should consider a move where they could reconstitute the enthusiasm they had developed originally in Bradford and resume the growing rate of Cub production they had before the fire. William Sr. was in favor of considering only those locations where the company would not have to compete with a labor force that was used to high wages, such as the West Coast cities with established aircraft manufacturing plants, or cities like Detroit and Pittsburgh with their steel and automobile high wages and unionized workers.

One of the aggressive towns that sought Piper's attention was Lock Haven, Pennsylvania, a small community in Clinton County on the flood-prone West Branch of the Susquehanna River, 85 miles south of Bradford. It had been incorporated as a borough in 1840 and was the terminus of the Pennsylvania Canal. It was named for its last canal lock and the safe haven across from it.

An enthusiastic young man named Jacob W. "Jake" Miller had learned to fly in a Taylor E-2 Cub and was a Cub distributor and flight service operator under the corporate name of Bald Eagle Airways, located beside Lock Haven's sod runway. He approached the Chamber of Commerce and suggested that the large Susquehanna Silk Mill, vacant since 1932 and on the other side of the airfield, would be ideal for making airplanes. It had a Pennsylvania Railroad siding on one side of the property and the airport on the other. The abandoned mill, with its long, narrow two-story building with about 100,000 square feet of space, was available. Most important, it was available at about 10 percent of its original cost.

Piper sent Ted Weld, the general manager, and Gordon M. Curtis, a financier and friend of the Pipers, to Lock Haven to check out the abandoned property. They liked what they saw and began negotiations with the Chamber of Commerce, the Lock Haven Trust Co., National City Bank of New York, and the realty firm in New York City that was seeking a buyer for the property. The asking price was originally $130,000, but was quickly reduced to $95,000.

The property included 16 acres of land and ten company-owned houses. The mill was constructed of steel, brick, and reinforced concrete, and had a sprinkler system installed throughout with a 50,000 gallon water tank as a reserve. The inside space of 100,000 square feet was more than was needed at the time. The West Branch of the Susquehanna River provided excellent facilities for seaplane flying. The City of Lock Haven agreed to construct a 2,000-foot hard surface runway if the company would agree to move. The Cub had found a new home.

***

Lock Haven had a 160-year history by this time and had been a lumbering town from 1830 to the 1880s. It had been known as Old Town during Revolutionary War days and was located in a broad valley between what one writer called "two brooding, misty mountains," with the Susquehanna River running between them.

The silk mill had begun operations just after World War I and had been an early victim of the Depression. The area had suffered a devastating flood in 1936, and the inhabitants who stayed would welcome a new business that would boost its economy. The cost of living was lower than in Bradford, which made it doubly attractive to the cost-conscious elder Piper. The town needed an industry, and Piper needed a sympathetic populace in a location with lower costs of operation.

The move from Bradford began in mid-summer of 1937 with the help of about 200 employees who had agreed to relocate. The production of the J-2 began as soon as possible in Lock Haven, and Piper told Jamouneau he wanted further improvements made in appearance, efficiency of operation, and comfort. While the J-2s continued to be produced into 1938 and more than 1,150 E-2s and

Bill Strohmeier (right) gives golf pro "Red" Richardson pre-flight instruction before a demonstration flight in a Cub Coupe. Strohmeier says "the deal was reciprocal." (William D. Strohmeier Collection)

J-2s were built, Jamouneau made subtle but effective changes in the design of the vertical stabilizer and elevators. One improvement from the pilot's standpoint was substitution of a tail wheel for the metal tail skid for easier taxiing and operations on hard-surfaced runways. The two hard plywood seats were enhanced with upholstered cushions, and all control wires were concealed from the interior. The instrument panel was improved with the addition of a magnetic compass, tachometer, oil pressure gauge, and an airspeed indicator. A better grade of steel tubing was approved for the fuselage and engine mount; the latter thus enabled heavier engines with higher horsepower to be installed. Again, a new model designation was required to reflect these changes.

The result was the J-3 Cub Trainer, which was introduced in the late fall of 1937 and was priced at $995 with the 40-hp Continental engine, the first new airplane ever to be sold in the United States for less than $1,000. The Cub buyer also had a choice of Continental, Franklin, and Lycoming 50-hp engines. Cub production in the company's first full year at Lock Haven totaled 701 aircraft, of which 687 were J-2s. The J-3 designation for the Cub and the aircraft designation by Douglas as DC-3 for its outstanding airliner would become the two most well-known aircraft numerical labels of all aircraft models in the world.

***

Tony and Pug Piper, the latter still in college but home for a vacation, were asked to see what they could do to design a tail wheel brake that would be operated by a cable from the cockpit, but it was unsatisfactory. They then worked on foot brakes for the Cub and helped devise the heel brake which, coupled with a swiveling tail wheel, enabled the Cub to operate more easily from hard-surface runways. The heel brakes were operable from either cockpit, but were not popular with most pilots and seemed unnatural compared with the toe brakes of other aircraft. However, brakes were greatly needed to make the Cub easier to taxi.

The most noticeable change of all during this period was the paint scheme for the J-3s. Instead of the silver, red, blue, or green colors used on the J-2s, the J-3s were painted in an overall bright yellow with a black trim stripe on both sides from nose to tail. The teddy bear logo was placed on each side of the vertical stabilizer. Later, the mustardy "Lock Haven Yellow" became brighter when butyrate dope replaced nitrate after World War II. This was then known as "Cub Yellow," and is one of the colors adopted by the makers of Crayola wax crayons used by thousands of kids today.

The color change made the Cubs more discernible to other aircraft in flight, especially in a training environment, where pilot visibility is limited because of the high-wing design of the Cubs. The bright yellow was also more easily seen if an aircraft were downed in a wooded area. The teddy bear logo became a standard addition on both sides of the vertical stabilizer.

A sales gimmick that was used by Cub dealers was the Piper Junk Box, which was sold or given to buyers. Made of tin like a child's lunch box, it contained J-3 consumables, such as bushings, bolts, cotter pins, etc. It is not known if any of these boxes survived but, if so, they are desired by the Piper Aviation Museum for display.

***

During this period of growth of light aircraft, engineers from the Lycoming Company and the Franklin Aircooled Engine Company proposed 50-horsepower engines that were made available to Cub buyers. Thus, the three engines—Lycoming, Franklin, and Continental—sold in nearly equal numbers from 1939 to 1941. However, when the Army later asked for planes to use in maneuvers, they were equipped with Continentals, since they developed a little more power than the others. All light planes delivered to the Army during World War II—the L-2s, L-3s, and L-4s—were powered by the same Continental engine.

The Continental engines were further improved and were made available in 40-, 50-, 60-, and 65-horsepower versions. The planes were offered to customers in three model versions, depending on the type of engine selected. The choices ranged from the Continental 40, Franklin, Lycoming, and Continental 50s, to the Franklin 60 and Continental 65. The end result was the emergence of three versions of the improved J-3 aircraft: Cub Trainer, Cub Sport, and later the Cub Sea Scout, which was a tandem Cub on floats. The variety of engines of varying horsepower available gave each model a different "dash number" indication and allowed higher useful loads to be carried, as the engine power was increased.

The Cub Sport was a plushed-up Trainer with wider rear seat, whipcord upholstery, an additional five inches of room in the front seat, a rear vision overhead mirror, and a streamlined instrument panel with cut-outs for more instruments that could be added as buyers requested.

Development was started on a new Cub with side-by-side seating that was faster and larger than the Trainer. It was labeled the J-4 Cub Coupe and was marketed primarily to private owners, rather than to flying school operators. It was first shown at the 1938 National Air Races in Cleveland, and production started in early 1939. Slightly larger and faster than the Cub Trainer, the Cub Coupe's most threatening rival was the Taylorcraft, which had begun its production following the side-by-side seating configuration as Taylor had done with the original Chummy. But the Piper J-4 was considered a step up in comfort, easier handling with hydraulic brakes, full-swiveling tail wheel, oleo shock absorbers, lights, compass, additional fuel capacity for four hours of flight, and space for over 100 lbs of baggage. Inside, it featured new standards of beauty and finish. It became an instant success.

The prices in 1938 ranged from the Cub Trainer ($1,098), Cub Sport ($1,148), to the Cub Coupe ($1,249). A three-cylinder Lenape

LM-3-50 radial engine also was used to power about a dozen Cub Trainers at $1,595. Seaplanes cost $1,793 upward, depending on engine power.

Spars and ribs used in the wings had been made of Oregon spruce, which was getting increasingly scarce. The substitute was an aluminum alloy that would resist corrosion and fatigue. The last of the J-2s and all J-3s used all-metal wing spars, which increased the life span of the Cubs and reduced the ever-present possibility of wing failures. Engine noise was reduced by the use of stainless steel exhaust mufflers.

Production methods were also improved and could be compared to Henry Ford's famous moving production lines for assembly of his automobiles. A rotating wheel arrangement was constructed in the Piper dope shop that held twelve wings and six fuselages; the wheel would rotate, and painters would spray each piece as it passed by. By the time one piece completed the cycle, it was ready for a second coat. Production was speeded up further when a monorail conveyor system was installed in the ceiling that enabled workers to work easily on their specific portion of a wing or fuselage and move it to the next station. This was an industry "first" in aircraft production.

At this time, according to the 1938 *Aircraft Year Book* that reviewed industry advances:

"...one of the most significant developments in the merchandizing of light aircraft was engineered by the Piper Aircraft Co. in

Piper publicists used cooperative Hollywood movie stars to spread the word about the Cub and its later models. Here actors Claudette Colbert and Ray Milland pose beside a Cub Coupe. It is not known if they took lessons in it. Women were advised to wear slacks for flying. (Paramount Photo)

the introduction of a successful finance plan with interest rates comparable to those charged for the purchase of an automobile."

A plane could be flown from Lock Haven with a down payment of $333 and the rest in easy payments; this included a flying course of eight hours of dual instruction, which was offered free, after which "the average person is ready to solo," according to magazine advertisements.

In a further unique promotion to call attention to Piper planes, a Cub Trainer with a Continental 65-hp engine was given away each Friday night in 1940 and 1941 during the "Wings of Destiny" program on a 92-station national hookup of NBC Radio.

Emphasis was not only placed on owning a Cub for pleasure, but for use by individuals for various business purposes. The possible ways that business enterprises could be developed using Cubs were by selling new ones, student instruction, charter flights, plane rentals, crop dusting, organizing flying clubs, aerial photography, passenger flights, aerial delivery service, and aerial advertising.

Sales were increasing as these improvements, changes, and opportunities were publicized widely, and the company announced that a total of 90 Cubs had been sold during August 1937 alone for a total of 452 since the previous January 1. This was compared to the previous production of Cubs that showed only 57 had been sold between 1931 and 1933, 70 in 1934, 211 in 1935, and 551 by the end of 1936.

Foreign shipments of Cubs were leaving the factory at a rate of more than two a week. Twenty-seven Cubs were shipped to Denmark in dismantled form, along with jigs and dies so that the balance of manufacture and assembly would be done there. Half a dozen Cubs were shipped to England, and a pilot named Charles Gardner won the 1936 King's Cup Race for light aircraft flying a Cub.

With an established agency representation in 40 countries by this time, more than 100 Cubs were in active service throughout the world. An assembly plant in Hamilton, Ontario, was preparing three Cubs a week for the Canadian market.

There were a number of competitors who were trying to give the impression that they were matching Piper's growth, as indicated by their advertisements in the aviation magazines. The public was made increasingly aware of such names as Luscombe, Rearwin, Porterfield, Aeronca, Waco, Interstate, Stinson, Welch, and Ercoupe.

By this time private flying for business and pleasure was increasing rapidly. Those who could not afford the price of a small plane or did not want the responsibility of individual ownership formed clubs whose members owned a plane in common. Air meets and races were frequent. Kits for making model airplanes were widely available; airplanes and air exploits of the stunt and racing pilots were subjects of specialized magazines. In spite of the Depression, young people were getting caught up in the exciting world of aviation.

The future depended on Piper's sales force to reach out and publicize the "New Cub" that was being touted in the aviation magazines. Bill Strohmeirer, a creative salesman, told of his experience in attracting public attention to the Cub's capabilities and safety. He had a prospective buyer in Cocoa Beach, Florida, who was interested in buying an Aeronca that was powered with a two-cylinder engine. To show the value of a four-cylinder engine versus an engine with only two, he disconnected the wire to one of his Cub's spark plugs and started the engine. He took off, circled the field and landed. He suggested to the prospect that he ask the Aeronca salesman to do the same and determine which plane he would rather fly. He sold a Cub that day.

Strohmeier continued his contacts with air show performers, and one of those noted for his precision aerobatic ability to perform unusual maneuvers in a Cub during inverted flight was Beverly E. "Bevo" Howard. He helped spread the name of the Piper Cub far and wide as few other pilots had ever done. A South Carolina native, he learned to fly while a junior in high school. He made his

One of the unusual acts at air shows was Mike Murphy's "Pick-a-Back" Cubs. This photo shows how the top J-3C was attached to the lower one. The bottom Cub's gear was strengthened to absorb the extra weight. (Peter M. Bowers Collection)

first parachute jump for the fun of it at age 17. He became a pilot for Eastern Air Lines flying Douglas DC-2s, and was one of the youngest airline pilots in the country at the time. He joined the Hawthorne Flying Service as assistant manager in 1932 and bought the company in 1936. It became one of the civilian-owned Army Air Force primary pilot training bases during World War II.

"Bevo" took up acrobatics and won National Lightplane Acrobatic Championship titles at Miami in 1939, 1940, and 1941 flying a 37-hp J-2 Cub. He was a featured performer at major pre-war air shows, such as the National Air Races at Cleveland, Miami All-American Air Maneuvers at Miami, the International Air Meet at Havana, Cuba, and other top shows. His act included two slow rolls immediately after takeoff, inverted 360-degree turns, inverted 4-point rolls, inverted snap rolls and spins, an outside loop, and an inverted ribbon clip. He concluded each show with an inverted glide and half roll to a landing.

Howard later used a J-3 "Special" with 3 1/2 feet clipped off at the root of each wing made by Piper to his specifications. It was originally equipped with a 75-hp Continental engine and a fixed-pitch propeller. In 1946 he installed an 85-hp Continental engine and a Sensenich controllable-pitch prop. The wing struts were heavier, with stiffeners inside them, and Piper provided a specially-built landing gear that was the experimental gear used on the PA-12 Super Cruiser. The engine fuel system was equipped with a fuel injector, and a floating line was installed in the gasoline tank so that the engine could run in any position of the plane.

Not only was Howard's show always a surprise to many who had believed a light plane would be incapable of such aerobatics, but it was especially awe-inspiring to watch, as the slow-flying plane seemed to float with an almost unbelievable grace through each maneuver. Howard disliked the term "stunt flying" and flew in a business suit and tie to project the image that flying could be safe, enjoyable, and within the reach of everyone.

"Bevo" Howard became one of Piper's greatest advocates before World War II and campaigned on his own to persuade the government to buy Pipers for training military pilots. In a magazine article in a pre-war issue of the *Dixie Air News* he said:

"Here is an airplane that has taught more people to fly than the Army and Navy put together in the last five years. Moreover, it has been the largest single factor in making the country air-conscious and getting more people into the air than any other airplane, and in my opinion, it is the airplane to use in this work.

"The Piper company in the Lock Haven plant can, if necessary, produce 1,000 Trainers a month. Compare this with the approximately 300 per month that is now being turned out by the manufacture of the trainer [the Stearman] that we are now using [at Hawthorne Flying Service]. Compare the price of $12,000 for one and approximately $2,000 for the other. Compare the fuel consumption of 12 gallons an hour against five. Then, of course, compare

performance and maneuverability. There is nothing that one can do that the other cannot do just as well."

"So, as you can see, it was through no effort on my part," Strohmeier reminisced modestly. "Air show pilots started using Cubs, and their acts helped establish the Cub as a household name."

Strohmeier joined Hawthorne Aviation as a flying instructor during World War II, and the two collaborated on a book titled *You Can Learn to Fly* published by Prentice-Hall of New York in 1944.

***

The 1930s were the years of record-setting, and many light plane pilots were vying to put their names in the aviation record books by setting endurance records. In June 1937, Norman B. Doerr established an endurance record with a 40-hp Continental-powered J-2 Cub by flying around Chicago for 24 hours, 2 minutes. He refueled by hauling up five-gallon cans of gasoline from a speeding automobile, a method that was used by succeeding record-setters. Two months later two Detroit pilots, Charles Davis and Gottlieb Bauer, set a new record of 25 hours, 21 minutes, also in a J-2. Their record was broken by Elmer Westerlund and Darrell Roote, two

Capt. Dick Schramm, Cub showman, always opened his show posing with a book purporting to give him flight instructions. (Author's Collection)

pilots from Jackson, Michigan, when they flew for 29 hours, 5 minutes. They had a 15-gallon tank installed in the belly of a J-3 Cub and departed the Jackson Municipal Airport to set a new record of 29 hours, 5 minutes, 5 seconds. The plane was refueled 43 times by contacting a speeding pickup truck on the ground with a dangling 32-foot rope used to exchange five-gallon gas cans back and forth. The pilot had to line up with the truck accurately, maintain a speed above stalling, and judge the proper altitude for the refueling man in the rear of the truck to catch the rope and make the exchange. This endurance flight was eclipsed by Russ Finefrock and Howard Naylor of Tyler, Texas, who used this refueling technique to fly a J-2 Cub for 36 hours, 18 minutes before calling it quits.

If it worked for these flights, perhaps it could be used to put Cubs in the news for more sensational news coverage. Someone at the Piper headquarters, probably Ted Weld, asked Kenneth T. Kress, chief pilot for Piper, who had the reported record of having tested more than 1,350 Cubs, if he would like to help celebrate the 20th anniversary of the first air mail service in the United States that had been started by the U.S. Army Air Service in May 1918. The plan was to fly from Newark to Miami in a Cub—a distance of more than 1,100 miles—and return without landing. He would be accompanied by Glenn Englert, a fellow Piper employee.

Kress and Englert agreed to try. Their plan was to equip a Cub J-3 with extra gas tanks and a three-cylinder Lenape Papoose radial engine and leave Newark on May 17, 1938. They practiced the fuel can pick-up many times from automobile-to-airplane, the same basic technique used by Westerlund and Roote. When satisfied, they took off after having previously made arrangements to refuel in flight at the Raleigh, North Carolina, Airport, then proceed to Jacksonville, Florida, for a second refueling. The fuel transfer worked satisfactorily at Raleigh and Jacksonville, despite windy weather, as volunteer helpers passed them the cans during each fly-by. It wasn't easy, as the Cub had to keep well above its 38-miles-per-hour normal stalling speed because of the extra weight, and the trucks had to accelerate to the plane's speed in the space of a 3,500-foot runway to make the exchange of cans and then stop before careening off the end of the runway.

The New Cub Sport J-3 was introduced in 1937 after the company moved to Lock Haven. It was remembered as the model that was eventually reduced to an all-time low price of $995 for J-3s in 1940. (Piper Aviation Museum)

It was now getting dark, and the ceilings were low after leaving Jacksonville. Their radio was not picking up clear radio range signals, so Kress orbited for a while before heading south, but became uncertain of their position in the poor visibility. He returned to Jacksonville and orbited around the dimly-lit city. Their refueling friends there had left when the last can of gas had been transferred and were not available to refuel them. Fortunately, a weather man at the airport had observed the refueling earlier and heard the Cub circling endlessly. He used his own pickup truck, and with the help of a friend supplied the gas so they could try again to proceed to Miami. They plunged on southward through uncertain weather and darkness.

Kress and Englert had not planned to refuel at Miami, but the Lenape engine company, anxious for them to succeed, had a man on the scene who had fortuitously arranged for fuel—just in case. They were supplied once more by an automobile refueler and returned to Jacksonville at daybreak, where they filled the belly and main tanks and took on several extra five-gallon cans, which Kress stored behind his seat. They also hauled up a new radio battery. However, during one of the passes at the airport Kress plowed through a tree top and broke the right wheel pant fairing. Fortunately, it did not interfere with the Cub's flying characteristics, and they plunged on northward under low ceilings for a final refueling at Raleigh. The thoroughly tired and deafened pair arrived at Newark at 8 PM on May 20 after flying 2,399 miles. They had been in the air for a world record mark of 63 hours, 54 minutes, despite the noise and teeth-shattering vibration of the three-cylinder Lenape engine.

The record did not last long. Two pilots (Ted Merrill and Mark Peters) set a new record of 67 hours in a J-3 Cub at Reno, Nevada, September 2-5, 1938. Not to be outdone, Merrill Phoenix, an airline pilot, and Harold Allen, a student pilot, took off in a Franklin-powered J-3 Cub named *Miss Dairylea* from the New York State Fair Grounds at Syracuse, New York, on September 2, 1938. One innovation was a small cot that had been extended back into the fuselage, a modification that was adopted to turn the Cub into an ambulance plane during World War II. An extra gas tank was added under the cockpit. They were refueled by friends from a speeding car at the Syracuse Airport and other locations. They shattered the other endurance records by flying 106 hours, 3 minutes, and estimated they had flown more than 7,000 miles on 287 gallons of gas that had been pulled in during more than 55 passes. They made an additional 25 contacts with their fast-driving friends for food and supplies.

Their record did not last long, either. Two months later Tom Smith and Clyde Schleiper, flying a J-3 Cub *The Little Bear* from Lancaster, California, in November 1938 set a new light plane world endurance record of 218 hours, 23 minutes. Smith got sick during the early hours of the flight and parachuted, leaving Schleiper alone until Harley Long climbed a rope ladder from a speeding automobile and joined him. Later, Schleiper bailed out and was substituted by Smith, who had recuperated.

In the summer of 1939, not to be outdone, the Moody brothers Hunter and Humphrey flew a Lycoming-powered Taylorcraft non-stop for 343 hours, 46 minutes, which was more than 14 days aloft. To outdo the Cub's chief competitor, this record was eclipsed in Muncie, Indiana, by Kelvin F. Baxter and Robert McDaniels, who finally decided to land their Cub Sport after being airborne for 535 hours, 45 minutes.

Between September 29 and October 29, 1939, Clyde Schlieper and Wes Carroll kept a Cub Sport seaplane named

Kay over southern California for 726 hours. They estimated they had flown nearly 55,000 miles, and had made 1,547 pickups that included 3,000 gallons of gas and 75 gallons of oil. They said they landed only because they were thoroughly worn out, not the engine.

By 1939 Piper had a lot to brag about, including this most recent endurance flight, and did so in full-page advertisements in several 1939 aviation magazines that read as follows:

• Biggest mass flight (185 Cubs) ever held of a single type of commercial plane, in a Light Plane Cavalcade to Miami, Florida, in January 1939. Over 350,000 aggregate miles.
• Production and sales record: 111 planes sold during August 1938. More than any company has produced and sold in any one month since the invention of the airplane in 1903.
• Long Distance non-stop light plane refueling record: 2,399 miles. Held by Kenneth Kress and Glenn Englet flying a Lenape-powered Cub New York-Miami-New York, May 19, 1938.
• First airplane to be used by a civilian training program by a state. Five bought by the Bureau of Aeronautics, Nashville, Tennessee, through its director, for training fifteen selected civilians per year in each of five major cities.

• For the past three years one-third of all aircraft sold commercially in the United States has been Cubs. Last year [1938] this proportion held, with the further distinction that of light plane sales, Cubs accounted for one-half, a record for commercial airplane production.
• Largest civilian mass flight ever held in Canada of one type of plane. First Annual Canadian Cub Tour with 51 Cubs to Hamilton and Toronto, September 1938.
• First airplane to feature free flying course with each plane sold. 5,872 hours were flown worth $38,168 at the average rate of $6.50 per hour for dual instruction eleven months after the offer was made.
• Cub factory [Lock Haven] is located in the "flyingest city in the world," where one out of every 90 inhabitants is a pilot, in contrast to the national average of 1 out of every 3,000.
• Most active flying club in the world uses the Cub. Piper factory employees club, averaging 80 members from month to month, has logged over 7,000 hours in three years.
• More than 20,000 student pilots are taking their training in Cubs—and this number is increasing daily.

Piper ads stated that the demand for Cubs was far exceeding the anticipated schedule of production. One ad boasted:

"Our volume of production has *gone up*; consequently, our unit cost of production has *gone down*. So, we pass on to you new and important savingsÖon many models more than one hundred and fifty dollars."

Experiments were conducted during the summer of 1938 on new 50-hp engines that were introduced by Lycoming and Franklin, as well as Continental. This meant that Cubs would have improved takeoff, faster speed, and better load-carrying capacity, and thus be more useful for the private pilot.

The side-by-side J-4 Cub Coupe was certified in 1938 in an effort to appeal to the private owner, rather than as a trainer for instructional services. The hinged door gave easier entry, and the contour of the fuselage was rounded. Subsequent models in the series had engines of 50- to 75-hp. The last of the series was the J-4E, which was sold in December 1941. (Peter M. Bowers Collection)

This year also saw the introduction of the Piper J-4 Coupe at the 1938 National Air Races, which was a new conception of luxury for light planes. It came complete with hydraulic brakes, lights, compass, and large gas tanks. It was powered with a 50-hp engine at first, then in the spring was approved for 65-hp engines, which gave it much-improved performance.

By the end of 1938 Piper had broken records for civil aircraft production when 737 Piper Cubs left the assembly line. Of that number, 81 were shipped abroad. At this time Piper introduced the concept of a 50/50 advertising campaign for dealers. Under this plan a dealer was given credit in the amount of one-half of one percent of his yearly business at the factory, which he could use for local newspaper advertising and radio plugs. A nationwide outdoor billboard campaign was also instituted, and Strohmeier introduced free matchbooks advertising Piper Cubs with a simple message: "Piper Cub—easy to fly, easy to buy. For only $333 down you can buy a new Piper Cub and learn to fly free." On the inside of each matchbook was a coupon that could be mailed to the company accompanied by a dime, which would purchase a Cub lapel pin or a tie clasp. Along with it would be a booklet titled "How to Fly a Piper Cub." More than 65 million books of matches were distributed nationwide at a cost of 40 cents per thousand.

As a former member of the National Intercollegiate Flying Club, Strohmeier enticed the organization to hold their annual Air Meet at Lock Haven in 1938 with Lock Haven State College as the host. The gathering attracted a large number of college clubs to send pilots and planes to compete for prizes in spot landing, balloon bursting, flour bombing, and other contests to test flying skills; most of the competing planes were Cubs.

The year 1938 had indeed been a banner year for Piper. It was also a year in which dramatic economic and political changes were taking place in all the industrial countries of the world. Piper and other light airplane manufacturers would soon have to vie for survival during a period when governmental emphasis was on building large, fast aircraft for the military services. However, 1,376 Cub Trainers were sold in 1939, in addition to the J-4 Cub Coupes, bringing the total for that year to 1,806. This represented over half of all the non-military planes built in the United States and 80% of all light aircraft.

Piper continued its aggressive promotions in 1940 and 1941. Large full-page color advertisements seeking to promote private flying on behalf of the entire industry were placed in magazines of wide circulation, such as the *Saturday Evening Post, Collier's,* and *Fortune.* Piper received over 75,000 inquiries as a result. An article in a spring issue of *Fortune* noted that Piper was building more airplanes "than any other manufacturer in the world."

Improvements in the Cubs were being made continually. Mufflers were added to all planes, reducing the engine noise to a point where it compared with an automobile traveling at 60 mph. Sound proofing was also built into Piper planes, and a self-starter was available, plus dual ignition, which added a safety factor.

Competition became intense, as more than a dozen manufacturers were marketing planes selling for under $3,000. Aeronca and Taylorcraft were producing embellished models that were also appealing to a public that was now recovering rapidly from the Depression. Piper introduced the three-place Cruiser with a 75-hp Lycoming engine to appeal to families or the businessman, and managed to keep the price under $2,000. At the same time, the side-by-side Cub Coupe was turned out in direct competition with the Taylorcraft, but with the object of improving eye appeal and passenger comfort. The improvements included a more sophisticated-looking instrument panel and upholstery in the cockpit, plus outside refinements from the enclosed engine cowling to streamlined wheel pants.

The self-starter in the Coupe and Cruiser models was a shock cord device weighing less than ten pounds. A shock cord ten feet long was attached to the rudder post and extended forward within the fuselage. It was attached to a cable that ran under the cockpit, then around a pulley to the starter, which had a few gears and a drum. Turning the crank in the cockpit developed tension which, when pushed in, turned the propeller two complete revolutions and started the engine. When not in use, the crank was removed.

Other experimental projects were undertaken which included the Cub Clipper, a four-seat version with a 115-hp engine. The word "Clipper" was brought to the attention of Pan American World Airways lawyers, who threatened suit against Piper. Pan Am's famous seaplanes of that time period were called Clippers, which they claimed was a trademarked name. Rather than fight a costly lawsuit, Piper gave in and renamed it the Pacer.

The company claimed a record delivery of 3,016 Cubs during 1940, 45 percent of all non-military aircraft built in the United States. This was made possible because of many improvements and additions to the Lock Haven plant. Floor space was increased to more than 180,000 square feet, and the monorail system was improved. A new two-story office building was built to house the sales, accounting, and engineering departments The work force was put on a 24-hour shift basis by October 1940, as Cubs were being produced at a rate of 100 a week.

The increased production required expansion of the plant. Recognizing that sales might diminish during the winter, W.T. Piper, Sr., ever the frugal entrepreneur, decided to build two new buildings, forty feet long and side-by-side, instead of one large building. Thus, one building could be shut down to save on heating expenses during the cold months. By the time these two and several other smaller buildings were completed, the Piper plant space had increased to nearly 200,000 square feet.

Another factor that contributed to increased production was the substitution of a lightweight, high strength alloy of aluminum that increased the strength of the Cub's wings. The use of the alloy cut the production time required to make wing frames from several days to two hours.

J-3S seaplanes are beached on the west side of the Susquehanna River at Lock Haven. The proximity of the Piper plant to the river made testing of float planes more convenient. (Piper Aviation Museum)

By this time there were 1,200 employees at Lock Haven. They were unionized under the American Federation of Labor (AF of L), and relations were amicable. The average employee earned 60 cents an hour, 20 cents above the minimum wage.

The Cub Flyers Club, an organization of Piper workers interested in learning to fly, had been formed in 1935 and grew to be the largest flying club in the United States, with 300 active members. It was established by Mr. Piper himself, who felt that workers would understand their jobs better if they knew what the end products were like and how they were used. He turned over one Cub to a small group of workers who were eager to fly. Instruction was free, and flying time was charged at only $1 per hour. More and more employees took up flying, and as sales increased in 1936, Mr. Piper told the club they could have a new Cub if the employees turned out 25 Cubs in a two-week period. If they did, the 25th Cub would be theirs. They could and did, and the club then had two Cubs. The company eventually supplied seven planes and three instructors at no cost to the club. Club members who had earned their licenses were authorized to deliver Cubs from Lock Haven to gain cross-country experience. They received a flat mileage rate, plus aircraft, pilot expenses, and insurance.

The U.S. Forest Service added a number of Cub Coupes to their fleet of planes that were used to detect and patrol forest fires in the Clark National Forest in Missouri. The Coupes were equipped with two-way radios and a 25-gallon gas tank that enabled them to fly for more than five hours. At the same time, the Department of Agriculture purchased a six-plane Cub fleet that was used by the Bureau of Entomology and Plant Quarantine for extensive survey work.

At this time delivery of planes became a problem, as individual buyers found they could not spare the time, or corporations could not send their executive pilots to come to Lock Haven to pick up their planes. Piper authorized employees who had earned their licenses to make the deliveries to individual buyers and distributors. They were reimbursed for their expenses and authorized an additional amount of per diem. Later, Cubs bound for Alaska were delivered dismantled three at a time via a DC-3 operated by Wallace Air Service of Spokane, Washington. They were also placed in box cars and shipped by train to a buyer's destination.

***

It had been three years since the Piper Aircraft Co. had moved from Bradford to Lock Haven, and the original building seemed at first to be considerably more than would ever be necessary for the construction of all the Cubs that would be ordered. Ever frugal in his planning, W.T. Piper, Sr., was hesitant about expanding the factory, yet it was obvious that more inside floor space was needed. Two new buildings were approved that would permit more efficient "straight line" production methods. A complete sprinkler system was installed, and the new buildings made the whole plant a complete unit. With new space for offices, the new plant area represented the largest facility in the United States devoted exclusively to private aircraft manufacture. This gave Piper the capacity to turn out 6,000 planes a year if that many were ordered. By the end of 1940 production reached 125 planes a week.

During that year the Piper Cruiser was added to the Cub Trainer and Cub Sport lines and marketed to airport operators for advanced student instruction, charters, and passenger-carrying. It was a three-place aircraft, with the pilot seated forward and the two passengers aft. Meanwhile, the Piper Coupe was available with a Continental 75-hp engine that gave it approximately a 100 mph cruising speed; added fuel capacity provided a range of over 500 miles. Besides dual ignition and muffler, it had door locks, wheel pants, a wind driven generator, a custom-built radio receiver, and a clock, plus a 105-lb. baggage compartment and two glove compartments.

The year 1941 was another record year for Piper. There were 3,016 aircraft produced, a figure that represented 46 percent of all non-military planes, and 59.8 percent of all airplanes under 100-hp built that year. November marked the month when the 10,000th Piper Cub rolled out of the assembly building at Lock Haven. Coincidentally, the 5,000th Lycoming 65-hp engine was completed and delivered to Lock Haven for installation in a Piper Cruiser.

But the final month of 1941 would be remembered as the time in Piper history when production of planes for civilian use would decline sharply. America was changed forever on December 7, 1941, as the news and the immediate economic impact of the Japanese attack on Pearl Harbor reached Lock Haven. Private plane production would quickly cease. The work force at the Piper factory was stunned, but everyone thought they would be engaged quickly in supporting the war effort by building more planes than ever before, and they would bear the insignia of the American military forces. There was disappointment ahead.

4

Cubs Prepare for War

At the beginning of 1939, most of the principal powers of the world, except the United States, had been striving to lead in the race for air supremacy. It was plainly apparent then that a war was imminent in Europe with each passing month. Germany's official spokesman had frankly boasted that it had a military air force second to none, and was threatening to go to war. Some of the other European nations had tried to disguise their military aviation build-ups by appearing to support civil aviation programs. This was especially true of Great Britain, France, Czechoslovakia, Poland, and other nations that had disclaimed any plan of intensive rearmament but were, in fact, rearming on an unprecedented scale.

These countries all had justification for doing so, as Germany, Russia, and Italy were not covering up their military aviation build-

An instructor congratulates a Piper employee after completing her first solo flight. The company encouraged employees to learn to fly in their time off and donated planes to the Cub Flyers Club, formed in 1935 at the Bradford factory. At one time the total membership of the club reportedly numbered well over one thousand, of which 130 were women. (Piper Aviation Museum)

ups. Adolf Hitler asserted that Germany's air force was capable of backing up any demands he might make against any of the other nations in Europe.

The United States was far behind in military aircraft development and pilot training. There were no national aeronautical training programs as there were in Germany, Italy, and Russia. There were fewer than 5,000 trained military pilots and less than 1,000 combat aircraft in the Army, Navy, and Marine Corps in the late Thirties. The Army Air Corps had three bases in San Antonio, Texas, to give primary, basic, and advanced pilot instruction; the Navy had similar bases at Pensacola, Florida, and Corpus Christi, Texas. Each service could train a maximum of 500 pilots per year. Official U.S. Bureau of Commerce records showed there were just over 23,000 certified civilian pilots and 9,700 civil aircraft, including about 400 transports, registered in the United States. In comparison with Germany, Italy, and Japan, the nation was not prepared for war.

The urgency to build American military aviation strength did not go completely unheeded in Washington. In a December 1938 press conference, President Franklin Roosevelt announced that he had approved a small-scale experimental program for the Civil Aeronautics Authority to promote the private aviation industry by giving flight instruction to a small number of college students. A total of $100,000 was authorized to set up a pilot project through the National Youth Administration to train 330 pilots in thirteen colleges and universities in the United States.

On January 12, 1939, the president asked the Congress for funds for "the annual training of additional air pilots." This training, he said, should be primarily directed to qualifying them for civilian flying in cooperation with educational institutions. He asked for $10 million a year to give primary training to 20,000 citizens.

After much haggling in Congress about the cost, the Civilian Pilot Training Program (CPTP) was officially established when the president signed the Civilian Pilot Training Act of 1939 on June 27. However, only $5.7 million was authorized for the fiscal years 1939

60

A new soloist undergoes the traditional shirt tail cutting ceremony by fellow Piper Cub Flyer members. Club members ferried new aircraft to buyers, and many women employees who built up enough flying time became WASP or WAFS members during World War II. (Piper Aviation Museum)

dents and provide a work force for an important and growing industry, as well as the military. However, one college president disagreed. Without any documentation, and probably thinking about the carefree days of the barnstorming and stunt pilots during the Twenties and Thirties, he said, "...the successful pilots of the country today are, in general, not college men."

The nay-sayers were a distinct minority. To lend personal support to the program, First Lady Eleanor Roosevelt took a flight in a Piper Cub that received wide news coverage.

With the funds now available, 404 universities agreed to offer flight training, compared to only 19 before the law was passed. Each named a local flying school to provide the aircraft, while CAA examiners determined their capability to sustain a training program. The CAA required at least one airplane of not less than 50 horsepower to be provided for the training of every ten students. The students were required to prove they were not aliens and could speak English, as were the instructors, who were flight-checked to determine their fitness and to standardize their teaching procedures and methods.

In addition to ground school courses in civil air regulations, meteorology, navigation, and aerodynamics, the students were to have a minimum of 17 hours of dual instruction and 18 hours of solo flying. The flying curriculum included stalls, spin recovery, landings in cross-winds and gusty air, simulated forced landings, power-on and power-off landings, and a cross country flight of 50 miles with landings at two different airports. Additional instruction was authorized for any maneuvers an instructor deemed necessary. When a student completed the course satisfactorily, he or she was issued a Student Pilot Certificate.

and 1940 to train 9,885 private pilots and provide refresher training for 1,925 instructors. The act was scheduled to expire on July 1, 1944.

A few university administrators felt that the federal government was dictating what they would include in their curricula and was unconstitutionally exercising a degree of illegal control over their domain. However, most agreed that the program could be beneficial by providing practical education that would benefit the stu-

One of the planes donated to the Cub Flyers Club by the Piper company has been preserved and can be seen at each annual Sentimental Journey fly-in at Lock Haven. (Photo by the author)

A lineup of J-5 Cub Cruisers awaits delivery orders at Lock Haven in the summer of 1940. (Piper Aviation Museum)

Piper Cruisers line up at Lock Haven before beginning a mass flight to Panama via Central American countries in January 1941. It was the first time that any light planes had made such a long-distance international ferry flight. (Piper Aircraft Corporation)

In 1941 48 Cubs, dubbed "Flitfires," were financed by Piper distributors and raffled off for the British Royal Air Force Benevolent Fund that provided benefits to disabled RAF pilots and crew members. Here they are lined up at Lock Haven for delivery to each of the 48 states. (Piper Aviation Museum)

The person who deserves major credit for the groundwork necessary to bring this legislation into being was Robert H. Hinckley, an Ogden, Utah, native with strong ties to the Democratic administration. In addition to many business interests, he had established Utah-Pacific Airways, principally a fixed base operation, and had become increasingly uneasy about the preparations for war. He served in the Utah House of Representatives, then was appointed an Assistant Administrator in that state for the Works Progress Administration (WPA), one of Roosevelt's New Deal programs to bolster the economy. He quickly became known as a leader in recommending the construction of airports as a productive way to spend government funds, and was persuaded to go to Washington to plan for the construction of a new airport for the nation's capital.

The Civil Aeronautics Act that had been passed in 1938 ushered in a new era for U.S. civil aviation. Sweeping changes were made that consolidated diverse functions in the Bureau of Air Commerce at the Department of Commerce and established the Civil Aeronautics Authority (CAA). Five men were named to head the CAA, and Hinckley was one of them. He was named chairman in April 1939, and thus became administrator of the CPT program, which he enthusiastically endorsed. He later was appointed Assistant Secretary of Commerce for Air.

This Flitfire, painted silver, often visits Lock Haven during the Sentimental Journey fly-in. It was authorized license number 1776 to correspond with the number of a Congressional resolution authorizing the British lend-lease program in 1941. (Photo by the author)

Piper conducted many experiments with Cubs to increase flying efficiency. This Cub Coupe J-4RX has a William Rose slotted wing fitted with slats, slotted ailerons, and flaps. It was not successful. (Howard Levy Collection)

Experiments were made by the Civil Aeronautics Authority in 1944 with this L-4B Cub to test cross-wind landing gear. The wheels swivel to compensate for strong winds on landing. (Peter M. Bowers Collection)

The CPT program was the nation's first full-scale, federally funded aviation education program, and one of the largest government-sponsored vocational education programs of its time. Simply put, it was intended to use the classrooms of American colleges and universities in collaboration with CAA-certified local flying schools to provide a pool of young civilian pilots who could potentially be available for military service in time of war.

Hinckley crusaded on a theme of "air conditioning" the youth of America into aviation, and appeared to have a mandate from the nation's universities to include them in the program, as well as support from the light plane manufacturers. Mr. Piper, Sr., projecting

such a program to the years ahead, was cautious and answered a newspaper reporter's query by saying:

"Any government aid which would increase private flying today would have to be perpetual, or the result would be an overproduction of planes and pilots when the subsidy was discontinued."

Of course, he had no way of knowing then how close the country was to being involved in the European war. And, although the company was the nation's leading producer of light aircraft, he could

The Applegate-Piper P-1 "Cub Clipper" with a 60-hp Papoose engine shown here was a spin-off from a home-built amphibian built by Ray Applegate. It had an all-metal hull, a set of J-3 Cub wings, rubber wing floats, and was tested with several different engines. A second prototype was flown, but the P-1 was not put into production. (Peter M. Bowers Collection)

To answer the call for a proposal from the Army Air Force for a two-place, retractable gear trainer, Piper designed the PT-1, the first Piper design with a low cantilever wood wing, slotted flaps, and control surfaces. Only one was built and failed to generate military interest. It has been restored for display at Lock Haven. (Piper Aviation Museum)

not foresee how his company might be able to support the war effort. After all, the major military aircraft expenditures were going for bombers, fighters, and transports, not light planes. Light planes were considered as those weighing less than 1,300 pounds gross weight and costing less than $2,000.

The Army and Navy were not particularly interested in the CPT program at first. Their bars were not let down for new trainees just because they may have completed 35 hours of light plane time or had a private license. But at least they learned the nomenclature of an airplane and had an elementary knowledge of turns, stalls, spins, takeoffs, and landings. Besides, the CPT program eliminated those who got chronically airsick or lost interest before they were admitted to military training schools, thus saving the services the cost and the time that would have been lost.

In spite of the opposition by some educators, isolationists, and those opposed to the New Deal programs in general, the CPT program became one of the most ambitious air training programs in the nation's history. During the first year 330 students completed

the course, while only a dozen dropped out. When the program was expanded, there were 10,000 students enrolled in 1939-40 who flew an estimated 96 million miles. By January 1, 1941, the CAA listed 63,113 pilots with licenses, an indication that Hinckley's "air conditioning" program was working. He was the first to sense the great need for early air education of the younger generation as the foundation upon which to build a sound and healthy industry.

At the beginning, there had been only one fatality in the first ten thousand students trained, and this ratio held throughout the program. Insurance premiums were lowered as a result. It was claimed that CPT trainees who went to the Air Force were found to be five times as likely to succeed as trainees who had not had CPT flight training. Hinckley's foresight gave the nation a reservoir of 105,000 pilots and instructors before the United States entered the war in December 1941.

The manufacturers of light planes were beneficiaries of the CPT program. While only 2,851 of all types had been produced between 1933 and 1937, 23,797 planes were turned out between

Out of a perceived public desire for new aircraft after World War II, Piper engineers designed the PWA-1 Skycoupe, a two-seat, side-by-side, low-wing model with a pusher-type engine, tri-cycle gear, and twin tail booms. It was not successful, nor was a later version. (Piper Aviation Museum)

Piper experimented with a single-seat aircraft, possibly calculating that former military pilots might be interested in owning it after World War II. Called the Skycycle, it was a low-wing monocoupe with fixed gear. It was built of plastic and aluminum with fabric-covered wings, and priced to sell at about $900. The fuselage reportedly was made from the drop tank of a Vought F-4U Corsair fighter plane to save production costs. (Piper Aviation Museum)

a spring 1940 issue of *Fortune* magazine reported that Piper was building more airplanes "than any other manufacturer in the world."

The burgeoning sales were the result of past and continuing efforts on the part of the aggressive sales force to make the Piper name and its planes known everywhere. Bill Strohmeier, promoted to Sales Promotion Manager, was sent to the New York World's Fair in 1939. He had arranged to have two Pipers on display when it opened. One was a centerpiece for the elaborate RCA exhibit; the other was outside the entrance to the Aviation Building. Cubs were being offered at that time for $995 and, although the company had been offered this latter choice spot, no advertising was allowed. This one was painted black, and the license number NC 995 was available and authorized.

"I flew NC 995 down to Flushing," Strohmeier said, "and with the help of a mechanic, took the wings off and towed it to the Fair grounds at dawn. After we assembled it we put it on display stilts and pulled masking tape off the wing and rudder, which revealed a dollar sign and the full license number as NC $995. Thus, the world knew that you could buy a Piper Cub for $995."

From then on, Piper salesmen displayed Cubs at any kind of show or exposition where they could obtain space. Since the planes were always an attraction, the space was usually at no cost to the company. At a major show at the Chicago Stock Yards, two Cubs were to be shown next to the Coliseum, which had to be flown in and landed on a very small car parking lot. This presented a challenge for Bill Strohmeier, who was "the Designated Lander" for both planes, and made the landings with a little room to spare:

"I had learned that Gabby Hartnett, then a popular manager of the Chicago Cubs baseball team, was going to visit the show," he recalled. "We alerted the press and persuaded Gabby to visit our

1938 and 1941. Piper, Aeronca, and Taylorcraft accounted for 17,727 of them, of which Piper sold 8,020, or 45 percent of the total. Other light plane makers trailed far behind and began directing their production to larger military aircraft or aircraft components for other manufacturers.

To meet this spurt of demand, Piper had led the way by increasing its production from 658 aircraft in 1938 to 1,698 in 1939 and 1,501 in the first seven and a half months of 1940. By this time there were over 2,000 employees on the Piper payroll. An article in

A suggestion for a post-war production four-seat aircraft was the Sky Sedan—shown here with fabric-covering and retractable gear—that first flew in March 1946. A second all-metal model was tested the following year, but the project was abandoned when the aircraft market collapsed in 1947. (Piper Aviation Museum)

Homebuilt enthusiasts made many variations of Piper Cubs over the years. This single-place Nelson N-4 was formerly a J-3C-65 Cub. Such extensive modifications were allowed before adoption of a federal 51% rule, which required a homebuilder to make 51% or more of the aircraft himself. (Peter M. Bowers Collection)

display. He did, and the resulting photograph was captioned 'Cub Meets Cub.' It received wide coverage in the sports pages across the country.

"Another event widely covered by the press was the Cub Convoy, which was first started in 1938," Strohmeier said. "I persuaded the Gulf Oil Co. to offer free gas to any Piper Cub owner who wanted to fly to the Miami All-American Air Maneuvers. We organized three air routes the Cubs were to fly from the northeast, midwest, and Texas. Hundreds of them took part. They converged first at Orlando for a big party, where every participant was made a 'Flying Alligator' by the Chamber of Commerce for having bravely flown over the Florida swamps to get there. They all then flew on to Miami. In subsequent years, Gulf opened the offer to other types of light aircraft and called it the 'Light Plane Cavalcade.'"

The Miami air shows were canceled after America became involved in World War II, and were resumed afterward for a short period. Mass Cub fly-ins have been held in recent years at Oshkosh, Wisconsin, and Lock Haven, Pennsylvania. The latter began in 1985, and the annual summer gatherings of Cubs there are known as the "Sentimental Journey."

There were several radio programs that gave away Piper Cubs to listeners. One, sponsored by Wings cigarettes, gave a Cub away every week for a year and a half. Piper donated the Cubs, and Continental donated the engines. Neither Aeronca, Taylorcraft, nor any other light plane manufacturer was able to match this publicity.

In a gesture to lure writers who were members of the Aviation Writers Association to report knowledgably about the Cub, the company offered to give free instruction to any newspaper or magazine

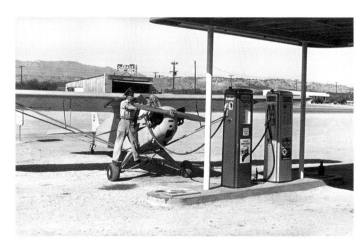

Ferry pilots often had to obtain gas for their Cubs from auto gas stations, as this one is doing in Arizona while en route to California. The Continental 65-hp engine could operate as efficiently on low octane automobile fuel as on the specified 73-octane fuel. (Don Downie Collection)

The first light aircraft procured by the Army Air Forces were designated "Observation" aircraft, and Piper Cubs were assigned as O-59s. In April 1942 the designation of all light planes was changed to "Liaison," and Piper Cubs became L-4s. This L-4 Cub in olive drab paint, actually a repainted J-3C-65, was one of the first shipped from Lock Haven. (Piper Aviation Museum)

aviation writer who would visit Lock Haven. One who took advantage of this rare opportunity was Devon Francis, the first reporter to specialize in writing about general aviation for the Associated Press. Strohmeier gave him the required dual instruction, and the day he completed the flight check for his Private Certificate, the two of them flew to Washington that evening, where Robert Hinckley, then head of the CAA, presented it to him.

To solve a critical shortage of ferry pilots that developed, Piper called on the Cub Flyers to help out. Interest in the club had grown, and by the end of 1940 had a membership of about 25 percent of the Piper work force, a fleet of seven aircraft, and three instructors paid by the company. Employees who had private licenses were given the opportunity to gain valuable cross-country flying experience by delivering aircraft to buyers anywhere in the United States.

A set of pontoons was donated to the club, and its members soon had the capability to deliver seaplanes directly from the seaplane base on the nearby Susquehanna River. This gave them the opportunity to gain experience in long-range navigation and landings on a variety of lakes and rivers.

Many employees left the company after getting their private and commercial certificates and joined the military forces, became flying instructors, or joined the growing airlines. Mr. Piper was never resentful about employees moving, and derived much personal pleasure in having provided the opportunity for young people to get ahead in the aviation career field.

The opportunity to ferry aircraft was extended to include members of the Aviation Writers Association, and first to receive an Honorary Ferry Pilot Certificate was Devon Francis, then president of the association. After he was presented the certificate by William T. Piper, Sr., he took off for Boston to deliver a new Cub.

Piper made news in aviation journals in January 1941 with a mass flyaway delivery of six Piper Cubs to Panama. It was the first time that light planes of any type had made an international flight of such a distance. The route took them from Newport News, Virginia, under the leadership of J.M. Hearn (a Canal Zone employee), through Mexico, Guatemala, Salvador, Nicaragua, and Costa Rica. At the same time, it was announced that four Cubs were being used in the Dominican Republic to deliver mail to outlying areas where ground transportation was slow and uncertain.

Another publicity event that Strohmeier instigated was a nationwide money raising campaign for the British Royal Air Force Benevolent Fund, which provided benefits for disabled RAF pilots and crew members. Strohmeier persuaded the Piper distributors from each of the 48 states to purchase a Cub marked with a British roundel on the fuselage and raffle them off. On April 29, 1941, 48 Cubs—dubbed Flitfires in contrast to the famous British Supermarine Spitfire fighters—were flown by Cub Flyers Club members in an impressive mass formation to New York's LaGuardia Field on Long Island, New York. Mayor Fiorello H. LaGuardia was master of ceremonies, and the 48 Cubs, painted silver, were christened by Harvey Conover models. They christened their assigned Flitfires by popping balloons attached to the propellers that were filled with "champagne gas," a name concocted by a reporter for carbon dioxide gas. The planes were then flown to distributors in the 48 states for raffling parties.

Strohmeier's idea had originated after the donation of a Cub by W. T. Piper, Sr., to the Fund. Painted silver, it had been authorized the government license number NC 1776 to correspond with the number of U.S. House of Representatives Resolution No. 1776, which had given American destroyers to the British as part of the

This YO-59, photographed at Hawkins Field, Jackson, Mississippi, was delivered in time to take part in some of the Army maneuvers in the fall of 1941. (Boardman C. Reed Collection)

government's lend-lease program. The plane would be raffled off as the grand prize at the La Guardia christening for the other 48 Flitfires.

"NC 1776 almost didn't get there for the festivities," Strohmeier told the author. "I decided to fly it from the factory to LaGuardia by way of South Dartmouth, Massachusetts, to visit my parents, and had to land on a golf course. It was equipped with a tail wheel but no brakes, so I had to jump out to stop it before hitting a row of trees. My face would have been quite red if I had to report that I had damaged this trophy airplane. This Flitfire is still flying today."

All of these Cub promotional events were carried out on a stringent budget and a very small staff at Lock Haven. Strohmeier's pay when promoted to Sales Promotion Manager was $27.50 a week. He and his wife rented a small cottage on the side of the Lock Haven airport at $25 a month. His next door neighbor was Mr. Piper himself, who rented his house from the same owner at $35. When Strohmeier got a subsequent small raise he was able to afford a telephone for the first time.

***

A J-3C is being refueled at a civilian gas pump in a southern country town during the Army's Louisiana maneuvers. The cross was for identification purposes during the war games. Also painted on the fuselage is a grasshopper cartoon, after an Army general referred to the Cubs as "Grasshoppers," and the name was adopted to include most liaison aircraft. (Peter M. Bowers Collection)

President Roosevelt made a special address to Congress on May 16, 1940, and asked that funds be authorized to produce 50,000 aircraft for the Army Air Corps. The following month, Hinckley announced an expansion of the CPT program to train 45,000 students with an appropriation of $37 million, a substantial increase over the previous year's $4 million. The program not only met the training goal, but claimed to have produced 57, 972 pilots during fiscal year 1941.

The encouraging statistics masked an underlying concern that the program was not benefiting the Army and Navy, as was one of its intentions. In a January 1941 press conference, President Roosevelt commented that the two services were not getting enough pilots out of the program. He admitted a "quite large" number of CPTP students declined to join either service, and added:

"It was a grand idea that we are going to teach everybody to fly, and now, from practical experience, we think we ought to do some pretty careful combing of the people so as to make them useful for military and naval work."

As a result of the president's remark and criticism from other quarters that the program was not contributing to the national defense effort, Congress cut the CPTP appropriation from the $37 million of the previous year to $25 million. But the disparagement may not have been totally warranted. Dominick Pisano, author of *To Fill the Skies with Pilots* (Smithsonian Institution Press), studied the numbers of students completing the Army Air Corps primary flying schools in 1941 who had completed CPTP training. He concluded that:

"...a higher percentage of those with CPTP training tended to complete the courses than those without CPTP training. This indicates that the CPTP was good preparation for military aviation."

In the summer of 1941 the program was divided into several phases at more than 800 training centers coast-to-coast, with 16,000 applicants. The phases were Private Course (college) and Private Course (non-college); Secondary Course; Cross-Country Course; and Instructors' Course. Applicants completing all courses would have flown 180 hours and have had 360 hours of ground school instruction.

There was disagreement at first about the value of the program from the leaders of the Army Air Forces (AAF), including its chief, Maj. Gen. Henry H. Arnold. He believed strongly at the time that the AAF should train its own pilots without outside pressures, such as having to give credit for prior training and thus shorten the period for training cadets after they enrolled at the regular AAF training schools. A compromise was reached when CAA and AAF officials agreed that the CPT Program would train AAF enlisted reserve personnel for non-combat duty as instructors, ferry, liaison, and glider pilots, and as commercial pilots for the Air Transport Command.

Although Navy officials appeared before Congressional committees opposing use of CPT training, posters were sent at the same time to CPTP schools saying that training was available at Pensacola for students ages 20 to 27 who had a minimum of two years of college. According to Pisano:

"...the navy did allow CPTP trainees to qualify as combat pilots, and used the program effectively to screen those who were unfit for pilot duty."

In his summation about the program, researcher Pisano states:

"One must inevitably conclude that before the war began, the CPTP was good preparation for military aviation. In the flurry of mobilization, however, quantity seemed to be more important than quality."

As it had been originally conceived, the CPT Program was to serve a dual purpose: prepare a cadre of civilian pilots as a war preparedness measure, and also help the Roosevelt Administration accomplish its New Deal economic goals by stimulating the light plane industry and airport construction projects. According to Pisano, these dual objectives ultimately contributed to its demise.

CPTP historian Patricia Strickland in

The Putt-Putt Air Force, published by the Government Printing Office in 1973, summarized the program more favorably as world events diverted the program from its original purposes:

The Civilian Pilot Training Program (CPTP) was established in 1939 under the Civil Aeronautics Authority (CAA) to train college students as pilots for possible use during a national emergency. About 20 percent of the enrollees were women. Here two women students at Lake Erie College in Ohio work on a Lycoming engine under the supervision of a male instructor. (Lycoming photo)

"Until the summer of 1941, the Civilian Pilot Training Program tried to keep its civilian identity, operating as a widely decentralized activity carried on in conjunction with the student's academic life. Its aims were essentially to give aviation a place in the educational system, and to awaken the country to the potential prosperity inherent in large numbers of civil pilots and privately-owned aircraft.

"As it was intended to do, all of civil aviation prospered from the CPTP. The fixed base operator learned to apply sound economic principles to his business instead of keeping the books in his head. He bought new airplanes, hired new instructors, and drew in additional—non-CPTP—money.

"Under the stimulus of the CPTP, hundreds of small airports were developed or reopened. Every field in the vicinity of a college was a busy little air center. Local authorities and private individuals helped build new airports and improved those already established."

When the developing world situation seemed more likely to involve the United States in the summer of 1941 the CPTP was forced to change. Women were no longer accepted, and a military pledge was required of all males. There were 16,000 trainees in the program, and when this group was about to graduate, the disaster at Pearl Harbor caused the CPTP to cease to exist for all practical purposes. President Roosevelt issued an Executive Order on December 13, 1941, directing that all pilot training facilities of the CAA were declared to be:

"...exclusively devoted to the procurement and training of men for ultimate service as military pilots, or for correlated non-military activities."

These changes gave the military services more control, and the name of the program was changed to the War Training Service (WTS) in 1942. During the following two years the CPTP-WTS trained more than 55,000 pilots for the AAF, but it was decided that its usefulness had declined and was not worth any further effort or expense. The navy concurred, and the CPTP-WTS agreement with the CAA was canceled in early 1944.

***

During those expansive years, W.T. Piper, Sr., was concerned about the future, and when Hitler's forces invaded Poland in September 1939, he felt an obligation to offer his voice to the growing feeling that the United States would be involved in Europe's war. He may have been encouraged to consider the use of light planes to supplement Army ground forces after receiving a letter from Texas National Guardsman Lt. Joseph M. Watson III in July 1940 asking if some Cubs could be flown to Camp Beauregard, Louisiana, the following month to demonstrate their use during maneuvers.

The idea of using light planes was not a new one for Watson. A licensed private pilot since 1936, he had thought then that light airplanes could be used to adjust artillery fire for his artillery brigade in the Texas 36th Division. He obtained permission from his commander to test his theories and rented a Cub at San Antonio's Stinson Field. He and Capt. John K. Burr, his superior officer, took along a bulky radio and began a private campaign to prove that the slow-flying Cub could radio his unit's artillery batteries and adjust artillery fire, as well as detect enemy forces that may be hiding under camouflage or in forested areas. During drill assemblies, Watson would land in small open places near the guns he was supporting and, when low on gas, obtained it from the nearest civilian gas station, or from a passing Army truck or command car.

Watson contacted Brig. General Robert O. Whiteaker, his division artillery commander, and asked if he could conduct a two-day test of his theory. Permission was granted, and Watson contacted Tom Case, a Piper employee, and asked him to fly a Cub to the brigade headquarters at Camp Beauregard, Louisiana. Case, accompanied by Jules Parmentier, promptly complied, and demonstrated the Cub's capability to land and take off in short spaces. The two pilots then flew missions with Watson along the route of the brigade's 90-mile convoy to its base camp to report accidents and warn of road blocks. The reconnaissance proved extremely worthwhile, and a favorable report was sent to Washington with a recommendation to consider that light planes should be added to Army units. It was difficult to take such a revolutionary idea up through Army channels and get any action immediately. The Army Air Corps had procurement authority for aircraft, not the Army Ground Forces.

Piper decided to see if he could get some reaction from Washington. In a letter to Secretary of War Henry L. Stimson dated February 18, 1941, he wrote:

"The Piper Aircraft Corporation, representing 50% of the Light Aircraft Production in the United States, is anxious to know what it can do to further aid in the defense of this country. Although I cannot speak for the rest of the industry, I am sure that their desire and willingness to help is no less than ours."

Piper attached a number of suggestions for the use of light planes to control and monitor troop movements, evacuate wounded, carry messages, ferry personnel, provide battlefield reconnaissance, drop bombs, and be used as trainers for instrument flying. Assistant to the Secretary of War for Air Robert A. Lovett responded that the ideas, such as controlling troop movement, carrying wounded, and ferrying personnel might be of interest to the ground forces, and the others could be considered by the air forces, but "neither personnel nor funds are at present available within the War Department."

The man who deserves much credit for changing the military mindset about the possible use of small aircraft for war missions was John E.P. Morgan, a member of the Piper board of directors and an imaginative thinker. He was a Yale classmate of Lovett who had been a naval reserve aviator, and had some light plane air time. Morgan was asked to go to Washington and try to persuade his friend and the War Department decision-makers to allow Piper to show what light aircraft could do for the Army Ground Forces, as well as the Navy and Marines. Morgan's friendship with Lovett would open many doors.

A meeting of aircraft manufacturers was called in Washington to answer questions about the 50,000-plane program that consisted mostly of fighters and bombers that the president had decreed would be built. The meeting was attended by Treasury Secretary Henry Morganthau, who turned it over to an Army general. When asked by one of the light plane makers if there would be any need for light planes by either of the services, the general responded that they were impractical and would not be required in any war production program for Army ground or air units:

"The Army has considered the possibilities of the light plane," he said, "but the conclusion is that it is impractical for military use."

When asked about possible use by the Navy, a Navy captain replied:

"The Navy can see no practical use for light planes for the same reasons the general has just given."

Piper and the other manufacturing representatives could not believe what they had heard. William Piper decided he had to say something:

"General," he began, "you and the Captain have just said that neither the Army nor the Navy wants light planes. As a maker of light planes I'm naturally a little disappointed. I know that our Air Force needs fighters and bombers before everything else, but it seems to me that the light plane hasn't been given a fair trial to show what it can do.

"Looking around the room, I see that all of the makers of light planes in the country seem to be present. I'm sure that they don't come down to Washington often because their expense accounts don't allow for it. But now that we're all here, we'd like to explain our side of the picture to somebody—some sergeant or corporal maybe."

Everyone laughed, and a later meeting was arranged, but the answer was the same: there would be no use for light planes for the Army or Navy.

The group of manufacturers decided that John Morgan would be their lobbyist to try to change the official opinions about the value of light planes in ground combat situations. It remained for Piper salesmen and pilots to show how they could be used to help win battles and save lives. Morgan encouraged them to take top ranking Army officers on flights, especially the colonels and generals, to show what a Cub could do.

In June 1941 extensive Army maneuvers were planned for that summer, and the Air Corps was asked to supply some aircraft for observation experiments. None were available, so Assistant Secretary of War Lovett asked John Morgan if he could arrange for some light airplanes to participate in maneuvers at Camp Forrest, Tennessee, from June 2 to June 28, 1941, at no expense to the government. Morgan immediately contacted Aeronca, Taylorcraft, and Piper managements. Seizing the opportunity, Piper promptly responded by furnishing ten Cubs, fifteen pilots, and two mechanics to fly to the maneuver area. Aeronca and Taylorcraft furnished two planes each. The Piper pilots were led by Ted Weld and included Thomas Piper, Jr., Howard Piper, and W.D. Strohmeier. John Morgan went along as an observer. The engines were all 65-hp Continentals, and the company sent two of their engine experts. The official Army Air Forces history of this period reports the arrangements this way:

"In June 1941 the Secretary of War informed General Arnold of ground force plans to use 12 Piper Cubs during the Second Army's June maneuvers in Tennessee. The Piper Aircraft Company made the original arrangements with the Second Army but, believing it wise for the three largest light airplane manufacturers in the United States to be represented, invited Aeronca and Taylor to participate in the tests. The commercial airplanes employed in this exercise were only rented from the manufacturers, and they were flown by civilian pilots who were manufacturers' representatives."

The group of civilian pilots selected by the three companies made many demonstration flights between June and September 1941 at other maneuvers in Louisiana, the Carolinas, New Mexico, Texas, and California. The planes were flown 12 to 14 hours a day, hedge-hopping over inhospitable terrain following orders from ground commanders. Morgan, following the "air conditioning" theme that Hinckley had propounded in the CPT Program, suggested that the pilots invite every high-ranking officer they could persuade to go on flights to demonstrate the planes' usefulness. Records of the maneuvers showed that about 500 colonels and 13 generals were given flights. Lt. Col. (later General) George S. Patton, who had a pilot license, used his own light plane for reconnaissance and was a staunch supporter of the use of liaison planes by his armored units. So was Major (later General) Mark Clark, who greatly depended on them later during the war.

Strohmeier reported in the November 1941 issue of *Poplar Aviation* that the pilots and planes were put through every kind of grueling test imaginable:

"...first in the hilly and wooded sections of eastern Tennessee, then in the sizzling high altitude desert country. In Louisiana, dur-

ing the largest maneuvers ever held in the nation, the light planes were landing almost anywhere, using roads mainly as landing fields. Filling station operators got used to having a plane drop in for gas. I landed at one lonely gas station expecting to be greeted as a hero, only to find that two other ships had been in that morning, and that they had sold more gasoline to airplanes in the previous several days than to automobiles!"

While at Camp Polk, Louisiana, Bill Strohmeier was assigned to fly an army lieutenant colonel, who said he had a private pilot license, along for a ride to check on his unit's bivouac areas. Always wary about those who claimed they could fly, Strohmeier asked where he had received his license. The officer replied that he had earned it in the Philippines in 1937 flying a Stearman trainer. Strohmeier let him fly wherever he wanted to go and recalled that "he was a good pilot and very good at using a map." The lieutenant colonel's name was Dwight D. Eisenhower.

 PIPER POINTS THE WAY WITH
...A PLANE TO FULFILL YOUR
EVERY FLIGHT REQUIREMENT

Piper is the plane for the people of America! On the U. S. Civilian Pilot Training Program, where thousands of pilots are being trained for national defense, Piper planes outnumber all other makes combined by more than 300%. In addition, men and women of all ages are finding their wings in these dependable, economical ships over every section of the country. And no wonder, for only Piper offers you a *complete* line from which to choose . . . a plane for every purpose. The famous Piper Cub tandem trainer is priced as low as $995, the roomy, three-place Piper Cruiser is but $2150 and the luxurious Piper Coupe is $2575 (all prices F.A.F. Lock Haven, Pennsylvania.)

FREE FOLDER showing all the new Piper planes will be sent you on request or may be obtained from your Piper Dealer. Or, if you wish a copy of the new Piper deluxe, full-color, 16-page catalog, it will be gladly mailed you, providing you enclose 10c in stamps or coin for postage-handling. Piper Aircraft Corporation, Dept. D81, Lock Haven, Penna.

FREE FLYING COURSE in his own plane is offered the purchaser of a new Piper. It consists of eight hours of dual flight instruction . . . take-offs, landings, taxiing and fundamental air maneuvers. At the completion of this free course the average person is ready to solo.

DOWN PAYMENT PRICES START AT
$333
EASY MONTHLY INSTALLMENTS

Tune in "Wings of Destiny" NBC Every Friday 10 P. M. (E.D.S.T.)
Continental "65" Piper Cub Given Away Each Week

A Piper advertisement in August 1941 issues of aviation magazines showed the three major planes then available: Piper Coupe, Piper Cruiser, and Piper Trainer. A course of instruction was offered free to buyers. During this period before World War II a Piper Cub was given away every week on an NBC radio program. (Aero Digest)

The following month, at Fort Bliss, Texas, the civilian pilots and their planes were invited to participate again, this time by Major General Henry H. "Hap" Arnold, then chief of the Air Corps, who had been persuaded that the idea deserved an opportunity to be tested. They were to report to Biggs Field at El Paso and conduct their missions from there. Although misunderstood at first how they could be used, the light planes and pilots proved their worth in temperatures that ranged up to 115 degrees. They flew in and out of unprepared rough desert areas for reconnaissance, message dropping, and personnel transport missions for the Army maneuver forces. There were a few mishaps, but repairs were quickly made. It was revealed that the civilian pilots had paid for their own gas and oil, food, repairs, and other charges.

At some time during this period of pre-war maneuvers, Major General Innis P. Swift, commander of the 1st Cavalry at Fort Bliss, Texas, referred to the light planes as "grasshoppers," and the nickname was used by the ground forces to identify all light aircraft during World War II, although it was officially applied to the Piper Cubs.

Bill Strohmeier described his reactions to the unusual experience operating with the ground troops:

"The first few days of this kind of flying, I'll admit, are pretty alarming—particularly if you've spent most of your flying abiding by CAA regulations and flying cross country at nice comfortable altitudes.

"First off, as a 'Grasshopper' pilot, you've got to forget entirely all the rules of flying except the fundamental common sense rules of safety. You've got to forget about the consequences of engine failure, either cross country or on takeoff. You've got to learn how to hedgehop like you've never hedgehopped before, so that the enemy won't see you while you're sneaking in to scout their position. You've got to forget about taking off always into the wind because you never have anything better than a one-direction 'airport,' and chances are pretty good you'll have a crosswind. You've got to forget all about neat pattern approaches, because you're seldom high enough to even wind back the stabilizer. You've got to learn how to bring them in on the ragged edge so that she'll quit flying the minute you close the throttle entirely—you've got to hit the edge of the field or run out of airport.

"You've got to learn just how much brake you can apply for maximum stopping in short spaces. You've got to learn how to raise the tail to flying position and then release the brakes just enough so you can always see over the nose and keep your wheels in the tire ruts, so that you won't catch a wheel in the mesquite. You've got to learn how to take off in a semi-circle around the side of a conical-shaped hill. You've got to get used to landing in fields and clearings which last year you wouldn't consider trying if it was zero-zero and you were running out of gas. From a casual glance you can draw the conclusion that flying a 'grasshopper' is not exactly a picnic."

Piper received a letter from Brigadier General Adna R. Chaffee, head of the Army's Armor School at Fort Knox, Kentucky. Chaffee asked if a Cub and a pilot could be loaned to see if an Army observer could direct armored columns on maneuvers and adjust tank firing. It was found that the observer could do both easily at low altitudes while remaining out of sight of opposing forces. The high wing of the monoplane Cub enabled the pilot and observer to see downward more easily than with the large Army Air Force low-wing observation planes like the ponderous North American O-47s and the Curtiss O-52s. Besides, these were grounded too often for maintenance and could not maneuver very well in the mountainous areas where the troops were operating. Furthermore, they required higher octane gas and were too fast to accurately give azimuth and range corrections to artillery units. Only experienced mechanics could work on them, while Cub pilots and auto mechanics with a minimum of training could do all necessary maintenance and repairs.

Strohmeier concluded that all of the Grasshoppers had shown their usefulness in the maneuvers, and that:

"the light plane is no longer the problem child of aviation. It has proven itself under the most grueling conditions and has shown the world that it's a tough little critter and not just a toy."

In 1941 Major General Robert M. Danford, chief of the Army's Field Artillery, had seen a demonstration of light planes operating in England with a field artillery unit. When he returned to the States he asked for permission to make field tests with light planes at Fort Sill, Oklahoma. No action had been taken on his request until December 22, 1941, fifteen days after the Pearl Harbor attack. At that time, the CAA agreed to send six flight instructors "of the barnstorming type" to Fort Sill, two of whom had participated in previous maneuvers. During January and February 1942 Tony Piper and Henry S. Wann, a Piper salesman in the western states, responded to the call, and about 24 Cubs were ordered to participate with civilian pilots from the CPT program.

To keep the Piper name in the news, the company announced a model building contest for young men and women ages 12 to 19. Prizes were offered that totaled over $100,000 in value and consisted of scholarships giving employment for a year at the Piper plant at regular salary plus 100 hours of flying time and instruction. At least one scholarship was to be presented in each community in which the competition was to take place.

Although it appeared to be the beginning of acceptance within the Army that light aircraft could fill a vital role for the ground forces, it would take time for the Army Air Corps (later the Army Air Forces) to complete the service tests required of all new aircraft. The urgency was not felt strongly at the time because bombers, fighters, and large transports were given priority. In any event, it appeared that there would be no requirement for a large number of Grasshoppers.

But there was a sudden break in the bad news. An undated Army Air Forces Historical Study tells what happened:

"The maneuvers of 1941 completely sold the light airplane to the ground forces. The Field Artillery, down to the lowest echelon, was enthusiastic. A mechanized Cavalry officer, speaking for that arm, asserted that the activities of the puddle jumpers with the mechanized regiment produced a 'realization among officers and men that such a type of plane is invaluable to ground forces.' The Armored Force was even more specific. Experience in the maneuvers led to the conclusion that it would require 15 liaison airplanes for each armored division and six for each armored corps headquarters."

In January 1942 John Morgan reported from Washington that his friend, Assistant Secretary Robert Lovett, had given him ad-

America's youngest licensed commercial pilot with an instructor's rating before World War II was Gertrude S. Meserve, 19, of Winchester, MA. Here she vigorously props a 55-hp dual-ignition Cub for one of her students. (Piper Aviation Museum)

vance information that an order for about 1,500 Grasshoppers had been approved, which was far less than the more than 4,600 that the ground forces calculated they would like to have. But the order to prepare bids for procurement was slow in coming. It was several weeks before an official order was received, but it was for 1,960 planes, all of them destined for the Field Artillery.

Meanwhile, in April 1942 the Secretary of War ordered the designation of "Observation" changed to "Liaison" for this class of aircraft. The Stinson O-49 became the L-1, and the Taylorcraft O-57, Aeronca O-58, and Piper O-59 became the L-2, L-3, and L-4, respectively.

After much wrangling in Washington, a memorandum dated June 6, 1942, was sent from General George C. Marshall, the Army Chief of Staff, to Lt. Gen. Lesley J. McNair, Commander of Army Ground Forces. It directed the inclusion of "organic air observation" for Field Artillery, and authorized the assignment of liaison aircraft at the rate of two per light and medium artillery battalion and two per division artillery headquarters. Personnel would be assigned on a ratio of one pilot and one-half airplane mechanic for each plane authorized. The memorandum concluded by saying:

"The airplanes will be commercial low performance aircraft of the 'Piper Cub' type."

This added sentence proved that the Cub by now had become well-established in the minds of military officials who would see service on the battlefield. The many months of promoting the Piper name by its salesmen had paid off. To prove the company's capability to respond to the order, Piper announced that the 10,000th Cub had just been completed in November 1941. It was a Cub Cruiser, and represented the final of 5,000 Cubs that had been completed in just the previous 14 months. By this time, 6,143 J-3 Cubs had been built between 1937 and February 1942, when their manufacture ceased in favor of fulfilling the military contracts. The L-4 variants were continually improved, culminating in the J-3C-65 model, and a total of 5,677 were built before the company resumed production of the J-3 after World War II ended. By the time J-3 production of all models ceased, including wartime L-4s and TG-8 gliders, 19,906 had been manufactured at Lock Haven, Ponca City, Oklahoma, and in Canada.

***

The Army's training of liaison pilots for the ground forces officially began on June 6, 1942, at the Army's Field Artillery school at Fort Sill, Oklahoma. Training started with a test group of 19 volunteers who had civilian pilot ratings. Flight training was also established at Pittsburg, Kansas; Denton, Texas; and Mineral Wells, Texas, for initial training before more advanced flying at Fort Sill.

Although Taylorcraft L-2s and Aeronca L-3s were used, the most widely used (and favored) of all liaison aircraft that were eventually procured was the Piper L-4. One of the reasons was, according to an Army Air Forces study:

"...throughout 1943, repeated accidents at Fort Sill led the Field Artillery to ground all L-2 and L-3 airplanes and request the Air Corps to replace these types with L-4s, the military equivalent of the commercial Piper."

Bruce Ihlenfeldt, chief check pilot at Fort Sill, Oklahoma, reported that, in the beginning, half of the pilots were trained on Taylorcraft L-2s and the other half on Piper L-4s. The L-4s were preferred because they could fly lower and could land and takeoff shorter than the L-2s:

"In all of the injury accidents that occurred at Fort Sill, all of them were in L-2s," he said. "I don't recall any in the L-4 that resulted in death or injury."

The AAF study added that:

"The Field Artillery believed that the L-4, a 65-hp airplane, was the 'ultimate in simplicity' and ideally suited to artillery use. True, its takeoff characteristics could be improved, but its maintenance was sufficiently simple for it to be accepted as ideal for Field Artillery operating conditions. The Air Corps, however, favored the L-5, a 185-hp Stinson, twice as heavy as the L-4, though equipped with slots and flaps which gave it some performance characteristics superior to those of the L-4. But the Field Artillery believed that these refinements were attained at the cost of increased

Many experiments were conducted by Piper engineers over the years to keep costs down and improve the various models. Piper salesman William Strohmeier demonstrates a shock cord engine starter in a Super Cruiser so the engine would not require hand-propping. (William D. Strohmeier Collection)

complication in operation and maintenance. The Army considered the L-5 far too difficult to keep in repair under field conditions with 'primitive equipment' and 'much too hot' in the air for Field Artillery pilots."

The basic argument against the use of small planes by ground forces had been their vulnerability to enemy fire. However, experience proved this to be a false assumption. Combat experience quickly demonstrated the fallibility of such dogmatic assertions. By 1944 liaison aircraft were officially designated to be used for artillery adjustment, reconnaissance and light photographic observation, troop and light-cargo transport, aerial evacuation, column control on the march, camouflage checking and wire laying for communications, "and a dozen other command, liaison, utility, and courier functions."

One of the reports that helped settle the argument was an Associated Press report from the front lines with the Seventh Army in Europe. It stated:

"In a recent battle, 'Iron Mike' [Maj. Gen. John W. O'Daniel, the division commander] watched from a Cub plane while a company took one position but hesitated to move forward without reconnaissance. The General's plane swooped low. He dropped a note saying, 'No Boche for two kilometers. Get moving.' The company moved."

As the debate subsided at the highest level of the War Department, more students were recruited to fly light aircraft, and training consisted of about 15 hours of dual and solo time before concentrating on flying in and out of small, constrained spaces, such as tree-lined roads and over obstructions. Ground school instruction included meteorology, navigation, aircraft maintenance, and experience as observers. Upon graduation, all were authorized to wear silver wings with an "L" superimposed on the shield in the center to differentiate the wearers from the graduates of the Army Air Forces flying training program. Originally, 80 percent of the graduates were to be enlisted men; the other 20 percent were commissioned. Beginning in April 1943, enlisted men were not eligible for liaison pilot training and were required to complete Officer Candidate School before entering the pilot training program.

In addition to the Army liaison training program, the Army Air Forces also trained approximately 1,300 pilots in light aircraft. Some had been previously eliminated from regular pilot training, but were judged suitable to fly light aircraft. They received advanced training at Lamesa, Texas. By the end of the war 28 liaison squadrons had been formed within the Army Air Forces, manned mostly by enlisted pilots.

***

By this time Piper was offering a Cub Coupe and a Cub Cruiser to civilian buyers with such improvements as a self-starter, better grouping of the instruments, custom-built radio transmitter, increased gas capacity, and a minimum set of blind flight instruments. The Continental 75-hp engine was standard and increased the cruising speed close to 100 mph. Gross weight allowed with two passengers was 1,400 lbs., with 105 lbs of baggage.

While the future for Piper to get any further substantial wartime contracts for military versions of the Cubs seemed in doubt, several experimental aircraft were developed between 1940 and the end of World War II that show the efforts made to contribute to the war effort. One was the P-1 Cub Clipper, a spin-off from a home-built amphibian with a pusher engine developed by Ray Applegate, who trucked it to Lock Haven to see if anyone was interested in producing it. Piper engineers thought an amphibian might be a salable model, but Applegate's home-built would have to be improved. A set of J-3 wings was substituted, and several engines were tested to replace the Essex automobile engine in Applegate's model. Several other engines were tried, and it was decided that a Franklin 130-hp engine was best. A second Cub Clipper was designed with retractable gear improvements, but the project was abandoned when there appeared to be no interest by the military.

A perceived need for a "3-in-1" trainer was expressed by Dave Long, a 27-year-old Piper engineer who had extensive instructional experience in the CPT Program. He visualized a light plane that could be used for primary, basic, and advanced flight instruction, and would be much less expensive than the heavier Boeing PT-17s, Fairchild PT-19s, Vultee BT-13s, and North American AT-6s then standard for the three phases of Army Air Force training.

To answer an Army Air Force bid request in early 1942 for a two-place tandem, retractable gear trainer, Dave Long and two other young Piper engineers designed the PT-1, the first Piper design with a low cantilever wood wing, steel slotted flaps and control surfaces, and powered by a Franklin 130-hp engine. Initial training in it could be conducted with the gear down; as a student progressed, more difficult flight maneuvers could be conducted with the gear up; and then it could be used as an instrument trainer. It underwent extensive tests and was not advertised until early 1943. Only one was built, and it failed to find any public or military interest. After the war, the company sold it and it went through a number of hands. It had made a wheels-up landing and, although in bad shape, was restored in 1978. It was donated to the Piper company and subsequently loaned to the Experimental Aircraft Association at Oshkosh, Wisconsin, until Piper had its own museum. It was trucked back to Lock Haven in 1998 for restoration to its original configuration and eventual display in the Piper Aviation Museum.

Piper engineers also experimented with a J-3C Cub in 1941 to determine if its speed could be increased. One, designated the P-5 (also called the J-3X), was built in 1944 that eliminated the wing struts, streamlined the fuselage, and had a full-cantilever wing with leading edge wing slots and flaps. Other minor changes to reduce drag were not successful and the project was dropped.

When the war in Europe was approaching its highest levels of activity Piper engineers directed their attention to some post-war products. One of them, designed in 1943, was dubbed the PWA-1 Skycoupe (for Post-War Airplane), and was a unique departure from all other previous Piper planes. It was an all-metal, low-wing, twin-boom, tri-cycle gear, single-engine pusher built for two side-by-side occupants. It, too, was abandoned when there was no apparent interest from the public.

Two more experimental models went under development at Piper. One was the Cub Skycycle, a single-place, low-wing monocoupe powered by a 55-hp engine; it would be made of plastic and aluminum with fabric-covered wings, and it was announced that it would be priced to sell between $900 and $1,000. Its fuselage was reportedly made from the drop tank of a Republic P-47 fighter.

The other was the PA-6 Cub Skysedan, a low-wing, four-place model with a 165-hp engine and constructed with tubing, skin-stressed metal, and fabric covering. Neither reached full production.

Piper engineers, disappointed with these models, continued to search for aviation-related products to manufacture that could fulfill a possible wartime or postwar need.

5

The Cub and National Defense

December 7, 1941, was a clear, crisp Sunday morning in Honolulu, Hawaii, the beginning of an ideal flying day, when Ray Buduick, a local attorney, decided that it was the perfect time for a solo hop in his J-3 Cub. He propped the plane himself and took off from John Rogers Airport, a civilian field east of Hickam Army Air Field and Pearl Harbor. He leveled off at about 1,500 feet and settled down for a leisurely cruise toward Diamond Head and down Waikiki Beach. Suddenly, without any warning, he saw several fast single-engine planes streaking out of the sky toward him. Fearing a midair collision, he dove toward the ground and was rocked by the turbulence as they roared past.

Looking toward Pearl Harbor, Buduick could see smoke rising, and more planes than he had ever seen in the air before were diving and releasing large objects. He reversed course and saw a single plane coming in his direction from the left with guns blazing with tracers. He gave the Cub full throttle, hedgehopped to the airport, landed hurriedly, shut off the engine, and ran toward the hangar. As he looked back at the Cub, he could see several bullet holes in the fabric along the fuselage.

Buduick quickly learned that the airport had been under attack by Japanese fighters and bombers, and that Robert Tyce, airport manager and Cub distributor for the islands, had been killed as he ran toward the hangars after cranking a Cub's propeller for a student pilot. At the same time Jim Duncan, foreman for a private contractor at Pearl Harbor, was taking lessons in his Cub from Tom Tommerlin, an inter-island pilot who instructed on weekends to earn extra money. They, too, had been attacked, and returned as quickly as they could to John Rogers Airport. They received no damage.

Roy Vitousek, with his son Martin, also was in the air for an early-morning flight in their bright yellow J-3 Cub. They were over the John Rogers Airport losing altitude to enter the traffic pattern when they saw the first explosions at Ford Island in the distance. Several planes with large red circles on their wings zoomed under them and roared off toward Pearl Harbor. Vitousek veered out to sea at a low altitude to escape detection and later returned to the airport to find out that the military bases around Honolulu had been attacked by a large Japanese force of aircraft.

Less than two weeks of Cub production is represented by the 171 Cubs lined up at Lock Haven Airport in late 1941. Security restrictions after December 7, 1941, prevented their delivery to new owners and distributors. (Piper Aviation Museum)

Congressional Flying Club student pilots race to their Piper Cubs at the civilian flying school at Congressional Airport, Rockville, Maryland, in 1941. (F. Clifton Berry Collection)

Piper's three-place training glider, the TG-8, is shown in flight. The instructor occupied the front seat, while students occupied the two rear seats and followed through on their controls. An order was placed with Piper for 250 in August 1942. (Jay Miller Collection)

Cornelia Fort, 22, an instructor with the Andrew Flying Service, was shooting landings at the John Rodgers Airport with her student, a defense worker named Suomala, when a plane with the emblem of the Rising Sun streaked by underneath them. Fort took the controls, landed hurriedly, and the two sprinted for cover as bullets blasted the plane behind them.

Two of the planes that belonged to the Andrew Flying Service never returned that day; they washed ashore several weeks later. According to Fort, it was "not a pretty way for the brave little yellow Cubs and their pilots to go down to their deaths," she said afterward.

These incidents were quickly forgotten in the aftermath of the tragedy that Sunday morning that thrust the nation into war. Suffice to say that these Piper Cub pilots were among the first civilians to witness the infamous attack on Pearl Harbor from the air. Bob Tyce was one of America's first victims in World War II.

***

It was painfully obvious in the immediate aftermath of Pearl Harbor that President Roosevelt's plan to manufacture 50,000 military and naval planes a year did not include a great number of light airplanes. Although they had proven useful in training civilian pilots, the manufacturers had been told that combat planes were needed, and any training planes procured had to be heavier and faster than the Piper Cubs, Aeroncas, and Taylorcrafts so pilots could make a quicker transition to heavy warplanes. The successful demonstrations by Tony Piper, Bill Strohmeier, Tom Case, and the other Piper salesmen had not stimulated official top-level interest sufficiently, and the manufacturers felt they could not afford to continue to supply planes, pilots, and maintenance personnel without compensation. Since the Army Air Corps (later the Army Air Forces) had the only authority to buy planes and the Army Ground Forces did not, John Morgan suggested the Army rent them. There were no funds to do this either, but the Army Air Forces, bowing to pressure from Congress, authorized the purchase of four planes from each of the three makers for service tests at Wright Field, Ohio. As

With civilian production of Cubs halted and military contracts below the company's capacity, one of Piper's wartime projects was the TG-8 Training Glider. It was a J-3C airframe with a new nose structure. Three seats with flight controls in each were installed. The landing gear was lowered, and the front cockpit had a hinged canopy. (Peter M. Bowers Collection)

The U.S. Navy experimented with an NE-1 Cub called a Glimpy that could be loaded with explosives, attached to a blimp, and guided to targets by radio control. During flight tests a pilot tested the Cub's radio control near Lakehurst, New Jersey. (David W. Lucabaugh Collection)

mentioned in Chapter 4, they were given AAF observation designations, such as YO-57 for Taylorcraft, YO-58 for Aeronca, and YO-59 for Piper. After the tests were completed the "Y" prefix (denoting service test) was dropped. Soon thereafter, light aircraft were re-labeled as liaison types and were renumbered with the "L" prefix. Pilots who later completed the liaison training program were authorized to wear silver wings with an "L" imposed in the center of the U.S. shield to differentiate them from the wings issued to Army Air Force pilots.

There were about 400 Cubs parked on the field at Lock Haven in the early months of 1942 that could not be flown to their new owners because of security restrictions. This meant the company was faced with an income shortage to repay a $150,000 loan to a New York bank. The bank was persuaded to lend more money when the Navy agreed to take some of the Cubs and the Army Air Forces the rest for training purposes.

Despite wartime restrictions, Piper advertised the company's support of the war effort by enclosing two packs of playing cards in each Cub crate shipped out. Included was a post card addressed to the Piper Aircraft Corporation on which pilots or mechanics could write a message and have it returned to Lock Haven. These cards are a valuable collectible now, and the Piper Aviation Museum is hoping some have survived and would be available for display.

The Glimpy was attached to a slightly modified Navy blimp's underside in front of the gondola, as shown here. Experiments were conducted with and without power. (David W. Lucabaugh Collection)

A radio-controlled release mechanism in a Glimpy could be triggered to release a depth charge on an enemy submarine or ship from a blimp. The depth charge is shown in the Cub's cabin. (Peter M. Bowers Collection)

Harry P. Mutter, Piper museum historian, is also looking for any surviving cigarette packages of the 17,500 packs the company sent overseas in 1942. Each pack had a message which read: "Best Wishes, Entire Piper Organization, Makers of Piper Cubs, Lock Haven, Pa."

Piper's later wartime plane production orders of more than 5,000 two-place military L-4 Cubs kept the Piper production facilities working at only about 50 percent of capacity. In order to keep the company afloat financially, defense work for other aircraft manufacturers was sought. Piper received contracts to make plastic canopies for Stearman and Fairchild trainers, wing and tail surfaces for Waco CG-4A gliders, and small parts for larger military planes:

"It may be surprising to some to learn that the bulk of our wartime work at Lock Haven was not the manufacture of airplanes but the building of radar masts" William Piper, Sr., revealed in his 1949 book. "At no time during the war years did we operate at more than one-fifth of our actual plane-making capacity. We were producing 20 planes a week when we could have actually been turning out a hundred. Our big war contract for radar masts, awarded us because of our experience in the welding of tubular steel, put our plant in the 'secret' category."

Piper produced the masts for the Army and Navy, most of them for the Army's Signal Corps. These consisted of large welded steel tube structures which, with their component electronic control parts, were the reflector screens of radar units used for aircraft detection. During peak production Piper turned out over 300 such units monthly. Toward the end of the war the company was awarded another contract for an improved radar system, the TPX. It was a reflector on top of a 17-foot mast that turned it in a 360-degree arc.

Piper also manufactured a parabolic radar reflector for use aboard ships by the Navy. Production of these units required aluminum fabrication and welding, as well as a large amount of electrical assemblies. All of this type of military work ceased quickly several weeks before V-J Day.

This kind of non-aircraft production gave the Cub engineering staff time to devote to improving the Cubs. Walter Jamouneau knew that the Army and Navy would probably want special modifications of the Cubs and began looking for ways they could be more useful. He took a Cub Cruiser with a Lycoming 100-hp engine off the line and converted it into an ambulance plane that might be used by either the Army or Navy as an ambulance plane. He redesigned it by placing a hinged, lift-up turtle deck from the trailing edge of the wing to the tail fin, providing access to a stretcher. The stretcher, equipped with wooden rollers, was put into the proper

The U.S. Navy conducted experiments in 1942 with a Piper "Glomb," designated the XLBP-1. It was a pilot-less glider made of plywood that carried a large bomb, and was towed by a fighter plane to a release point and guided to a target by radio control. Three were produced and 100 were ordered, but the order was canceled, as World War II was ending. (Piper Aviation Museum)

position with the patient strapped down. An experimental model was produced that could carry two litters, one above the other. The Navy liked the air ambulance idea and bought a number of J-5C Cub Coupes under the designation HE-1 (later changed to the AE-1 for "air ambulance). About 230 J-3C Cub tandem trainers were also bought by the Navy for use as utility planes and designated NE-1s.

Then there was the development of a glider designated the TG-8 (for training glider) from a J-3 airframe. It was a three-seat tandem model with a longer canopy, tow hook, and a rounded nose that replaced the engine. The tow hook could be released from any one of the three seats. The Army Air Forces ordered 253 gliders; three of them were transferred to the Navy for experimental purposes. After the war, a number of the gliders that survived were sold to civilians and, with new engines, some were converted into Cub variants.

Experiments were conducted with controllable pitch propellers, a single blade propeller, castoring landing gear for cross-wind landings, a cantilever wing, slotted flaps, long-stroke landing gear, and larger "greenhouse" areas for better observation purposes. Several different radial and in-line engines in the 40- to 65-horsepower range were installed with varying degrees of success, the most popular being the Continentals and Lycomings. Models of the J-3 series were mounted on metal, plywood, or pneumatic floats and called Cub Sea Scouts.

One of the unique experimental programs that Piper was involved with was the pilotless glider called the Glomb, for "glider bomb," with a fuselage made of plywood covered with steel framework. The one-piece 34-foot wing was of wood construction with fabric covering. The Glomb, carrying a large bomb, was towed by an aircraft larger than a Cub. It was to be released and guided to the target by remote radio control by the tow ship. The Navy designated the glide bomb as XLBP-1, and three were produced and flight-tested under a contract calling for 100 Glombs. The first Glomb test flight was made with a pilot at Fort Dix, New Jersey, in January 1945, and was towed by a Grumman Wildcat fighter. Further tests were abandoned when the war neared its end in the summer of 1945.

Another experiment involving a radio-controlled Cub was used in combination with a Navy blimp. A pilotless Cub, labeled a Glimpy, was suspended under a blimp with a depth bomb in the cockpit. When released, the Cub was to be controlled by radio from the blimp and directed to an enemy submarine or ship. Initial test flights were made under power with a pilot aboard. It, like the Glomb, was also abandoned toward the end of the war after a few experimental flights.

Meanwhile, William Piper, Sr., decided to go public with his concern on behalf of all the light plane manufacturers that the value of small planes was still being largely ignored by the government.

Another view of the Glimpy taken at Lakehurst Naval Air Station in March 1944 showing the attachment mechanism. Note how the blimp was modified to allow clearance for the propeller. (David W. Lucabaugh Collection)

An in-flight view of a Glimpy attached to a Navy blimp. After the engine was started the pilot climbed out and the Glimpy was released and guided under radio control to a target. (David W. Lucabaugh Collection)

He wrote a Guest Editorial in the November 1942 issue of *Aero Digest* under the title "Light Planes Being Overlooked" that pointed out the jobs that light planes could do, not only on the industrial front, but also with armies in the field:

"Recent unofficial reports stated these light airplanes have repeatedly proven their worth under combat conditions at places like Port Moresby, where American initiative has put them on a hitherto unthought-of task. They are being used to pick up American pilots and crewmen who have been forced to bail out over jungles impregnable to ground transportation. However dense the forest or unsuitable the terrain, these Cubs can usually find a nearby spot to land and rescue the stranded airmen.

"The armed forces are using them quite successfully in directing artillery fire and for communicating among various unit command posts. Since the success in all battles is largely dependent upon coordination of action, which can be accomplished only by swift and positive messenger service, light planes can perform an important job, as they have proven so many times on Army maneuvers.

"It is highly significant that, during the last hours of the struggle for Bataan, light liaison type aircraft operated continually between the peninsula and Corregidor Island till the available gasoline supply was exhausted. Do we need further proof of their military value?"

Piper pointed out that the Navy had been using their HE-1s as "ships of mercy" when they were dispatched to the scenes of crashes and carried the injured to hospitals. Light planes could augment the work of the larger transports by bringing in the wounded from the front lines so the bigger craft could carry them to a higher level of medical attention:

"We have capitalized on the light plane to this extent," he wrote, "but we have failed to take full advantage of its possibilities. For example, a few hundred of these 'Grasshopper' planes might have turned the trick at Dieppe by putting a large force of men on the ground *behind* enemy positions and then acting as their source of supply from the mainland."

Piper then presented a sample scenario where "a few thousand" light planes with three men in each could rendezvous inside France with commando equipment. They could then harass the enemy, cut their communication lines, take over gun emplacements, and attack, strafing enemy positions. He was the first to coin the term "air cavalry" and said:

"We cannot help but believe that the first nation to pioneer this type of fighting unit will have a potent and extremely effective fighting force.... All that light planes need to step into this, their new and important role, is a field trial."

Piper stressed that low-flying light planes could supplant motorcycle and automobile scouts more readily by spotting enemy anti-tank guns concealed in roadside foliage:

"If motorcycles and scout cars are expendable," he wrote, "why are not light planes, which have so much better chance of spotting the enemy and warning the rear by radio while making good their own escape? Their chances of survival are far better than those of the motorcyclists.

"At home, we bemoan the fact that despite the rubber, material, and gasoline shortages, the Army still insists on giving primary training in planes requiring more than twice as much material. Standard primary trainers used for the *ab initio* pilots consumes about 15 gallons of gas an hour, while the same training can be given for the first 35 to 40 hours in a Cub burning less than one-third that amount of fuel.

"Experience has proven that light planes deserve a place in the nation's transportation system. Many times we have seen the Piper assembly line waiting for a shipment of instruments, batteries, etc.,

The Civil Air Patrol was officially formed on December 1, 1941, sparked by the concern of Gill Robb Wilson, an aviation editor and president of the National Aeronautic Association. Owners of civilian aircraft like this Piper Cub, now preserved in an Arizona air museum, was one of several hundred that served in various ways during World War II. (Photo by the author)

which might have been brought in by light plane. A short time ago we saved two days by dispatching one of our own craft a few hundred miles away for radios to be installed in aircraft scheduled for delivery to the Army. These planes left in the morning and were back in time to permit the night shift to complete the installation. During recent floods in Pennsylvania our aircraft provided the only means of reaching one important factory in the inundated area. Although bridges and railroads were washed out, the light planes delivered the material."

Piper also suggested that light aircraft could be used for the transport of industry executives in the United States when rail and air travel required priority ratings and automobile travel was limited by a 35-mile-an-hour speed limit, in addition to gas and tire shortages.

"The Civil Air Patrol has advocated such use of the light plane to no avail," he added, "and yet every pilot knows the potential value of such means of communication."

Piper also noted the work of the light plane for coast and forest fire patrol, but added:

"...no matter how often their story is told, there is the same unreasonable opposition from the proponents of the high horsepower craft."

He concluded that the potential of the light airplane had not been discovered yet, and new uses were continually being revealed:

"It seems ironical that in a war of transportation, with an exclusive system of transportation conveyance at our fingertips, we still have to avail ourselves of its utility. Why can't we do something about this *now*."

***

One answer to Mr. Piper's concern was the formation of the Civil Air Patrol, which he had heartily supported. It was formed officially on December 1, 1941, six days before the infamous attack on Pearl Harbor. In Europe, civilian aviation activities ceased when World War II began in 1939. But a group of American aviation enthusiasts was determined that general aviation—non-military planes and their pilots— had a role to play in this country's defense.

One man who had observed the buildup of airpower in Germany under Adolf Hitler and the aviation training of young German males was Gil Robb Wilson, the *New York Herald Tribune's* aviation editor and president of the National Aeronautic Association (NAA). The earnestness and knowledge of the youths made a deep impression on him. "Surely there was nothing like this any-

This three-bladed propeller logo was adopted as the insignia for the Civil Air Patrol during World War II. (Photo by the author)

where else in the world," he wrote in his autobiography *I Walked with Giants*. "Hitler was not drafting an air force—he was raising it from the cradle!"

Wilson was firmly convinced that Germany was far ahead of the United States in the development of air power, and was perhaps even beyond overtaking it. Although the American aircraft industry was accumulating a wealth of knowledge, he felt that time was against overcoming the head start that Germany had:

"It was at this point that I began to think of the private and business pilots and the miscellaneous fleet as shock troops to gain

Civil Air Patrol volunteers prepare for submarine patrol off the East Coast during World War II. CAP members flew 86,685 patrol missions in 244,600 hours of flying. (Civil Air Patrol Archives)

time should the United States be attacked," Wilson wrote. "I had never heard anyone suggest that this segment of aviation might be a national resource."

David Harold Byrd, a Texas oil man, claimed that he and Wilson had formulated the basic idea on the back of a menu card at the Peacock Terrace of the Baker Hotel in Dallas in September 1941. The basic theme they agreed on was that:

"...a large potential of unused flying talent would go to waste, in the event of hostilities, unless those pilots who were too old or otherwise not qualified for military duty could be mobilized."

Wilson began a research program in his home state of New Jersey and set up an experimental organization he called the "Civil Air Defense Service." Pilot and plane rosters were compiled, experimental patrols were flown, emergency situations simulated, and indoctrination classes were set up. Three hundred members volun-

teered, and Wilson went on a speaking tour to tell civic and veteran groups of the nationwide need for such an organization. As the NAA president, he had an office in Washington and contacted members of Congress to lobby for his plan. He headed a committee in September 1941 that presented a plan for the formation of a national organization to be known as the Civil Air Patrol under Fiorello LaGuardia, then Director of United States Civil Defense and former mayor of New York City. LaGuardia had been a pilot during World War I and recognized the merits of the plan. He forwarded the plan to the War Department in Washington, strongly recommending approval. Late in 1941, a board of Army Air Corps officers approved the concept to organize the many civilian pilots into squadrons based at airports throughout the country under the control of the Office of Civil Defense.

On December 1 La Guardia signed a formal order authorized by a Presidential Executive Order creating the Civil Air Patrol. A charter was written and approved that set forth the voluntary nature of the organization and made clear that its source was the deep

Painting by an anonymous artist depicts a CAP aircraft banking to make a bombing attack on an enemy submarine off the East Coast in early 1942. (Civil Air Patrol Archives)

The New **PIPER PATROL** Is Ready!

Reporting for Active Duty with

THE CIVIL AIR PATROL

The transparent cabin enclosure provides unparalleled visibility for Civil Air Patrol flying.

Here is the ideal plane for use in Civil Air Patrol . . . recommended by pilots, built by Piper and especially suited for patrol flying! The new Piper Patrol is an adaptation of the Piper L-4A, built for the U. S. Army. It has visibility all around the compass and a reversible seating arrangement for the observer with a desk shelf upon which observation reports can be written while in flight. Like all Piper planes, it can be flown by any pilot, and with traditional Piper economy of operation. Dual controls permit the Patrol to be used as a trainer when not on CAP duty, thus doubling its utility to the flying service operator. Available in standard Piper colors with CAP insignia on fuselage and wings. See it and fly it at your Piper Dealer's.

FREE CATALOG showing all the Piper planes may be obtained from your Piper Dealer. Or, if you wish, we will gladly mail you one of these handsome, deluxe catalogs which portrays all the new Piper ships in full natural color, providing you enclose 10c in stamps or coin for postage-handling. Piper Aircraft Corporation, Department D72, Lock Haven, Pennsylvania, U. S. A.

PIPER POINTS THE WAY TO WINGS FOR ALL AMERICA

JULY 1942   7

Piper took advantage of the establishment of the Civil Air Patrol to advertise the capability of Cubs for CAP duty. Piper offered them with the CAP logo on the fuselage and wings. (*Aero Digest*)

desire of the citizen airmen to serve the country. The charter established a broad classification for membership, provided for an oath of allegiance, and stated in general terms the nature of the services to be performed.

One of the fundamental services that Wilson foresaw came from a remark that a German major had made during Wilson's pre-war visit to Germany: "Your East Coast is the best submarine hunting ground in the world!" Thereafter, coastal reconnaissance would be given number one priority. Wilson argued that:

"The civilians might not be able to do combat with submarines, but they could carry smoke bombs to mark their sightings; and their very presence would be a threat to submarines."

The first national CAP commander was Brigadier General John F. Curry, who immediately began the daunting task of mobilizing and training a volunteer force of civilian fliers for military operations to function effectively as an aid to the Army and Navy. When war was declared a week later the seeds had been planted, and the Civil Air Patrol was destined to show what non-military light planes and pilots could do to solve an immediate problem. In March 1942 Major (later Colonel) Earle L. Johnson succeeded Curry and continued the work of setting up the organization.

Tankers carrying gasoline from Texas to the East Coast were being blown up almost daily after leaving Texas refineries headed for northern ports by German submarines in sight of land! Freighters bound for Russia and England were sunk soon after departing American ports. The requirement to attempt to stop the losses was urgent, but the Army, Navy, and Coast Guard lacked the equipment and personnel to handle the overwhelming menace.

Sinkings rose from 12 in January 1942 and increased to 52 by May, threatening to prevent the U.S.' ability to carry the war to

Europe. German submarines menaced the entire length of the Atlantic and Gulf coasts from Halifax, Nova Scotia, to Tampico, Mexico. The ship losses became so frequent that shipping was stopped until convoys with Navy protection could be organized.

When Major Johnson, executive officer to General Curry, was appointed the CAP commander, he had other pressing concerns about civil defense. He caused a national furor when he "went public" with his deep fear that an enemy saboteur could steal a plane from an unguarded airport and use it to bomb a war plant. To prove his point, Johnson took off in his Cub one evening and dropped bags loaded with flour on a defense plant to show how easy it would be for a saboteur in an airplane to drop explosives:

"It gave me the creeps," he said, "to think what a hundred determined Germans could do to a hundred factories in just one night. They could land their planes in a field, walk away, and never be caught."

As a result, U.S. airports were placed under armed guard, civilian pilots were required to prove their citizenship and loyalty, and no planes were allowed to take off without obtaining flight clearances.

After the United States officially entered the war, the week-old Civil Air Patrol was hastily organized to prepare for whatever duties it might be called upon to perform. The plan was to organize a wing in each of the 48 states that was responsible to a national headquarters in Washington. Each wing consisted of squadrons of 50 to 200 members. Each squadron, in turn, was divided into flights of 10 to 60 members.

Directives issued by CAP headquarters emphasized the importance of training. Each squadron was to give its members all the ground school instruction needed to obtain a private pilot's license,

Civil Air Patrol members flew identification missions with volunteer ground observers during World War II. CAP planes were also used to search for submarines, lost hunters, wrecked aircraft, searchlight tracking, and target towing. Twenty-five different types of planes were used by the wartime CAP. (U.S. Air Force photo)

Young members of the CAP attend ground school classes during World War II. CAP non-rated members helped to improve airfields, worked with the civil defense organization as spotters, flew as observers, and helped service aircraft. (Civil Air Patrol Archives)

plus a certain amount of military drill and lessons in military customs and courtesies.

Any U.S. citizen over 18 years of age of good moral character and proven loyalty could enlist in the CAP. The first call was for men and women who had pilot licenses or some other specialized skill, such as knowledge of radio or mechanics. However, there were many other positions established for non-fliers, such as office work, sentry duty, control tower operators, and communications.

From the very beginning the Civil Air Patrol proved that civilian pilots flying light aircraft could serve the country in the best Minuteman tradition. To guard hundreds of miles of coastline and protect essential shipping, the United States had only a small force of five World War I anti-submarine escort vessels, called Eagle boats, three ocean-going yachts, less than a dozen small Coast Guard cutters, four blimps, and a few military planes. With some misgivings the Army and Navy turned to the Civil Air Patrol for help. Could the CAP help out for a 90-day period until more men and equipment were made available for the military?

Answering that call was the beginning of the most spectacular of the Civil Air Patrol's wartime missions—coastal patrol. But, although the German submarines were sinking American ships at will, there was skepticism among military leaders that they should turn over coastal patrol to civilians flying small land-based planes. They insisted that the CAP needed more time to get organized and, besides, patrolling at sea was not a job for amateurs.

In March 1942, despite the resistance of the military, experimental CAP bases were established at Atlantic City, New Jersey, and Rehoboth Beach, Delaware. The first light plane patrol flights were made on March 6, 1942. A third base went into operation at Lantana, Florida, the following month. Major oil companies established the Tanker Protection Fund and donated $40,000 to support

the administrative costs of coastal bases. Government funding did not come through until the middle of 1942. Meanwhile, CAP members volunteered their time and had to buy their own gasoline and borrow or beg for ground equipment to keep planes flying.

One of the first instances that showed the unarmed light planes could be exceptionally useful was when a Cub patrol plane caught a German U-boat close inshore off the east Florida coast and so frightened the skipper by diving at it that he ran the sub into a mud bank. While the Cub circled above, frantically sending radio hurry-up calls to summon cutters, destroyers, or bombers to the scene, the sub squirmed free after an hour and escaped before Army bombers arrived.

When General Henry H. "Hap" Arnold heard about this he contacted Gil Robb Wilson:

"I asked Gil if he thought the CAP pilots, dressed in civilian clothes and having no military status, would object to carrying bombs on their puddle-jumpers," Arnold said in *Global Mission*, his wartime memoirs. "As usual, Wilson was enthusiastic and asked, 'Where do we get them?'

Lookout towers were built by Ground Observer Corps volunteers during World War II. Civil Air Patrol members flew missions to give observers practice in identifying aircraft. The GOC later received official status during the later Cold War period under the Air Force Air Defense Command. (U.S. Air Force photo)

WAFS pilots from their base at Love Field, Dallas, Texas, study the recommended route to deliver twin-engine Beechcraft AT-11 trainers to a World War II bombardier training school. (Beech Aircraft Corporation)

"Accordingly, I had special bomb racks built at one of our depots—bomb racks that could be attached to these small planes in a very short time. We also built a cheap bombsight, and thereafter most of the CAP planes carried bombs—fifty pounders that pilots could drop on the submarines, knowing full well that if they were taken prisoner in civilian clothes they could not be considered part of our armed forces, but guerrillas."

Some of the larger planes were equipped with stronger racks to hold one or two demolition bombs and an attachment for a depth charge. Several technicians designed a bombsight with tin cans and other scrap metal and claimed it was so accurate that one light plane's explosive reportedly hit a U-boat on its conning tower.

A patrol of two light planes that were following two tankers off Cape May, New Jersey, spotted the CAP's first submarine on March 10, 1942. It looked like an upside-down ship at first, but when a closer look showed that it was a submarine, the pilots of both planes dove on it at full throttle. They scared the sub commander into thinking he was under attack. He dove rapidly out of sight and abandoned the attack on the two tankers.

Other sightings by CAP followed and further proved that light planes, although unarmed at first, could prevent sinkings just by being in the air. Soon, many qualified civilian pilots in the country reported voluntarily to the East Coast bases with their light planes, many of them Cubs, and the necessary ground equipment. The thought of flying over the ocean at a few hundred feet and as far as 50 or 75 miles from shore was something most would have considered suicide a few months earlier.

From dawn to dusk the civilian pilots patrolled the shipping lanes, where sinkings had become almost daily occurrences. Flying in pairs for mutual protection, they reported subs to armed military planes. The mere appearance of single-engine planes overhead

sometimes frightened a U-boat away just as it was about to attack a slow-moving tanker or cargo ship. In addition, the planes saved lives by radioing the positions of ships in distress and the location of survivors floating in life rafts.

Major Hugh R. Sharp, Jr., and Navy Ensign Edmond Edwards, who were CAP members before both were commissioned, were presented Air Medals by President Roosevelt in a White House ceremony, the first time this decoration was awarded for civilian service. Both were on coastal patrol when a CAP plane went down 20 miles off shore with two men aboard. The observer, Edward Shelfus, was lost—the first fatality in the CAP's sea patrolling. The pilot, Henry Cross, was able to inflate a life raft, despite a broken back and gasoline burns. Sharp and Edwards made a rough-water landing in a Sikorsky amphibian and rescued the paralyzed Cross. At the White House ceremony Major General George E. Stratemeyer said:

"These two men exemplify the spirit of the Civil Air Patrol, in cooperation with the Army Air Forces, in the flying of many types of special war missions necessitated by our war effort. Their activities have made possible the releasing of Army pilots and Army airplanes for combat service."

The citation accompanying the award stated:

"This difficult mission of great responsibility required outstanding initiative, resourcefulness, and a high degree of courage. The superior manner in which all duties were performed will establish high traditions of service for the Civil Air Patrol."

Before the 90-day trial period was up, the CAP Coastal Patrol had proven the wisdom of the use of light aircraft against the undersea raiders. Major Al Williams, widely known racing pilot, summarized their efforts in his syndicated newspaper column. He likened the CAP volunteers to the early American patriots who volunteered for the War of Independence and brought their own rifles and shot. He told his readers that the CAP pilots were making themselves indispensable to the regular air services:

"They bought their own uniforms," he said. "They bought their own planes, tools, and spare parts. They equipped their planes with suitable radio sets and recruited their own mechanics to service their ships. In addition, the CAP pilots have raised so much cain about being permitted to equip their planes with bomb racks that now they are going to patrol with their own punishing armament on board."

By the fall of 1942 21 CAP bases had been established extending from Bar Harbor, Maine, down the East Coast to Florida and around its West Coast to Brownsville, Texas. They ranged from such fairly well-equipped airports as Pascagoula, Mississippi, and

Beaumont, Texas, to the barely livable facilities at Grand Isle, Louisiana, where a highway was used for takeoffs and landings. The living quarters there were in an abandoned hotel that had no electricity. In Parksley, Virginia, CAP members scraped out a runway with local farm equipment and converted a chicken coop into an operations center.

To these bases came men and women from every profession and occupation—lawyers, shoe salesmen, barnstormers, mechanics, brokers, plumbers, teachers, nurses, doctors, and millionaire sportsmen. Many of the men, who were in their 30s, 40s, and 50s, were exempt from military service for physical reasons. Some of the younger male and female volunteers went into the services later. No physically-qualified male could be excused from military service just because of his CAP affiliation. The only restriction was that women were not to fly missions over the ocean, since there would probably be adverse publicity if they were lost.

The CAP was not intended to be a flight training organization. Its training program was to advance the skills of licensed airmen, but also encourage those with little or no experience to take flying lessons in light aircraft. Each member was required to take ground school subjects necessary for a private license. The basic course of 80 hours stressed such topics as military drill, discipline, first aid, gas protection, and signaling. The advanced course of 150 hours included air navigation, meteorology, and practice missions simulating CAP wartime assignments.

By mid-1942 the CAP had recruited 63,000 members, and its members were flying about 4,000 planes, a majority of them Piper Cubs. In addition to the coastal patrol, CAP planes began surveillance missions along the Mexican border looking for foreign agents and saboteurs. For eighteen months, beginning in October 1942, the CAP's Southern Liaison Patrol helped the Mexican government, the U.S. Immigration and Naturalization Service, the FBI, and the U.S. Army thwart illegal border crossings. During 4,720 patrol missions they reported 176 unidentified aircraft and 6,874 unusual ground activities to the federal authorities.

Another wartime mission for the CAP was providing assistance to the Ground Observer Corps/Aircraft Warning Service. After the raid on Pearl Harbor there was an immediate public outcry for a national air warning system but, although few realized it, an aircraft warning system was in being on Pearl Harbor Day, and civilian volunteers had hurriedly manned their observation posts along both coasts when they heard the news. An Aircraft Warning Service had been formed in April 1941 under the jurisdiction of the Army Air Forces and was associated with the interceptor commands that protected both coasts. New filter and information centers were established with both civilian volunteers and military personnel; however, as the war progressed, fewer military personnel were made available.

On July 15, 1942, the War Department formally designated the civilian volunteers as members of the AAF Ground Observer Corps (GOC). On May 7, 1943, the War Department reorganized the GOC volunteers in the filter and information centers into the AAF Aircraft Warning Service to assist in "the assembly, evaluation, and display of information concerning all planes in flight within certain areas." To help in the training of the volunteers in aircraft recognition, CAP aircraft flew missions to test the system and evaluate the ability of the volunteers to identify the type (known or unknown) and number of aircraft, approximate altitude, speed (slow, fast, or very fast), and the direction of flight they were headed. In May 1944 the Aircraft Warning Service was absorbed into the Army Air Forces' air defense installations that were training fighter-interceptor pilots.

Coastal patrol operations by the CAP ceased when the Navy took over the protection of the shipping lanes on August 31, 1943. During eighteen months of patrols the civilian flyers had flown more than 24 million miles over water, spotted 173 subs, dropped bombs or depth charges against 82, and reported 17 floating mines, several of which were in the paths of troop ships. They located 363 survivors of ship sinkings or aircraft ditchings, reported 91 ships in distress, sighted and reported 36 bodies, and rescued 129 air crewmen at sea.

William T. Piper, Sr., visited a Women Airforce Service Pilot (WASP) graduation in 1943 at Avenger Field, Sweetwater, Texas. Many graduates had their initial training in Piper Cubs at Lock Haven. (Piper Aviation Museum)

Official records show that the CAP was credited during this period with two submarine kills. Its sub hunters flew 86,685 missions in 244,600 hours of flying. Unfortunately, there were 26 fatalities, all resulting from engine failures that ended in a ditching at sea; seven others were seriously injured, and 90 planes were lost or damaged beyond repair.

As the CAP units phased out of their over-water mission, General Henry H. Arnold, chief of the Army Air Forces, lauded them for what they had done:

"The Civil Air Patrol grew out of the urgency of the situation. The CAP set up and went into operation almost overnight. It patrolled our shores—performed its anti-submarine work—at a time of almost desperate national crisis. If it had done nothing beyond that, the Civil Air Patrol would have earned an honorable place in the history of American Air Power."

Most CAP pilots that had been performing sub hunting duties continued their service by taking part in search and rescue missions, a job just as important to the war effort. It was a role especially suited for the light planes and their pilots, who had done so much with so little. The slow-flying aircraft of the CAP were particularly well-suited for searching downed planes and lost hunters in mountainous areas. Unlike the larger, faster military planes, with their low wings that prevented pilots from seeing beneath them, the high-winged Piper, Aeronca, and Stinson monoplanes could linger over an area, maneuver easily in and out of canyons, and fly low enough to allow observers to look under trees and up into shadowy canyon recesses.

These were the official wings authorized for WASP graduates for Class 43 W-8 to 44 W-10 that ended a controversy about whether or not they should wear Army Air Force wings. Women pilots originally flying for the Women's Auxiliary Ferrying Squadron (WAFS), directed by Nancy Love, wore wings with the Ferry Command logo in the center until they were incorporated into the WASP. (U.S. Air Force photo)

The huge buildup of air forces of the Army, Navy, and Marines meant that hundreds of military planes were constantly in the air day and night from the several hundred training fields that dotted the country. It was inevitable that some would be lost. The Civil Air Patrol members had a special advantage when participating in search and rescue missions. The crews knew every inch of their home territory, and their light, slow planes were ideal for making detailed aerial surveillance, especially over areas of rough terrain. There were many instances where this local knowledge saved lives.

In December 1942 an early winter blizzard struck northern New Mexico near Taos. An Army Air Force B-24 bomber had made a "controlled crash" in which nine of the ten men aboard had survived. They made a shelter from the twisted wreckage, built a fire, and huddled together, hungry and cold, as the storm raged.

Three days later they heard the welcome sound of airplane engines. It was a B-17 Flying Fortress circling the area. The wreckage was sighted, and bundles of rations, blankets, and first aid supplies were dropped. But the bundles fell into huge snow drifts more than a half mile away. It would have been suicidal for the marooned men to try to fight their way through the towering snow, icy wind, and rocky terrain to dig them out. The B-17 crew, disappointed at their poor marksmanship, radioed the location of the wrecked B-24 and headed for its base.

It was the next day that the huddled crew heard the sound of an aircraft engine. Instead of the deep-throated roar of four engines, it was a sound much like that of an outboard boat motor. It was a light plane loaded with rations and blankets piloted by CAP pilot Norman Kramer and his observer, Arthur A. Mosher.

Mosher pushed the bundles out the door and almost into the hands of the men on the ground. The two headed back toward their base at Alamosa for more supplies. They returned, and after dropping supplies again, Kramer decided to land on a flat area where

William T. Piper looks at the WASP wings presented to him by Jacqueline Cochran (left) at graduation ceremonies in October 1943. Mrs. Barton K. Yount, wife of the commanding general of the Army Air Force Training Command, represented her husband during the activities. (Piper Aviation Museum)

the winds had swept the ground bare. He dragged the area and made a cautious approach. When he chopped the throttle, the tiny craft plopped to almost a dead stop. The high wind plus an uphill grade acted like a brake.

The nine wrecked airmen watched the landing in awe. They made their way to the plane and had a conference with Kramer and Mosher. It was decided that the nine men would wait for a ground rescue party that had begun a slow climb up the mountain. In the meantime, Kramer promised to keep the men supplied with rations as long as the weather was favorable. They made six more trips before the rescue party reached the crash scene.

While persistence in searching for lost planes or people played an important role, luck and hunches sometime paid off, too. Capt. Bill Mueller of the El Paso, Texas, squadron proved this one day in 1944 when an AAF P-47 fighter failed to arrive at its New Mexico destination after departing Biggs Field, near El Paso. Mueller and four other pilots from the Roswell, New Mexico, squadron logged over 300 hours searching in their Cubs without sighting the fighter. Mueller was about to call off the search when he had an idea. He had seen a number of hunting parties during his missions; perhaps they could help.

Mueller loaded some rocks in his plane and tied notes to them asking the finders to watch for airplane wreckage. When he spotted hunters below, he dropped the rocks near them and watched as the men recovered the notes, read them, and then waved their acknowledgments. The idea worked. A short time later one of the hunters sighted a scrap of shiny aluminum and located the wreckage in an arroyo that could not be seen from the air. The pilot was found alive nearby.

These are only two instances of the value of light aircraft on the home front during World War II. The CAP flew more than 24,000 hours of search and rescue missions, many of them in Piper Cubs, during that time. While no accurate record was kept of the number

WASP members Betty Jane Bachman and Betty Whitlow check the Form IA of the P-40 that one of them will ferry to a combat unit in the United States. WASPs and WAFS pilots ferried every type of training and combat aircraft during World War II, from Cubs to the Boeing B-29 Superfortresses. (Curtiss Aircraft Corporation)

of downed aircraft spotted or the number of survivors located, CAP searchers reportedly turned up at least a hundred missing planes.

Another CAP duty was target towing for the Army. In March 1942 the Army Air Force could not spare large planes or crews to tow targets for Army anti-aircraft units to practice shooting, so the planes of the Illinois CAP wing took over the task. They flew over the anti-aircraft guns at Fort Sheridan, Illinois, trailing improvised targets. Cub pilots piled up hundreds of hours towing the target sleeves back and forth.

Target towing and searchlight tracking by CAP planes was canceled in March 1944 after flying more than 19,000 missions totaling more than 44,000 flying hours. It had been hazardous flying, as some planes returned with jagged shrapnel holes through their fuselages. Seven members had been killed in various parts of the country and five were seriously injured. Nineteen planes were lost.

WASPs are greeted by Army Air Force officers after ferrying Piper L-4s to the Army Air Force's test facility at Wright Field, Ohio, for service tests in 1942. WASPs were paid $250 a month after graduation from training and paid for their own food, uniforms, and lodging. (William D. Strohmeier Collection)

Target towing was a daytime operation, but some CAP units were assigned tracking missions at night for anti-aircraft artillery searchlight units. The planes flew a predetermined course, on instruments, while the searchlight crews tried to find them and hold them in the glare of the searchlights so the gun units could track them.

The CAP pilots also carried out missions to exercise the Aircraft Warning System, participated in mock air raids, and dropped leaflets reminding a community that "THIS COULD HAVE BEEN A BOMB!" War bond and blood bank drives were highlighted by CAP planes flying overhead towing banners to remind the public of the need to participate.

CAP units had other wartime tasks. One was the care and maintenance of airports, and sometimes their actual construction. No less than 215 airports were owned, operated, or managed by local units of the CAP.

On December 1, 1942, the little known CAP Courier Service was officially established to carry key executives and urgent shipments, such as machine parts, in light planes between air bases, Army posts, and defense industry facilities. An example of this need had occurred in early 1942 when a war plant in Kalamazoo, Michigan, was shut down because it lacked a shipment of only 100 pounds of vital parts from Oil City, PA. The CAP unit at Detroit received the urgent phone call at noon. A Cub was dispatched, and by seven PM the plant was back in operation.

The regular courier service carried out by Cubs and other light CAP planes proved especially valuable in Illinois, and at its peak flew 60 regular flights from Scott Field, Illinois, to Ephrata, Washington, and intermediate bases between the two locations. An operation in Kansas involved sixteen daily flights by two female pilots from Kansas City to bases as far away as Clovis, New Mexico. The courier station at Cleveland, Ohio, delivered vitally-needed small truck parts from the Thompson Products Co. to a plant at Sidney, Ohio. There was no airport nearby, so the packages weighing up to 50 lbs. were dropped from Cubs using strong paper para-

chutes perfected by CAP Lt. Dean H. Robinson. Virginia Wing pilots tested and proved that blood plasma bottles could be dropped by those paper parachutes without damage to the containers.

In an experimental test conducted by the Pennsylvania CAP Wing at the Army Air Force's Middletown Air Depot, five large planes were reported as having flown more than a million pound-miles of cargo to Army Air Force bases. In its first year of operation the Kansas CAP Courier Service reportedly flew 725,000 miles during a total of 9,907 hours in the air.

In May 1942 a plan was developed with the U.S. Forest Service and National Park Service for CAP planes to fly forest observation and fire patrols. Under the agreement the two agencies provided compensation for the CAP pilots and observers and rental for planes engaged in forest patrol missions.

By the beginning of 1943 the nationwide CAP fleet consisted of no less than 25 different types of aircraft, ranging from the Aeroncas, Taylorcrafts, Stinsons, and Piper Cubs to the larger, heavier, longer-range Beech, Spartan, Fairchild, and Sikorsky types. They flew so many official missions that the three-bladed CAP insignia could be seen transiting on official flights at almost every airfield in the country.

Reconnaissance missions made during flood periods was still another CAP task. In April 1943 a flood along the Missouri River, the worst in more than 60 years, devastated a large area. CAP members flew many missions in Kansas to report river conditions and spot marooned people and livestock; on one mission, flyers discovered a huge break in an interstate oil pipe line.

CAP planes from the Iowa Wing ferried doctors, nurses, food, plasma, and serum to communities cut off by rising waters, in addition to patrolling 1,000 miles of levies along the lower Mississippi River. In Oklahoma, a tornado near Pryor took more than 70 lives and left 350 injured, and 16 CAP Cubs and other light planes flew tetanus and typhoid serums to the stricken area.

CAP aircraft in other states were dispatched to check reservoirs, dams, power lines, waterways, and irrigation canals for dam-

WASP pilots march past a row of Vultee BT-13 basic trainers. After checking out in light aircraft, such as Piper Cubs, WASP trainees transitioned to BT-13s and North American AT-6s. They also received military drill instruction, in addition to courses in meteorology, navigation, and Morse code. (U.S. Air Force photo)

Many WASPs ferried Cubs from the factory during World War II. A group of WASPs, known as the Order of Fifinella, who returned to Lock Haven in 1946, consult the map before departing in a mass formation, ferrying Cubs to buyers. En route, they visited the Cleveland Air Races. (Piper Aviation Museum)

age. Camouflage and smoke screen effectiveness was checked from the air. Flying over cities at night, they checked for blackouts, dim-outs, and smoke sources. Those without radios used carrier pigeons to relay urgent messages back to their bases. War shortages of essential materials resulted in missions to spot waste metal, and there were many reports of unused railroad tracks, forgotten mining machinery, unused steel bridges, and abandoned vehicles located in former lumbering areas; in one case, an abandoned locomotive and carloads of steel were found parked at a deserted oil field.

CAP planes were also called to the scenes of car accidents, train wrecks, and large building fires. A CAP emergency first aid station was established at the municipal airport in Omaha, Nebraska, to assist victims of air, highway, and water accidents. In New Hampshire, CAP pilots located a lost three-year-old boy after an extensive ground search had failed. In Wheeling, West Virginia, a CAP patrol circled overhead for hours with their Cubs to keep watch over convicts from a road construction crew that had escaped and were preparing to cross the Ohio River. In Maine, CAP flyers located and helped in the capture of a Canadian draft dodger who had lived in the woods for more than a year by robbing camps and had murdered the father of the man who finally captured him.

In Oklahoma and Texas, CAP pilots flying J-3 Cubs killed wolves and coyotes from the air that were causing the loss of thousands of head of livestock. The coyotes, especially, were on a rampage in northwestern Oklahoma during World War II, and a special hunt was organized in 1944 in which the state game wardens and state police also participated.

Shooting coyotes from the air was not new to Oklahomans, but this was the first time official permission had been given for an organized hunt. The Cubs were piloted by men who had a commercial license. The gunners were expert marksmen and knew the dangers involved in shooting from an aircraft at very low altitudes. Gunning down a wily coyote called for perfect coordination between the two Cub occupants. The records show a kill of 230 coyotes in the ten days permitted for the hunt. Governor Robert Kerr estimated that 2,300 head of livestock had been saved by the Cub pilots.

There was one small group of CAP members that actually served in an overseas combat area. They were 20 volunteers of the First Air Ambulance Squadron of the American Field Service under the command of Major George Wilson. They were recruited by the American Red Cross for service with the British 14th Army in Burma in 1945. Their mission was the evacuation of wounded troops and newly-released sick prisoners-of-war in L-4 Cubs from battle areas to airstrips in the rear.

As the war progressed and was entering its final phase toward the victory in Europe, the CAP's active duty missions slowed down. The CAP Courier Service, towing, and tracking were phased out, but the search and rescue operations continued. In addition, CAP units became active in developing interest in air marking, so that every city and town could be identified from the air by painting the names on water towers, roofs of large buildings, or laying out tiles on the ground that spelled out the towns' names in large, open areas.

When the war was over, General Carl A. Spaatz, commanding general of the Army Air Forces, paid tribute to the Civil Air Patrol at a press conference in March 1946. He said:

"The Army Air Forces recognizes and is grateful for the many wartime contributions of anti-submarine patrol along our shores; towing and tracking missions invaluable to our anti-aircraft training; searches for lost aircraft that saved the lives of our aviators; courier service whereby parts and materials necessary to the war effort were delivered to the right place and at the right time; recruiting of cadets for air crew training; and an excellent cadet training program which interested our young people in aviation and performed a service so important to our country in time of war."

The accomplishments of the Civil Air Patrol during World War II were not without a human price. Fifty-six members were lost on wartime missions. A total of 825 Air Medals and 25 War Department certificates for Exceptional Civilian Service were awarded as tokens of high esteem from a grateful government.

Fortunately for the nation, the Civil Air Patrol did not cease to exist when the war was over. The status of the CAP was formalized on July 1, 1946, when President Harry S. Truman signed a national charter approved by Congress designating the CAP as a civilian-sponsored, educational, non-profit organization. Rep. Hatton W. Sumner of Texas gave a ringing speech of praise to the CAP in the House of Representatives and concluded:

"My interest was aroused in this organization because of its demonstrated unselfish, self-reliant willingness-to-do-something-about-it, fit-to-live-in-a-democracy sort of spirit—the sort of spirit which makes free government possible."

At the press conference where General Spaatz gave his talk, he announced that the Army Air Forces would continue to support the Civil Air Patrol. On May 26, 1948, the 80th Congress passed Public Law 557, establishing the CAP as the civilian auxiliary of the U.S. Air Force and authorizing its members to wear the Air Force blue uniform with certain identifying changes in insignia. This law formalized its status to carry out non-combat missions.

Legislation in the aftermath of the tragedies caused by terrorists on September 11, 2001, has substantially improved the Air Force's status with the CAP by providing the Air Force greater authority to use and support the organization. Federal agencies, such as the Federal Emergency Management Agency, the Drug Enforcement Administration, and the U.S. Customs Service, may also use this Air Force auxiliary capability. The Civil Air Patrol has proven over more than six decades that its members and small non-military planes, like the ubiquitous Piper Cubs, are capable of responding rapidly and with patriotic dedication to national emergencies in the 50 states at any time.

***

Another wartime group that was influenced by the presence of Piper Cubs in their lives was two organizations of women pilots recruited to relieve the shortage of male pilots in the Air Transport Command (ATC) at the beginning of America's involvement in World War II. Nancy Harkness Love and Jacqueline Cochran were two experienced women pilots with the same idea. Love was hired by the Army Air Force in September 1942 to recruit 27 of the most qualified women pilots in the country to ferry military aircraft from the factories to the point of embarkation or training bases in the U.S. All had to have a commercial license and at least 500 hours flying time. Most were CPT or War Training Program flight instructors, and almost all had flown Piper Cubs at some time during their flying careers at that point. These women comprised the Women's Auxiliary Ferrying Squadron (WAFS) and have been called "the Originals," because they paved the way for women who are flying military and commercial aircraft today. At the same time, Cochran was put in charge of training a large group of women to be qualified to ferry military aircraft. That unit was called the Women's Flying Training Detachment (WFTD). Some of those who graduated first from this training were assigned to the WAFS.

On August 5, 1943, the WAFS and the WFTD were merged and re-designated the Women's Airforce Service Pilots, or WASPs. Cochran was appointed Director of Women Pilots, and Love was named WASP Executive of the Ferrying Division of the Air Trans-

port Command. Pilots of the latter were checked out in several types of aircraft before they were assigned to their bases.

Acceptance into the WASP program for those with lesser flying experience required that the applicants be 21-35 years of age, possess a high school diploma, a commercial pilot license, and a minimum of 200 hours of pilot time. They took six months of ground school courses that included meteorology, aerodynamics, engine operations and maintenance, navigation, and military and civilian air regulations. Flight training was conducted at Hughes Field in Houston, and later at Avenger Field, Sweetwater, Texas. Many of the WASPs learned to fly in Piper Cubs, first in the CPT program at their respective colleges or at Lock Haven (they called it "Sweetwater Prep"), and subsequently moving on to the Texas base when they had accumulated sufficient flying time.

The flight training at Sweetwater was in Stearman PT-17s, Vultee BT-13s, and North American AT-6s. After graduation, some found themselves back at Lock Haven and assigned to ferry Piper L-4s to Army posts and Air Force bases throughout the country. Unlike the Women's Army Corps, the WASPs were denied military status by Congress and remained on Civil Service status throughout their service. They were, however, entitled to the privileges of officers when on a base, wore a distinctive Saratoga-blue uniform, and had to conform to military regulations while on duty. They had

WASPs gather for a final briefing before their mass formation flight to Ohio, and then to final destinations in 33 states. (William D. Strohmeier Collection)

a special insignia consisting of silver wings surmounted by a silver diamond-shaped lozenge. They were paid $150 per month while training and $250 a month when placed on operational status. No WASPs piloted aircraft overseas or to Alaska, although a few ferried them from Romulus, Michigan, to RCAF bases in Canada.

Vivian Gilchrist Nemhauser recalled those days during a 1995 WASP reunion at Lock Haven:

"When I was in the Ferry Command at New Castle Army Air Base near Wilmington, Delaware, the orders were first to go out and gather up 400 beat-up Cubs (L-4s) and take them to Rome, New York. There they made 300 good ones, which we then had to pick up and deliver to Newark Airport. Then they were wrapped in protective covering and shipped overseas to become the little 'Grasshopper,' or spotter planes, which the enemy could not detect. They liked to have the WASP ferry those planes because the fellows who were returning from Europe were having a great time flying these planes under telephone wires or other antics and sometimes cracking them up. We were so happy to have anything to fly that we flew the straight and narrow path. I picked up three planes to deliver to Rome and delivered 17 planes to Newark."

Besides ferrying aircraft, records show that 637 WASPs served at a number of Air Training Command bases in the aircraft maintenance sections testing repaired trainers and "slow-timing" engines. One hundred and eighteen performed various courier duties, eleven were assigned to fly meteorologists for weather observations, and three were assigned to the Army Air Force Proving Ground to make specialized tests on planes and equipment, while another three performed special research flying for the Air Technical Service Command.

When the need for pilots lessened, the WASPs were officially disbanded on December 20, 1944. They had ferried 43 different types of aircraft in the AAF inventory, including all models of bombers and fighters; two women had checked out in the giant Boeing B-29 Superfortress. When announcing the disbandment, General Arnold praised them, saying:

"I am proud of the WASP and their record of skill, versatility, and loyalty. They have not only performed highly essential service, but also established previously unknown facts concerning the capabilities of women in highly specialized military jobs. This knowledge will be of inestimable value should another national emergency arise."

In another statement he said that women could "fly wingtip to wingtip" with their brother pilots, and "it is on the record that women can fly as well as men."

Nearly 25,000 women had applied for the WFTD program; 1,830 were accepted, and 1,074 women graduated. It was estimated that the WAFS and WASPs flew 60 million miles on ferrying duty; 11 died in crashes during their service. Two former WASPs—Margaret Latta and Judy (Keiles) Seltzer—returned to Lock Haven after their release from duty. Both ferried planes for Piper, and Latta

A Civil Air Patrol Cub is "propped" for a search mission from Hyde Field, Maryland. The CAP is now an official auxiliary of the U.S. Air Force. (CAP Historical Foundation Archives)

Chief Warrant Officer A.W. Schell, Jr. (right), with an unidentified observer before an over-water search mission from Westminster CAP Field, Maryland. At the beginning of World War II life vests and other types of survival equipment were not available for CAP crews. (CAP Historical Foundation Archives)

also worked as an airport clearance officer for four years; Seltzer also flew as a co-pilot for a company that flew cargo and executive transport aircraft. Latta recalled that:

"We never made much money flying planes from Lock Haven, and if we were forced by weather or other circumstances to remain over night, we'd call Bill Piper, Jr., and he'd send us money. We were paid seven cents an air mile, which averaged out to about $25 a week."

In September 1946 William Piper, Sr., invited the WASPs back to Lock Haven for their first reunion. After a business meeting they competed in spot landing and bomb dropping contests with lime bags, and were given the opportunity to fly new models they had not flown before. The next day 83 Cubs were flagged off in quick succession in groups of three flying several models of the Cubs (mostly J-3s) to the airport at Akron, Ohio, via Dubois and Clarion, PA. It was the greatest formation of civilian planes in the country at the time. As they approached the city the tower operator gave an incoming airliner the weather as high broken clouds and warned of "lower scattered Cubs." A total of 276 formation takeoffs and landings were made on narrow runways and short fields without incident or accident. The total distance flown that one day was estimated at 20,700 miles.

The WASPs were bused to Cleveland to attend the National Air Races and then returned to Akron. They took off and scattered to the four winds on their way to buyers in 33 states in what was the largest mass delivery of aircraft in the history of private flying.

Vivian Gilchrist Nemhauser was assigned to fly a J-3 to a dealer at the DePonti Aircraft Co. at Minneapolis after the air races. En route over Wisconsin, she said the engine began to "sound funny." She checked the magnetos and found that the left one was inoperative. She continued flying on the right magneto and landed at Rochester, where a mechanic assured her that she should have no problem continuing to Minneapolis. He removed the left magneto and handed it to her:

"The flight to Minneapolis was fine," she said. "I walked into the office at DePonti and said, 'Here are the papers, and here's the left mag.' The dealer was astonished.'"

In August 1995 another WASP reunion was held during the 10th annual Sentimental Journey at the William T. Piper Memorial Airport for those who had flown Cubs at Cub Haven during World War II. Fifty women pilots, mostly in their 70s and early 80s by then, were able to attend. B. Kimball Baker said in an *Aviation Quarterly* magazine article:

"These women earned their wings when flying was considered far too dangerous and unladylike for a woman. But for them, the challenge and excitement of flying—those feelings of getting above it all, which every pilot knows but few can describe—were magnets too powerful to resist."

The WAFS and WASPs had made American aviation history during their brief service, and Piper Cubs had helped them make it.

6

Light Planes Join the Fight

On May 15, 1942, the Army Air Forces announced the establishment of an extensive glider training program for civilian pilots who had not been eligible for aviation cadet training. Such a program was necessary to catch up with developments in Europe. The Germans had used hundreds of gliders to haul troops and equipment in the 1940 invasion of Belgium. Later, they startled Allied war planners with the seizure of Crete in May 1941 using hundreds of gliders carrying infantry, field artillery pieces, ammunition, and cargo. German glider forces were used against Russian objectives on the Black Sea, and their gliders had supplied their armored units in Libya.

The U.S. glider program could be said to have begun when the Army Air Forces accepted delivery of its first glider in July 1942 at the 12th annual National Soaring Contest at Elmira, New York. It was a two-place Schweizer all-metal glider that was tested by Major Fred R. Dent, the Army Air Forces' first qualified glider pilot. At a banquet after the contests, Lt. Gen. Henry H. Arnold announced

his intention to build a glider force "second to none." He declared that the Army must be prepared to use glider-borne troops as well as parachutists—the airborne infantry—and "not by the hundreds or the thousands—but by the tens of thousands."

A program was inaugurated to produce 6,000 glider pilots, and the word went out quickly to Army recruiting offices. Volunteers between 18 and 35 who could meet the physical requirements were required to possess a private pilot's license or better, or have completed at least the elementary CPT course. They could not have been eliminated for flying deficiency previously in Army, Navy, or CAA pilot training courses.

Training began at a number of civilian flying fields, mostly in the Midwest. Trainees received basic instruction on light airplanes like the Piper Cub J-3 or the military L-4. The training then concentrated on power-off landings from various altitudes, glides, and angles until the student attained maximum proficiency at landing on specified areas on the field. For those who had flown Piper Cubs

One of the advantages of the Piper L-4 was that it could be easily dismantled for inspection and maintenance in the field by automobile mechanics with minimum instruction. (U.S. Army Aviation Museum)

Marine General W. H. Rupertus and other wartime leaders used the L-4 to visit front line troops in the South Pacific during World War II. (Peter Petras Collection)

L-4s were used by many of the Allied air and ground forces during World War II. This one is in Australian war colors at Brisbane. (Lang Kidby Collection)

before entering the glider program this proved to be relatively easy, and they quickly transitioned to gliders.

Following a two-month course in dead-stick landings, students moved on to two-place Army gliders at advanced schools. They learned four methods of launching: straight auto pull, pulley tow, winch tow, and airplane tow. Airplane launchings could be single, double, or triple, which required different lengths of rope. Graduates of the program went on to fly large, troop-carrying gliders. All volunteers who successfully completed the glider training program were appointed staff sergeants with a glider pilot rating and flying

Piper L-4s and Stinson L-5s proved their mettle in the South Pacific during World War II. This was the scene at Sandburg Field, in the New Hebrides, in 1944, as two Cubs stood by on alert at an airstrip that had been cleared for air operations. (Bill Stratton Collection)

LST No. 386 launches an L-4 to reconnoiter the coast before landings on Sicily by Allied forces in June 1943. (Bill Stratton Collection)

A number of LSTs were converted to launch Cubs for reconnaissance missions, but landing on them safely was not possible. An L-4 is recovered from the ocean after a bad launch from an LST at an undisclosed location in the Pacific. (Fred Boucher Collection)

pay. The silver wings of the Army glider pilots had a "G" in the center of the U.S. shield to differentiate them from graduates of the pilot training program of the Army Air Forces.

One problem was quickly apparent as qualified candidates were selected and ready to begin training. There was a severe shortage of gliders. Since neither the Army nor Air Force had any glider pilots, the services commandeered sailplanes from civilian owners and quickly ordered new ones. However, it was obvious that the sailplane manufacturers could not turn them out quickly enough; be-

sides, there were too few civilian glider-qualified instructors. The Army Air Forces immediately looked to the three major light plane makers for the training gliders.

Piper designed its first glider by removing the engine of a J-3 Cub and modifying the nose and fuselage to meet the government specifications. A contract was awarded for three prototypes, designated the TG-8, followed by an order for 250 TG-8s on August 15, 1942, plus three for the Navy designated as the XLNP-1. The first TG-8 prototype was rolled out for testing at Lock Haven on June 17, 1942. The unit cost was estimated at $2,100 each.

S/Sgt Frank Perkins poses nonchalantly beside *Super Snooper* in Tunisia in 1943. Pilots flying Cubs on reconnaissance missions at low altitudes rarely wore parachutes and carried only a .45 caliber automatic pistol for personal protection. (U.S. Army Photo)

Just as the Army Air Force's fighters and bombers were permitted to have "nose art" on their aircraft, many Army Cub pilots also decorated theirs. Here a pilot and observer express their feelings about when they might return to the States from an overseas war zone. (U.S. Army Photo)

Two Army liaison pilots proudly pose with their Cub *Sad Sack* somewhere in Europe. Enemy soldiers did not like to see L-4s observing their positions, because their presence soon meant bombardment by Allied field artillery. (Bill Stratton Collection)

The approved Piper training glider had three seats in tandem with controls in each. The engine was replaced by an extended nose, and a skid was installed underneath; internal modifications had to be made to adjust for the change in the center of gravity. The cockpit was made longer, with a hinged-up canopy for the front cockpit; the wing included spoilers to be used as brakes. A modified cross-axle landing gear replaced the normal split-axle arrangement of the J-3. The TG-8s that survived the war were easily converted back to J-3s with deactivated wing spoilers.

Larger troop-carrying gliders were on the drawing boards, and graduates from the light glider schools would eventually transition into them. However, these had to be manufactured from scratch and were not yet available. Meanwhile, the graduates flew the available light planes to maintain their flying proficiency. When they completed training in the large gliders they were expected to take into battle, they continued to fly the light aircraft assigned to their units.

The exploits of the glider pilots during World War II have been told in books by the participants. Many brave men piloted the fragile canvas or plywood motorless aircraft into Sicily, Normandy, southern France, Holland, and across the Rhine to deliver guns, jeeps, and reinforcements for embattled paratroopers who had landed before they did. They endured not only the enemy's flak, but foul weather, inexperienced tow plane pilots, and gliders that tended to disintegrate in turbulence. After their usual crash-landings in the combat areas, few pilots returned to their takeoff bases to fly gliders on subsequent missions. They were expected to join the men they had transported, and many died fighting on the ground after their piloting role was concluded.

The question is often asked in hindsight if the price the glider crews suffered was worth it. One pilot's answer says it all:

"It was a job. We volunteered for it, we were selected for it, we trained for it, and finally we did it—and lost a lot of good friends. But, in the end, it was just another lousy job that someone had to do."

***

The value of small, light planes for observation purposes by U.S. Army ground troops had been proven by the civilian salesmen from Piper, Aeronca, and Taylorcraft during the summer of 1941. They could be operated from unprepared landing grounds, were

A launch by an Army L-4 goes awry during a cross-wind takeoff from a Navy LST somewhere in the South Pacific. LSTs could not always maneuver quickly enough to turn into the wind for safe takeoffs. (Peter M. Bowers Collection)

LST 906 was one of several landing ships converted to small aircraft carriers with 200-foot decks. Rudders were removed from parked aircraft to provide takeoff clearance. (U.S. Army Aviation Museum)

easily maintained, and could be made quickly available in large numbers. After the War Department approved the assignment of light planes to each Field Artillery battalion and division, basic flight training was given at civilian flight schools at Denton, Texas, and Pittsburg, Kansas. Advanced operational flight training and maintenance instruction were given at the Field Artillery School at Fort Sill, Oklahoma. At its peak about 200 L-4 Grasshoppers were assigned there for the training of artillery officers as pilots in artillery fire direction.

Piper, Taylorcraft, and Aeronca planes equipped with 65-hp Continental engines, and two-way radios made up the majority of the liaison training force, with Cubs leading the list. Stinsons were designated L-5s and were equipped with the Lycoming 185-hp engine. A reported 3,590 light planes were procured, and nearly 500 were transferred to the Navy and Marines for observation purposes; these were designated OY-1s.

It was decided early that the Piper L-4 was to be the standard liaison aircraft to be used overseas to avoid procurement problems with spare parts supply and maintenance. The first real test of the L-4s in combat came in the invasion of North Africa on November 8, 1942, when American forces landed on French soil. Three of them took off from a Navy carrier to spot for ground units going

Piper converted the J-5C Cub Coupe into an ambulance plane for the Navy, which was first designated the HE-1, and later the AE-1. The rear fuselage was enlarged to allow space for a stretcher patient to be carried. The rear turtleneck is hinged to allow easier patient placement. (David W. Lucabaugh Collection)

A patient is loaded into an HE-1 at the Corpus Christi Naval Air Station in December 1942. (David W. Lucabaugh Collection)

ashore. Since there had been no advance notice of their arrival and their profiles had not been illustrated in aircraft recognition manuals, two were shot down by American forces and one by the French. All six occupants escaped unharmed.

The first American plane to land successfully in North Africa was a Cub named *Little Lucy*, later to become one of the most used "aerial jeeps" of the Mediterranean Theater of Operations for flying more than 1,500 hours. Major Edward Gordon had departed in it from a Navy carrier 60 miles at sea and flew into an airport north of Casablanca.

It had not been an easy landing. German planes had bombed and strafed the field only five minutes before, and French ack-ack gunners already set up to defend the field had not expected a light plane to lead the American invasion. Gordon slid in for a landing and the Cub was not damaged. In subsequent weeks the Cubs proved themselves many times over. Their slow speed was an advantage

when attacked by enemy fighters, and their low altitude gave enemy anti-aircraft gunners difficulty because they could not lower their guns down far enough to aim and fire. This success, however, made them special targets for roaming Messerschmitt 109 and Focke-Wulf 190 fighters. Fortunately, casualties suffered by the Cubs and their pilots were relatively low.

When the war moved into Italy and Europe the Cubs continued to show what they could do to assist artillery units. Typical of all the Cub planes that accomplished their jobs in the European War was

Janey, assigned to the American 3rd Infantry Division. Though many men flew J*aney* (an L-4B) in her two and a half years of combat, she was originally the plane of Capt. Alfred W. "Dutch" Schultz, and was named for Jane Willis Reese, his college sweetheart and future wife. He flew it more often any other Cub pilot during the division's battles from Casablanca to Berchtesgaden. His

The Navy assigned HE-1s/AE-1s to the blimp units as a transport for injured personnel, but also for additional submarine patrols when needed. (U.S. Navy photo)

Many L-4 Cubs were ferried across the English Channel on D-Day by borrowing gas cans from Jeeps for additional fuel. All aircraft were painted with white invasion stripes for identification. (U.S. Army photo)

excellent book, titled *Janey*, tells of his experiences taking General George Patton on dangerous flights to observe ground fighting, to check out German glider fields, and to meet wounded soldiers as they were being evacuated.

Janey's life under fire is also reported by Major Harold W. Wellinger when it was assigned to the 7th Army in Europe:

"When the 3rd Division landed on the coast of Africa on November 8, 1942, *Janey* flew from the U.S. aircraft carrier *Ranger*, 20 miles at sea, and landed at Port Lyautey, Morocco. Following the fall of Casablanca, *Janey* returned to her original landing strip in North Africa to spend the next months in training for her next mission.

"After a short time at Arzew in April of that year, the 35th Division was alerted to move into the line at Tunisia. Then, for the first and only time, *Janey* was late for an appointment with the enemy. She arrived on the scene just one hour after the Italian and German forces unconditionally surrendered in North Africa in May.

"A Mediterranean cruise was next on *Janey's* prolonged European tour. She made the voyage on an LST after being dismantled and placed on a truck. On July 10, 1943, her cruise ended abruptly when she touched down on the short field at Licata, Sicily, at H-plus-3 hours. A few hours later she was flying over difficult mountains. Here she began piling up her impressive list of 'firsts.' She was the only plane to land at Palermo and the first Allied plane to direct fire on the Italian mainland. At this time, she received the Purple Heart for wounds inflicted from accurate German anti-aircraft fire.

"After a short rest at Trapani, Sicily, she again received the truck and LST treatment, and this time rolled ashore at Salerno, Italy, on September 18, 1943. Mountains were again passing under *Janey's* wings as she went about her daily business of looking for enemy installations—and finding them. While parked on the ground one day, an enemy shell crashed nearby and *Janey* received an Oak Leaf Cluster to the Purple Heart for wounds received in action. After assisting in the crossing of the Volturno River, she got a short

This AE-1 was used by the Navy for malaria control on Guadalcanal in 1945. (David W. Lucabaugh Collection)

The U.S. Navy procured several Cubs for each of its naval air stations. This one was assigned to Anacostia Naval Air Station, Washington, D.C. (David W. Lucabaugh Collection)

relief in the vicinity of Naples. On the eve of the 1944 New Year, a violent windstorm came up and *Janey* took a flight by herself. She ended up in the top of a tall tree and was badly damaged. But the crew chief made her available soon after for more combat service.

"January 22, 1944, was a day that will be long remembered in military annals. In the early light of the morning, troops of the 3rd Division landed at Anzio, one of the bloodiest battlefields of the war. *Janey* took off from an LST that had been converted into a 'baby flattop' for the specific purpose of carrying Cubs. She was the first plane to land on the Anzio beachhead. During the hectic four months that followed, she was wounded two more times, once by anti-aircraft fire and once by bomb fragments. Then came the break-through and the rush to Rome. When it started, the 3rd Divi-

sion had nine Cubs in addition to *Janey*. When Rome was finally taken, there were only two left. Of course, one of them was *Janey*.

"Next came the chance to visit France. She was there when the 3rd Division landed on the shores of Southern France on August 15, 1944. Again taking off from an LST, she was the first Cub to land in the sector near St. Tropez. Then came the pursuit of the German 19th Army from Brignoles over the Vosges Mountains all the way to Strasbourg. *Janey* was active during all of these moves.

"*Janey* was wounded again over the fortress of Neuf Brisach when German gunners caught her in their sights. When the 3rd Division spearheaded the attack on the Siegfried Line, *Janey* did more than her share. She flew Major General J. W. O'Daniels to reconnoiter the division's advance. *Janey* landed between the U.S. troops

General Dwight D. Eisenhower, Supreme Commander of Allied troops in Europe, grins as his pilot, Major T.J. Walker, taxis in after a flight to visit a front line unit. Many Army generals depended on the Piper L-4 for short distance transportation during World War II. The future president learned to fly while stationed in the Philippines, 1935-1939. (U.S. Army photo)

General Mark Clark debarks from an L-4 for a visit to a combat unit somewhere in Italy. Senior Army officers had L-4s assigned to their headquarter's units for quick inspection trips. (Piper Aviation Museum)

An L-4 is off-loaded from a Navy ship in the South Pacific as Army soldiers wait for the command to debark. (Piper Aviation Museum)

Pilots and their observers study a map before a reconnaissance mission over a jungle combat area. Although flying low and slow, they were usually not easy targets for enemy ground fire because of the dense foliage. (Piper Aviation Museum)

and the Germans so that he could send back needed information to his troops. Then came the crossing of the Rhine, across Germany to Nurnberg, Augsburg, Munich, Salzburg, and Berchtesgaden. When the European War ended, *Janey* was still in flying trim, having accumulated more than 650 combat hours."

***

Many civilian-owned Cubs flown in the northern United States, Canada, and Alaska were equipped with skis from the days of the E-2s; however, they were not so equipped by the military until the 1943-44 winter Army maneuvers in northern Michigan. Approximately 100 Ground Force Cubs were ski-equipped during the winter months in Europe after the 1944 invasion in Belgium and France.

They were generally used when operating in deep snow until landing strips could be bull-dozed and normal wheel operations could be resumed.

Floats were attached to Cubs when units of the Fifth Army flew from the Naples area to the Anzio beachhead. The Cubs were required to fly four or five miles out to sea and proceed northwest, paralleling the enemy-held coast until they reached Anzio. Courier and passenger flights were made almost daily over a two-month period. Here is an official report from one unit during the Anzio engagement:

"On 5 December 1943, between the hours of 1220 and 1240, three artillery observation planes were attacked by four Me-109s. The Cubs were attacked simultaneously by two Me-109s from

Army liaison crews wave to unit members arriving in their L-4s over their base at an undisclosed location in Italy. (Piper Aviation Museum)

An L-4A lines up for takeoff from the *USS Ranger* off French North Africa in November 1942. The Cub's pilot has been ordered to fly to a beachhead for naval gunfire spotting and reconnaissance. (U.S. Navy photo)

Some pilots outfitted their planes with hand grenades on the wing struts, as on this L-4 Cub. Several pilots attached rockets, which proved to be more effective against ground targets. (Peter M. Bowers Collection)

above. One plane was hit by a 37 mm cannon, damaging the left strut and tearing holes in the plane's fabric. Another plane was hit with .50 caliber machine gun fire in the wing but no serious damage occurred. When the enemy fighters attacked, the artillery planes were put into a dive. They were able to recover from the dive and elude the Germans. However, when they pulled out of the dive, two other Me-109s at a low altitude made another attack. They were also outmaneuvered by the artillery planes which then returned to their airfield with only slight damage and no injury to personnel.

"The third plane was attacked a few seconds later but was able to outmaneuver the Me-109s by flying toward the center of a circle that was being made by the attacking planes. At the same time, this plane was losing altitude and working its way toward home. This plane also landed safely and without damage.

"Friendly troops viewed the above activity and were evidently so astonished that not a round of ground fire was given to help the 'flying box kites.' The elapsed time of the battle was ten minutes."

The point of this report was that the Cubs had a capability not appreciated before, and the German Luftwaffe was concerned. Their pilots were offered points toward a medal for shooting down Allied planes. Three points were awarded for knocking down a four-engine bomber, two points for an escorted two-engine bomber, one point for a fighter, and two points for a liaison plane. Ground troops were offered fifteen days' leave for knocking down a Cub.

The L-4 Cubs soon became valued by U.S. battlefront troops, as they called in artillery fire adjustments on enemy gun emplacements, troop positions, and camouflaged areas. The observers reported what they saw to artillery direction centers, and in a matter of minutes, the heavy fire power of several battalions would descend on the targets they identified. One German prisoner com-

mented after his unit was the target for such a barrage that the most nerve-wracking effect was after a liaison plane was spotted;

"The Bird hovers over our positions," he said, "and if we make the slightest move—hell breaks loose."

General Linnarz, chief of the crack German 26th Panzer Division in Italy, agreed wholeheartedly:

"The really demoralizing experience for the ground soldier," he said after the war, "is the sight of the artillery-directing aircraft

An improved model of the L-4 Cub was developed toward the end of World War II at the request of the War Department. It was the L-14A, which was equipped with a 125-hp Lycoming engine, electric starter and generator, controllable propeller, long stroke landing gear, and a set of instruments for blind flying. (Piper Aviation Museum)

Another Cub improvement was this YL-21 being tested at Lock Haven with a Whittaker four-wheel tandem landing gear. The Army and Air Force ordered 150; none were used in combat. (Piper Aviation Museum)

circling over your position for hours. You know for a certainty that if you make one move, you will have a shell within your foxhole in two minutes."

General James A. Van Fleet, commenting on this virtue of the Cubs, stated:

"If one of our World War II infantry groups found itself under German artillery fire, it called for either counter-battery fire or a Cub plane. Either was enough to silence the German guns. The Germans conserved their guns and crews, and never wanted to give away their positions. One little Cub was enough to stop their fire; we sent Cubs up time after time and they never failed."

A letter found on a dead German soldier fighting in the Italian mountains confirmed the effect the Cubs had on their morale. Freely translated, it said:

"It is very cold and damp here in the caves where we are now quartered. It is terrible, *lieber Papa*, not to be able to go outside for whole weeks at a time. But we have no choice. When the weather is stormy, we cannot go outside without being soaked to the skin. When the weather is clear, the damned (*allgegenwärtiger*) Cubs are flying around overhead. When if we so much as show our noses the whole American Army starts shooting at us. So we stay inside. Heil Hitler!"

This tri-gear experimental YL-21 was towed aloft and flown as a glider to study air flow and boundary layer control. (Peter M. Bowers Collection)

A profile of the hooking mechanism of the Brodie System on an L-4 in flight. Planes could take off or "land" on an overhead steel cable. The system was invented and perfected by James H. Brodie. The device is on display at the Smithsonian's Udvar-Hazy Center museum, near Dulles International Airport. (Paul Bowen Photography, Inc.)

An L-4H is shown with the mechanism that was used to launch and retrieve aircraft on a Navy ship equipped with the Brodie Device. Army pilots radioed information to Navy destroyers to adjust their gunfire. Retrieving the aircraft was the most difficult part of the operation. (Peter M. Bowers Collection)

Amphibious operations also showed the value of the Cubs in all theaters of operations. They were flown from Navy carriers and LSTs on which decks had been constructed for Cub takeoffs, but were too short for safe landings. The Cubs were so simply built that they could be disassembled, loaded in Curtiss C-46s or Douglas C-47s, and reassembled when the transports arrived at forward fighting areas.

The Cubs took part in the Normandy invasion in June 1944. With tail surfaces and wings removed, a large number were loaded on two-and-a-half ton trucks and carried ashore on LSTs to be reassembled farther inland. Others were flown across the English Channel by pilots who had auxiliary fuel tanks installed in their rear seats. They landed, removed the tanks, picked up their observers,

and flew to find their assigned areas. Approximately 1,000 such Channel crossings were made with no losses. It was not uncommon for flights of 15 or more liaison aircraft flown by artillery pilots to cross the Channel to join their units. Many others were ferried to their respective units by Ninth Air Force fighter pilots who had previously flown light aircraft. On New Year's Day 1944, a loose formation of 50 Cubs crossed from Friston to St. Valery.

Once the Allied troops had completed the invasion, the L-birds became more valuable than previously thought. General George S. Patton, famous gung-ho leader of the Third Army, had conceived a plan called Operation Canary, which was to augment forces crossing the Rhine River during darkness at the earliest possible time by flying in reinforcements in light planes. Four fields were selected

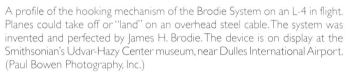

An L-4H is shown engaging the Brodie Device on a ship after a reconnaissance mission. Army L-4 pilots and observers were directed by the Navy to scout unseen enemy ships and enemy-held islands beyond the horizon in advance of an invasion. (R. L. Cavanagh Collection)

An L-4 approaches the Brodie Device to make a shipside landing during combat operations in the South Pacific. The Piper Cubs were used to reconnoiter for Navy task forces before assaults on enemy beaches. (Jim Brodie collection)

just west of the river, and 25 Cubs and pilots were assigned to land at each field. At first light one pilot was to fly to the far shore and select similar fields. Other light planes with radio equipment were to be dispatched to the fields to provide communications and assist in air traffic control.

Elements of the 5th Division were to begin the river crossing after dark, and it was estimated that one battalion would secure a beachhead and force the enemy back far enough to eliminate the hazard of small arms fire on the chosen airstrips. Practice runs were

made beforehand behind the American lines with men and equipment in light aircraft, ferrying them the approximate distance required, unloading the planes, and returning to their bases. This test showed that approximately one infantry battalion (about 800 men) could be ferried in two hours' time, using 90 aircraft. The traffic was spaced so that a plane would roll to a stop, turn off the landing strip, unload, take off, and return to base for another load.

When the operation began, three battalions had crossed the river and met no resistance, so that it was not necessary to have the fourth battalion ferried by air. However, Patton was pleased. He had proven that the 65-hp Cubs could do an unprecedented troop transport job if needed.

Light plane units were also active during the famous Battle of the Bulge, dropping emergency supplies, including maps, homing pigeons, food, first aid packages, and ammunition. According to one report, when the besieged garrison at Bastogne radioed on Christmas Eve 1944 that it had more than 500 casualties, many of whom faced imminent death unless they received immediate medications, Lt. Kenneth B. Schley, an artillery observation pilot, risked his life to fly a supply of life-saving penicillin into the beleaguered city:

"To do so," the report stated, "he defied darkness, intense enemy fire, an unknown and possibly non-existent landing strip, and an official order not to leave the ground, but he insisted on carrying the precious Christmas gift to the entrapped men."

Another instance occurred during the Moselle River crossing. After two companies of infantry had crossed, enemy fire and rising water prevented any re-supply. It was decided to try to use artillery

The Army experimented with the Brodie Device in jungle areas where takeoffs and landings were hindered by trees. The system was used to conduct clandestine missions in Japanese-occupied areas and retrieve wounded from battle zones. (Piper Aviation Museum)

Stinson L-5s were also launched and retrieved by the Brodie Device. This one was photographed during experiments in Florida. (Air Force Museum)

An L-4 has just been released from the Brodie Device for flight as mechanics watch from the boom. Note life preserver available for use if needed. (Army Aviation Museum)

liaison planes, because heavy enemy anti-aircraft fire prevented drops of supplies by parachute from troop carrier planes. A drop zone was marked by cloth panels, and L-4s flew 150 sorties, dropping K-rations, blankets, medical supplies, and ammunition.

A similar re-supply mission was carried out near Metz, France, when two isolated battalions were supplied by low-flying Cubs for five days without the loss of a single plane. And another took place at St. Tropez in southern France when a 12-foot snowfall prevented ground transportation from providing supplies. Artillery L-4s performed all re-supply for about five days by simply flying over the top of the famous ski slopes and dropping their loads, which skidded downhill to the stranded troops.

Don Carrell, an enlisted pilot with the 8th Armored Division, took his initial Cub training at Stillwater, and then at Fort Sill, Oklahoma;

"We'd fly over barriers and make the landings shorter and shorter," he recalled in *Flying Through Time* by James M. Doyle. "We landed on curved roads. We'd do ninety-degree takeoffs. If you've got a field that is too short and you can run around a course— you learned how to take off that way.

"The Cub is a fantastic airplane. I've operated out of cornfields that just weren't big enough to get anything into. The approach needed for that is called a power stall. You stall the airplane al the way to the ground, with power to get the shortest possible landing. We used to carry a roll of toilet paper. When we'd get into a small field, we'd go in as short as possible. But the takeoff was always a longer run. You'd walk it if necessary and use the toilet paper to mark the various stumps and whatever else was in your way."

The L-4 became a fighter plane when Major Charles "Bazooka" Carpenter, a pilot with the 4th Armored Division, with the help of a

Ninth Air Force Service Command ordnance specialist, fashioned two sets of three bazookas and attached them to the wheel struts mounted on *Rosie the Rocketer's* L-4H. On an observation mission, he saw many enemy tanks lumbering along unmolested. He dove on them and pulled a lanyard to fire the deadly rounds. It was reported that he demolished five German tanks and an ammunition truck during several attacks. After the latest kill, he said:

"...word must be getting around among those krauts to watch out for Cubs with bazookas. Every time I show up they shoot at me with everything they have."

A ski-equipped L-4J takes off from a field in Europe during the Battle of the Bulge in 1944. American troops liked to see the Cubs overhead, because it meant that the enemy would be lying low, knowing that if they were sighted, a heavy artillery barrage would follow. (U. S. Army photo)

lery-spotting Cub. The pilot flew straight up the valley, snapping pictures as he went and, based on these photographs, the assault began."

The first victory by a Cub over a German fighter was credited to Capt. V.J. McGrath, a flying officer with the British Royal Artillery who was attached to the U.S. Fifth Army fighting in the Italian mountains. He had been chased several times by a marauding German Messerschmitt that had peppered his Cub with bullet holes but had not hit him or any vital plane parts. Tired of this harassment, McGrath decided to set a trap. He circled over the mountains waiting for the lone gunman and, true to form, he showed up. When McGrath sighted him, he flew into a ravine. The Me-109 followed him with flaming tracers trying to find a mark. At the end of the ravine McGrath made a vertical 180-degree turn that the fighter could not match and watched his opponent plow into the face of a cliff.

Cub pilots sometimes had their special problems while making routine flights between friendly bases. Lt. Bud Friesell of the 635th Field Artillery Battalion recalled his experience running into a headwind on a courier flight from Cognac to the French coast:

"I suddenly detected from watching vehicles on a paved road that I did not seem to be moving forward. I went up higher, hoping the wind might be more favorable, but not so—it was worse, as I was now moving backwards! I had noticed an artillery airstrip about five miles back, not far off the road, with three Cubs tied down and a pyramidal tent, and hoping someone would be there I decided to try to make it into that field. I put the nose into a slight down position with the throttle almost wide open, so that I was moving backwards at a rate sufficient to reach the strip at a height of several hundred feet. I knew I could not turn around for fear of being blown beyond the landing strip and not being able to get back to it.

"My plan worked! As I got close to the strip, I kept looking to the rear. To my delight, four men in army fatigues were waving their arms wildly, indicating that I should get down as quickly as

The Piper L-4, nicknamed the Grasshopper, was noted for its capability to land almost anywhere. An observer "props" the engine of the plane for his pilot after landing on a road in Italy in 1944. (U.S. Air Force photo)

Another pilot rigged a bomb rack that carried ten hand grenades. As he flew over his targets at a low altitude, he pulled a cable to arm them one at a time and then let them drop. Several pilots put hand grenades in Mason jars after they found that the grenades often exploded before reaching the ground. The weight of the jars as they pulled the cable to release the pins would make them fall faster.

Photo reconnaissance was sometimes required of the Cub pilots. A report from the Fifth Army in Italy demonstrates that capability:

"When appalling bad weather grounded the regular photo-reconnaissance planes during the Volturno offensive, the whole Fifth Army, massed for the battle, waited for several days. Finally, unable to wait any longer, yet unwilling to advance without photo-reconnaissance, Major General Lucian Truscott sent up an artil-

Cubs were easily dispersed in wooded areas after landing from artillery spotting duty in Europe during World War II. (U.S. Army photo)

possible. They must have been reading my mind as to how I was going to accomplish this—by varying both throttle and nose-down attitude, I gently backed into the field. Upon touching the ground, very slowly going backwards with the tail up, two men on each side grabbed the wing struts. I immediately cut the engine switch and jumped out to help. All five of us eased the plane to a parking area and tied it down."

The success of the Cubs in combat did not mean that there were no casualties, but there were for a number of reasons. Lt. Joseph F. Gordon explains in his book *Flying Low*:

"We had no airports most of the time, flying into and off of unprepared fields of grass or anything that was somewhat level. Some planes and pilots were lost going into fences, ditches, and trees—even haystacks. Our low-level observation position, especially in landing and taking off, made us vulnerable to ground fire from civilian rifles and shotguns, as well as military weapons. A thin layer of fabric enclosed our cockpit, providing zero protection. The floor was a sheet of 3/8-inch plywood. Our own artillery brought down a few of our planes. We often flew in marginal weather with no instruments better than our eyes. The instrument panel had an altimeter, airspeed indicator, tachometer, compass, and fuel gauge, but we relied heavily on the seat of our pants.

"When possible, we wore steel helmets, carried a shoulder-strap .45 Colt automatic pistol, and had a parachute, either seat pack or back pack. I heard of only one observer parachuting from a Cub in combat when the pilot was killed. The observers were, of course,

exposed to all these same hazards, with the added disadvantage of not being in control of the aircraft."

The first known death in a Cub attributed to enemy ground fire took place in the fighting at the Kasserine Pass in North Africa. The pilot, badly wounded by enemy machine gun fire, was captured and died later in a prison camp. In Sicily, Sgt. James J. Smith, Jr., and his observer died when their Cub's wing was clipped off by a German fighter. Ernie Pyle, famous war correspondent, reported another tragedy from Italy:

"The saddest story I've ever heard about a Cub happened here on the Fifth Army beachhead. A (friendly) 'Long Tom'—or 155 mm rifle—was the unwitting villain in this case. This certain gun fired only once that entire day—but that one shell, with all the sky to travel to, made a direct hit on one of our Cubs in the air and blew it to smithereens."

Ironically, Pyle's last flight was in a Cub to cover the fighting at Ie Shima in the Pacific in 1945. He flew off a Brodie Device from a ship to the shore and was killed shortly afterward on the ground by a Japanese sniper.

Many ground force generals used Cubs during the war, including Generals Dwight D. Eisenhower, George S. Patton, Omar Bradley, Mark Clark, and George C. Marshall. Prime Minister Winston Churchill flew in a Cub at least once, as did Britain's King George in a Royal Air Force version of the Cub. General William "Wild Bill" Donovan, head of the OSS, reportedly flew in an L-4 about 150 miles into enemy-held Burma on an inspection trip.

Teamwork between Army armored units and radio-equipped Cubs is implied in this photo, taken somewhere deep inside Europe during WWII combat operations. (U.S. Army photo)

Joe E. Brown and Bob Hope, famous comics who flew to the battlefronts to entertain the troops, also flew in Cubs. Hope called them "Mustang fighters that wouldn't eat their cereal."

In addition to its many "firsts," during World War II in Europe the Piper Cub also had a noteworthy "last." An L-4 named

Miss Me scored what is reported as the last air-to-air "kill" in Europe during late April 1945. Lt. Duane Francis, one of the pilots assigned to the 5th Armored Division, and his observer were on an observation mission when they spotted a German Fieseler Storch below them. They dived on it and shot it down, firing from the side windows with their .45 caliber automatic pistols. The Storch crash-landed and the Cub followed; the Germans were quickly captured. The Storch was the only plane shot down by a handgun since World War I.

The end of the war in Europe in May 1945 also meant the end of active L-4 pilot combat days for Lt. George Ledermann of the 205th Field Artillery group. He describes what he saw on May 3, 1945:

"The location was just outside of Lubtheen, and the occasion was the collapse of the German nation in that part of the country. For a long time I flew back and forth, looking down on thousands upon thousands of Germans—young and old, men, women, and children, soldiers and civilians—streaming to the west on foot, in wagons, in vehicles of all kinds, some with animals, but all fleeing from the Russians, who had swept in from the east. They were now seeking safety, taking their chances with the Americans. It was history. Although it was not official until May 8, it was the end of the war in Europe."

***

William T. Piper, Sr (left), chats with Army Captain Michael J. Strok, a former Piper employee, who learned to fly Cubs through the company's program. He won a commission in the Army and served as an air operations officer with the Fifth Army in Italy. He designed a release device for the L-4 to drop supplies to marooned troops. (Piper Aviation Museum)

At least one Piper L-4 with D-Day invasion stripes visits the annual fly-in of Cubs each year at Lock Haven. Note the extended window section to enable the observer in the rear seat to see downward more easily. (Photo by the author)

The Army's L-4 Cubs also were used to adjust naval gunfire, and it was a common sight in North Africa, Sicily, Normandy, and in the South Pacific to see the little planes flying up and down off-shore from a strip of beach radioing coordinate information of inland targets to destroyers cruising offshore. A Cub assigned to an Army artillery unit took on the role of a fighter plane in the Pacific theater on August 17, 1944, when 12 Japanese soldiers were sighted attempting to escape from an island in two native canoes. The pilot and observer returned to the base camp, secured machine guns and hand grenades, and returned to strafe and bomb the escapees. Three Japanese were killed, and the others were captured by a Navy PT boat crew.

Light planes made the headlines in the United States when General Douglas MacArthur returned to the Philippines as he had promised. Several Cubs were the first Allied planes to fly over the capital city of Manila, specifically to spot enemy artillery and fortifications. An L-4 had scored a previous "first" when it had been the first Allied plane to land on Okinawa.

***

One of the most interesting developments to assist in light plane operations during World War II was known as the Brodie System or Brodie Device. Named for Capt. James H. Brodie, it was a mechanism that enabled a pilot to take off from ships or from jungle areas without any runway. It consisted of a cable 500 feet long that was stretched between two 65-foot masts. A hook was mounted on top of the fuselage that permitted an aircraft to take off and land while suspended about fifty feet above the water or ground. A steel cable and a loop of nylon was suspended from a taut, horizontal cable. In landing, a plane snagged the loop with an overhead hook, and a friction brake gradually halted it. In taking off, the friction brake

A Navy ship with a Cub attached to the launch arm of the Brodie Device. Another Cub is readied on the forward deck for attachment. (U.S. Navy Photo)

held the aircraft until sufficient power was applied, which allowed the plane to run down the cable until the pilot yanked a lanyard, releasing the hook from a stirrup attached to the nylon loop. He would then be free to proceed with his mission. All equipment and a nine-man crew could be carried in cargo planes and landed by parachute.

It was not the first time such a system had been tried. Adolphe Pegoud, a French pilot, had made a takeoff and landing in a Bleriot XI from a wire in 1911. Although he was successful, the idea was abandoned because it was thought that only a pilot with great skill could accomplish such a feat.

Brodie had conceived the idea on his own during the dark days in early 1942 when German submarines were sinking American ships off the Atlantic and Gulf coasts daily. An engineering graduate of the University of Minnesota, he drafted the plans for a rig and obtained $10,000 in government funds, but only after many conferences with officials in Washington, many of whom thought the idea was too far-fetched to merit any interest. Assigned to redesign cargo ships for the Army Transportation Corps, Brodie began to build his first device on his own time at New Orleans in April 1943, which he simulated being used on a ship.

Brodie's principal problems were development of adequate brakes and the reduction of shock during the process of getting the landing trolley accelerated. He finally got satisfactory braking performance by use of an aluminum reel, two standard hydraulic automobile brake assemblies and automatic brake delay screw, a tension adjuster, and a gauge for determining line tension. The delay screw permitted rotating parts to become accelerated to airplane speed upon contact with the landing sling.

Brodie designed the trolley in a half-moon shape, which allowed the lower half to pendulum forward before the trolley wheel

was set in motion. The hook arm swung to a horizontal position and then telescoped outward about two feet upon contact with the landing sling.

A plane would be suspended by the hook on its top to a heavy nylon sling that dropped down a trolley on a cable. The pilot would give the plane full throttle, speed down the cable, and yank a lanyard to break free of the hook. When returning, he would maneuver the plane into position to engage the hook, cut the throttle, and be slowed down to a stop.

Lt. C. B. Wheeler, an Army service pilot, made the first takeoff from the device in late August 1943. The first round trip from takeoff to a successful landing was made by Major James D. Kemp on September 3, 1943. By mid-September, the first regularly assigned Brodie system test pilot arrived. He was Sgt. (later Flight Officer) Raymond A. Gregory, fresh from maneuvers as a liaison pilot in Louisiana. He made more than 300 landings and takeoffs from the rig and was convinced that any pilot capable of handling a plane in normal flight could use the Brodie system.

Late in 1943 Brodie obtained use of the *City of Dalhart*, a 5,800-ton cargo ship, for experimental use, and a series of successful takeoffs and landings in L-4 Cubs and Stinson L-5s were made off New Orleans in the Gulf of Mexico.

Although Brodie designed the system to assist in tracking enemy submarines, the Navy saw its potential usefulness to launch light aircraft for reconnaissance in support of amphibious landing operations. When he heard about it, Major General William J. Donovan, head of the Officer of Strategic Services (OSS)—forerunner of the Central Intelligence Agency (CIA)—also planned to use it to launch liaison planes to support espionage, sabotage, and psychological operations behind enemy lines in Europe and Scandinavia, but never did.

One of those who tested the device was Tony Piper, who was curious about how much the drag would be reduced on a Cub when launched with the wheels removed. There is no record of what his purpose or conclusions were.

In November 1944 the Brodie Sytem was used at Jasoore, India, to support British clandestine missions, such as dropping saboteurs and guerillas into Japanese-occupied areas. The British also equipped two hospital ships with the device to retrieve wounded and bring them to the ships operating off the Burmese coast. However, they were never used, as the fighting in Burma had ceased when the Japanese fled. The system was not used in Europe, although the British had been sent a system for possible use in the invasion.

Ship operations first began training in the use of the Brodie System with L-4s and L-5s off San Diego in the fall of 1944. By March 1945 eight LST vessels were converted to use the Brodie Device. Although the L-5 had an electric starter, the L-4 had to be started by hand. However, thanks to the Cub's side door opening, the pilot could climb out with one foot on the right wheel and do his own "propping." On the LSTs without a carrier deck, the pilot and observer had to climb out on the Brodie derrick assembly and lower themselves onto the plane and into the cockpit.

One of the most outstanding examples of the use of the Brodie System was accomplished during the battle to occupy Okinawa. Sgt. John C. Kriegsman, a liaison pilot assigned to the 77th Infantry Division Artillery, tells of his experience with the device during the battle for the island:

"Through rumors and grapevine we found we were to secure a group of islands. It developed that they were near Okinawa, wherever that was. About two weeks before we were to leave we found out we were going to leave a week before the main task force to establish an anchorage. About that same time we were issued two of the craziest-looking hooks we had ever seen on any aircraft. Along with the hooks were instructions how and where they were to be mounted on our Cubs. We figured we were to hook something, but we didn't know what!

"Somehow, word came we were to operate off an LST. A Navy commander would arrive on a transport to explain how the hooks were to be used. Several days passed and the transport did arrive. The Commander was extremely vague. He was unable to supply a

EYES UPSTAIRS!

On many fighting fronts of the world, our tank destroyers often count on the Piper L-4 "Grasshopper" to help spot enemy tanks. Serving as the "Eyes Upstairs," the Piper L-4 flashes instructions by radio to the tank destroyers, directing their courses and fire.

The plane's ability to fly low, land quickly almost anywhere and hide easily enables it to play an important part also in the Artillery, Cavalry and Infantry. It acts as a scout, directs troop movements, transports officer personnel and delivers messages.

The advantages of the Piper L-4 in wartime will prove invaluable also in peacetime. Then, in your smart, new Piper Cub you'll hop around the country on vacation and business trips with the greatest of ease, pleasure, safety and economy.

FREE BOOKLET ON HOW TO FLY. Send today for your copy of "You, Too, Can Fly!" If you also want the full-color Piper catalog, enclose 10c in stamps or coin for postage-handling. Piper Aircraft Corporation, Dept. NA93, Lock Haven, Penna.

16mm. SOUND FILM—"The Construction of a Light Airplane." For distribution points write: Supervisor, Audio-Visual Aids, Extension Services, Penna. State College, State College, Penna.

PIPER *Cub*

Points the Way to Wings for All Americans

Cub advertisement that appeared in major aviation magazines in 1943. (*Aero Digest*)

picture or even a sketch how the LST was to be fitted to hook a Cub, or why it was necessary in the first place. He did say the LST was used at Iwo Jima by the Marines, who had L-5 Stinsons. They were much heavier than our Cubs. They waited on board until an airstrip was secured on shore, which took two precious days. Then they took off and never returned."

A Brodie Device finally arrived and was mounted on the deck of LST 776 on the day before the convoy was to leave. Several of the 77th air section, including Kriegsman and Lt. Montgomery, went aboard. The crew told them how to use the device and get their Cubs on board without damaging them. Next day, the convoy assembled early to move out for the Kerama Retto Islands— six small rocky islands with no beaches located about 20 miles west of Okinawa. An anchorage was to be established for supplying the invasion forces for Okinawa. If the islands were occupied by the Americans, it would have been almost impossible for the enemy to penetrate into the anchorage and damage the ships:

"Our LST was in the convoy, and we had no chance to practice landings or takeoffs," Kriegsman continued. "Lt. Montgomery and I were expected to get on that ship. The LST would accommodate only two Cubs. Initial observation of those islands was extremely critical. With the convoy under way we were the show of the day. All eyes and field glasses from nearby ships were on us as we gingerly flew around the LST, valiantly trying to hook the 3-foot by 4-foot loop. From the curve of the hook to the top of the propeller we had about 20 inches to "play" with. Lt. Montgomery was the first to hook the loop. I managed in five passes. Thanks be to God, we did not damage our precious planes.

"LST 776 was a strange-looking craft, but very simple. Forward was a steel pole at the 10 o'clock position. It was the same aft of the ship, with the arm projecting out at about the 8 o'clock position. The ends of the arms had a cable on top that was sort of a receiving platform for the [Brodie] crew to stand and manipulate the trolley.

"When a plane was to land, a trolley device would roll aft on the cable. A nylon rectangle about three feet wide and four feet long would be dropped from it. The LST would be turned into the wind at full speed. The LST had little or no keel. As a result, the ship would roll grandly. This meant those 50-foot arms over the side would make an arc maybe 30 feet high. The pilot would approach this loop in sort of a porpoise fashion. It was necessary for the pilot to get the rhythm of the ship as he made his approach so when he hooked or missed the loop, the arm would not come crashing down on him.

"Cubs are trail-draggers. When one made a three-point landing, he pulled the stick into his belly. It was as natural as pulling on your trousers. Not so when you hooked the loop. You had to remember to jam the stick ahead at the slightest tug to indicate that you were hooked. That kept the nose down, so the prop would not go up into the cable and get chewed to pieces.

"Probably the worst thing that could happen was to think you were hooked when you were not, and you jammed the stick forward. Diving 30 feet straight down would make a big problem. Without any practice or instructions, extreme concentration was required.

"When securely hooked, the trolley would roll down the cable. The ship's crew would stop the roll. At the forward end of the cable, the crew would transfer the Cub to the cable going on to the ship and lower it to the deck for refueling.

"To take off, a small nylon loop about 12 inches in diameter was installed in the small eye at the top of the hook. The pilot, passenger, and Cub, with its propeller turning, would be lifted up, hooked on the trolley, and transferred to the larger cable. The crew would pull the trolley aft as far as it would go. It would be held there while the LST headed at full power into the wind. The pilot would apply full RPM for takeoff. When he checked his magnetos and was ready for takeoff, he signaled the crew and they would release him.

"The cable was about 300 feet long. When the pilot arrived at the 250-foot mark, he would pull the release chain like flushing an old-fashioned toilet. If he didn't have enough airspeed, he would use the 30-foot drop to pick up enough airspeed just before he hit the water. From then on it was normal flying until time to land and refuel.

"We did not feel it was a risky operation at all. Some did. However, we were concerned that we did not have a chance to practice, since we were the only two Cubs that could observe the initial landings."

As the 77th Division convoy approached the islands on March 26, 1945, and were about 30 miles away, they could not yet be seen over the horizon by the enemy. Kriegsman took off from the LST with his observer and headed toward the islands. When asked if they saw anything unusual, he reported an unusual sight. All the islands had dozens of caves with railroad tracks going from the water to the caves. There was nothing else around.

It was found later that the caves contained about 350 small boats with at least one depth charge in each. Apparently, the Japanese did not contemplate that the American force preparing to invade Okinawa would pay any attention to the railroad tracks and made no attempt to camouflage them. Their plan was to pilot these skiffs at night kamikaze-style into the rudders and propellers of the convoy. The ships would have no chance to escape, and dozens of ships could have been immobilized by this type of attack. As a result of the discovery, the American destroyers fired hundreds of shells into the caves before a single skiff was launched. Unfortunately, several members of a landing party sent to inspect the caves were killed when an explosion occurred which had been set off by surviving Japanese hiding in the caves. Kriegsman's report was said to be the most important observation made by a Cub pilot in the Pacific War.

After operations on Okinawa, the 77th Division prepared for the invasion of Kyushu, Japan. A meeting was held to decide if the LST 776 with its Brodie Device should participate. There would be high cliffs at the assigned invasion site, and early observation by liaison planes would be required. However, the atomic bomb explosions at Hiroshima and Nagasaki made the operation unnecessary. As far as Major General A.D. Bruce, commander of the 77th Division, was concerned, "The Piper Cub was the secret weapon of the war in the South Pacific."

It has been reported that LST 776 was named the *USS Brodie* as a tribute to the system's inventor, but Navy records do not reflect this. However, Brodie was honored when he received the Legion of Merit in 1945 for his invention. He never knew how it had been used during the war after it left his control until many years later. However, he thought it had commercial use and could be built to

L-4s are lined up at Fort Sill, Oklahoma, one of the major training sites for Army liaison pilots during World War II. The Cubs had the lowest accident rate compared to the other light planes, and were chosen as the primary liaison plane for use in overseas areas. (U.S. Army Photo)

Graduates of the Army glider training program were authorized to wear these wings during World War II. Most training was conducted power-off in Cubs before transitioning to gliders. This aeronautical rating is no longer effective. (Kevin K. Hudson photo)

Army pilots assigned to fly missions to observe enemy activities, usually in conjunction with artillery units, were authorized to wear the "L" wings. (Kevin K. Hudson photo)

handle cargo planes weighing up to 7,000 pounds. The rig takeoff could reduce the amount of fuel consumed between landings and thus increase the payload that could be carried. He thought ranchers and farmers in remote areas would find the rig useful in wooded or mountainous areas.

Several years ago the Brodie System was offered to the National Air and Space Museum. Curator Major Robert C. Mikesh, a former Air Force pilot, accepted a complete kit of the device from the manufacturer. It can be seen with a Stinson L-5 liaison plane attached at the Stephen F. Udvar-Hazy Center near Dulles International Airport in Virginia.

In early 1945 a two-stage pickup system was developed for L-4s and L-5s to snatch up 100-pound cargo packets from isolated ground units to eliminate the bulky reels that were used by planes for glider pickups. The equipment included a hook on the end of a springy nylon rope attached directly to the airplane's fuselage, a conventional double-pole ground assembly, and an arrangement of valve springs and wooden buffer blocks.

As the aircraft approached, the pickup line hooked onto the nylon loop stretched between the two ground poles. The ground loop was jerked taut, catapulting the cargo container forward along a guideline at one-half its tug speed. Springs and buffers at the end of the line threw the cargo packet free of the ground, increasing its upward surge to full tug speed, resulting in two stages of acceleration. Once the cargo was lifted from the ground it could be pulled into the plane by hand. Lightweight winches were later devised for reeling in heavy packets.

***

The U.S. Marines also used Cubs in the South Pacific. Retired Col. Theodore A. Petras was a captain then and personal pilot for Maj. Gen. Archibald A. Vandergrift, commander of the 1st Marine Division. Petras told this story for the International Liaison Pilot and Aircraft Association (ILPA):

"After Guadalcanal we were deployed to Australia for reorganizing. Then we were sent to Goodenough Island, off the New Guinea coast, to stage and train for the next operation at Cape

Gloucester. While there my crew and I noticed the Army had so many Piper Cubs. We talked to Lt. Col. Ken Weir, the division air officer, who agreed it was a good idea to get a few for our use.

"General Vandergrift had me get a plane ready, and we flew to Brisbane, MacArthur's headquarters. His request [to acquire some Cubs] was granted. We were delivered eight Cubs that were flyable and four in crates."

A group of pilots, observers, and mechanics was formed as the 1st Provisional Air Liaison Unit and saw its first action during the landing at Cape Gloucester. Two Cubs were put on floats and used for reconnaissance. Brig. Gen. W.H. Rupertus, deputy division commander, used one of the Cubs to obtain an overall view of the landing and made daily use of it for reconnaissance. To the despair of his staff, he decided one day to contribute personally to the action by carrying along a bag of hand grenades and dropping them over suspected enemy positions. As in Europe, the Japanese troops quickly realized that if they were spotted by the Cub pilots, horrific artillery fire would descend on them.

The L-4s were found very useful when the Owen-Stanley mountain range confronted the troops who landed in and around Port Moresby, and it was essential that bases be established on the other side of the mountains. Air Force General George C. Kenney did not hesitate to use whatever undercover personnel and facilities were available to locate level strips upon which the Cubs could land, loaded with such hand tools as they could carry. While the Cubs returned to their base, the passengers would make contact with the natives, and soon an air strip would be started. It would not be long before a C-47 transport would land with larger equipment, and the air strip would be further extended until bombers and fighters could land and thus be based closer to their distant targets.

Liaison pilots flying L-4s in the Pacific Theater had different kinds of problems than the other theaters of war. In December 1943 the Third Air Task Force had a squadron known as the "Guinea Short Line," attached to an Army Air Force fighter unit at New Hollandia in the East Indies. The squadron was involved in many searches, and in the first 12 months of operations had rescued 15 pilots and aircrew members that had crashed or bailed out in the impenetrable New Guinea jungle. The Cubs, protected by fighters, flew to the crash sites through Japanese fighters and anti-aircraft fire so they could drop food and rescue equipment. They also strafed enemy encampments with automatic machine guns and dropped hand grenades. But it was the rescue of stranded air crews that taxed their skills and ingenuity. T/Sgt. Allen Lockwood was one of those assigned to the Guinea Short Line at Port Moresby in December 1943. He tells what it was like in a classified narrative:

"It was a serious and systematic business. First, you had to locate the crashed plane, and that was no cinch when it was among 12-foot kunai grass or dense rain forest. Next, you had to drop messages to the guys down there on the ground telling them to stay put and not get panicky. If they wandered off, if the Nips didn't get them, something else would. Best way to get them to stay put was to drop food, guns, blankets, and stuff to make them sort of cozy.

"Then we had to figure the best way to get them out. Sometimes we worked with them from the air to prepare an emergency strip, if it was kunai grass. If that couldn't be done, we reconnoitered and mapped the best route for them to walk out. Other times, if they were near a river, we dropped life rafts and floated them out.

"Some A-20s out of Gusap got into a hunk of bad weather coming back from a mission. Three of them were straggling and almost out of gas. The flight leader told them they were on their own...and they were. They came down in different places in the Ramu Valley; that was unexplored jungle, with Japs all around.

"When we [Lockwood and Sgt. Walter James] got the word, we went up in two L-4s along with some P-40s to try and locate them. Walt spotted the first wreck and then the others. We dropped supplies and messages telling the crews to remain where they were, not to make too much noise, and to avoid contact with the natives."

Two P-40s guided by Lockwood dropped belly tanks filled with gasoline in the kunai grass in a selected spot near one of the A-20s where the pilot and gunner waved that they were alive. The P-40s then strafed the area with incendiary bullets and ignited the gasoline. It didn't burn well enough, so they returned later with detonators attached to the belly tanks, and this time burned off a landing area. However, there were trees in the way, and Lockwood dropped notes telling the two men to cut them down. When this was completed a day later, Lockwood dropped a note asking that when he flew over to lie down on their backs with their heads in the direction the landing should be made.

"You had to be careful about that," Lockwood reported. "Those guys were lonely down there, and at times got a bit too eager for company; they would signal a strip was in good shape when a toy glider couldn't land on it."

Lockwood risked a landing, and as he touched down gingerly, he found that the strip was too soft and muddy. He tried an immediate go-around but ended up with his prop churning kunai grass.

Luckily, it didn't damage the plane. The three of them worked for two days lengthening and widening the makeshift strip:

"I tested it again, solo, and this time I got into the air, but it was nip and tuck," Lockwood reported. "A repeat performance, especially with a passenger, wasn't my idea of a picnic exactly. I sure was tempted to stay up there and wing it back to Gusap, but those guys were counting on me. I came in for a landing, and a couple of minutes later was off again, this time with the pilot, who had a bad scalp wound. Next day, Sgt. James went in and got the gunner out."

Sgt. Glenn Basset was assigned to a liaison squadron in India after learning to fly in the CPT program. He had been unable to qualify for regular pilot training, but was accepted as a liaison pilot. He recalled his first operation flying the L-4:

"A veteran pilot crawled into his plane and told me to follow him. That was the briefing. I got on his tail and followed him over the hills, and we went down on a little jungle strip. We picked up some wounded Chinese infantrymen and flew them to a hospital.

"That was pretty good, but it wasn't dropping bombs. I still had an idea you had to drop bombs from an airplane to make it worthwhile.

"From that day forward I seemed to be flying all the time. I hauled supplies to the front and brought out wounded Chinese, Ghurkas, Africans, and Indians. I learned to do things with that little aircraft. I could feel my way along the bottom and fly when the ceiling was almost on the trees. I was flying day after day when bombers and fighters were sitting on the ground.

"I began to realize what I had when bomber pilots came around, hoping to get a ride. Sometimes they would take a plane up and wring it out. One of them said, 'Sergeant, flying this thing is a pleasure. When you sit down at the controls of a B-24 you're in big business, with all the worries.' By that time I wasn't feeling too bad about being rejected for pilot training. I had come to think of my Cub as something personal—all mine.

"Then one day I was assigned to go into northern Burma and bring out some wounded boys who were part of Merrill's Marauders. On the way back, one infantryman with a serious leg wound called to me. The plane was so quiet that we seldom used the com-

Experienced civilian pilots were commissioned during World War II and qualified to fly USAAF aircraft, but not in combat. Those who passed a qualifying flight examination were authorized to wear these Service Pilot wings. The rating was discontinued after World War II. (Kevin K. Hudson photo)

munications system. 'Hey, Pilot,' he said. 'Back in the States I used to hate your guts. Especially when I'd see you Air Force guys sailing over me during maneuvers. Now I take it all back. How long before we get to a hospital?'

'Two hours by air,' I said proudly. 'By other means, three weeks.'"

***

Other nations flew Cubs in combat during World War II. It is not generally remembered today, but Brazil was one of America's allies. The Brazilian Expeditionary Force was organized after the country declared war on the Axis forces and arrived in Italy in July 1944. It was comprised of an infantry division, a fighter-bomber group, and a liaison squadron equipped with L-4H Cubs.

When the war was over, the unit history of the light plane squadron showed that they had flown 2,400 hours on 684 missions, most of them target spotting and fire direction. Each pilot flew an average of 62 missions. Not a single plane or pilot was lost.

***

Although the L-4 was the dominant liaison model used by the military forces during World War II, there was a subsequent Piper military model built—the L-14A, an improved larger version of the L-4. Piper had answered an Army requirement for a more versatile and powerful model of a liaison plane to compete with other liaison types, such as the Consolidated-Vultee L-13, Boeing's L-15, and the Aeronca L-16. Five L-14s were ordered by the Army and put through successful service testing at Wright Field, Ohio, in May 1945.

The L-14 was equipped with a 125-hp Lycoming engine with electric starter and generator. With a complete panel of blind flying instruments and a controllable pitch propeller, it had provisions for four occupants, including one litter case. Production began in June 1945, and several L-14As were shipped to the Pacific theater, where they were flown during the final days of the war. A total of 850 were ordered, but procurement was canceled when the war ended.

According to Bill Stratton, editor of a newsletter for the International Liaison Pilot and Aircraft Association (ILPA), the Piper L-14 was an:

"...end-of-war/post-war attempt to maintain [Piper's] number one liaison aircraft manufacturer's spot that they had maintained throughout World War II."

The tally of L-4s and L-14s accepted by the Army Air Forces was 5,611. A total of 3,590 Stinson L-5s were also procured, which together constituted more than 65 percent of the 33,558 liaison-type planes accepted by the services between June 1940 and August 1945

***

When World War II was concluded with the official surrender of the Japanese in 1945, several thousand liaison planes were declared surplus and could be bought through the War Assets Administration at much less than the original cost to the government. Some

Navy HE-1s used to transport casualties during World War II were clearly marked with a red cross on the fuselage, as well as the U.S. star insignia on the wings. (David W. Lucabaugh Collection)

were converted to crop dusters, but a large number were bought by clubs or individuals in the U.S., while many were transferred to the armed forces of Belgium, France, Denmark, Norway, Czechoslovakia, Switzerland, and Poland. A few L-4s, some reclassified as J-5Cs, and others that were stripped of all excess weight down to a micro-light status, are still flying in Europe today.

Ken Wakefield, in *Light Planes at War*, states that the life expectancy of these aircraft during World War II was considered very short, not only because of the hazards of combat, but because of the risks involved in operating from short, rough airstrips and few maintenance facilities. He concludes that:

"...few people, if any, could have foreseen that many of these cheaply-produced, expendable 'flying Jeeps' would still be in existence some 55 years later. And not merely in existence as immobile museum pieces, but actually flying, lovingly restored and highly valued in an historical sense by wartime veterans and younger generations alike. Long may this state of affairs continue, above all as a mark of respect for those who built, flew and serviced liaison aircraft during World War II."

Lt. Joseph Furbee Gordon, a spotter pilot with the 65th Armored Artillery who was shot down twice, adds this final comment in his memoir *Flying Low*:

"The Piper Cub, the artillery liaison pilots and the observers performed a service that had not been available to our military forces before then. The airplane was ideally suited for the job at that time, considering the weaponry and tactical theories practiced in the days before helicopters, jet engines, computers and the whole array of materiel of modern warfare."

It is interesting to note that about 1,000 Piper employees served on active duty during the WW II years, many of them as pilots in one of the military services. A number of them flew the L-4s they had helped to build, and 34 lost their lives. By March 1946, 516 veterans were back building Piper planes again.

***

The invasion of South Korea by communist troops from North Korea on June 25, 1950, caught the rest of the world unprepared for another war. American troops were hastily ordered to move to Japan and from there to Korea. The aviation section of the U.S. Army's 24th Division, part of the occupation force in Japan, was unprepared for combat when it had been transferred to South Korea on June 19, six days before hostilities began.

Some Piper L-4s and Stinson L-5s had been retained by the Army after World War II, and a few of both types were assigned to the two infantry divisions stationed in Japan. When the war began as North Korean forces pushed south, the post motor pools in Japan were ordered to strip gas tanks from some of their Jeeps and fit them into the rear seats of the L-4s for the flight across the Sea of Japan. Fortunately for Capt. James C. Goode, the extra gas saved him a ditching as he approached Korea. The weather deteriorated, and he had to use that fuel to return to Japan. This hurry-up measure was a repeat of the invasion of Normandy, when Jeeps had loaned their tanks for the same purpose and regained them when they arrived on the Continent.

Although war-weary and short of spare parts, the L-4s and L-5s were promptly assigned observation missions when the North Koreans began their advance southward. Both types carried messages, mail, and maps, and evacuated wounded during American troop landings at Inchon. There was a shortage of aviators throughout the Army, and pilot training in light planes was hurriedly increased from 100 per year to 100 per month as reservists were called to active duty and sent to Japan and Korea.

Although the number of L-4s in Korea was limited, they proved their usefulness at the outset. In his book *Operation Grasshopper*, Dario Politella, a courier pilot during that war, told what it was like as American and other United Nations forces arrived in greater numbers to combat the invaders:

"With the arrival of increasing numbers of Army aircraft in the Korean Theater, the task of plotting the movements and dispositions of enemy forces became less difficult. Division commanders were relying heavily on information received from the Army Aviators who were flying the front from morning until night. Because of the rugged terrain and the lack of engineering equipment, their

After World War II, hundreds of military aircraft were ferried to aircraft "boneyards" for storage or sale. Here Navy AE-1s are lined up with war-weary fighters at the Clinton, Oklahoma, surplus storage site for disposal in 1945. (David W. Lucabaugh Collection)

air strips were small and rough. From the outset, Division commanders had requested that the aviation sections operate from fields as close to their command posts as possible. Commanders who had previously plotted their tactics from their command posts and had observed the war from their Jeeps began to use the Army aircraft almost exclusively for orientation, planning and operation.

"Because of the congested and hazardous road conditions, field commanders also used the light planes as expeditious means of supervising the activities of their troops in zones of action. The communications difficulties during this period would have been insurmountable were it not for the light planes. The greatest percentage of information on the front line activities was supplied by Army Aviators and more than 75 percent of the artillery missions were fired [coordinated] by air observers. In addition, surveillance missions were flown over a vast area to detect any possible beach landings or flanking movements by the enemy. And the pilots averaged 100 flying hours a month for the first three months of the war."

The pilots were not immune to enemy fire, however. On July 14, 1951, Lt. Woodrow W. Brown had three feet of his left wing shot off by enemy ground fire, but he was able to glide back to safety and landed only 50 yards behind the United Nations outpost positions.

Capt. Alexander P. Bolding found that his L-4 Cub was prey for enemy aircraft when he was jumped by two North Korean Yak-9 fighters. He and Lt. Robert C. Adams, a pilot/observer, were observing the withdrawal of two U.S. infantry regiments across the Kum River when they were attacked by gunfire from above. Adams, then at the controls, quickly made evasive turns close to the ground; one of the Yaks, pursuing too closely and unable to follow, lost control and crashed into a mountain. It was the only enemy aircraft in the Korean War that was credited to an Army aircraft—a Piper Cub.

Three rocket tubes were attached to this L-4 for experiments, but it is not believed rockets were to be fired through the propeller arc. They were probably used to transport rockets from the rear to forward areas. (U.S. Army photograph)

As the war progressed, the L-4s and L-5s were eventually phased out by the U.S. Army units, although the South Korean Air Force continued to use L-4s throughout the rest of hostilities. These L-4s were the last of the older model Cubs ever to operate in a war environment. In November 1950, Turkish Air Force units arrived with several new Piper L-18 Super Cubs, equipped with flaps and electric starters. These were the envy of the American pilots, as they were the most modern type of single-engine liaison aircraft to arrive there since the war had begun.

Other single-engine types that replaced the L-4s and L-5s included North American L-17 Navions, Cessna L-19 Bird Dogs, and DeHavilland L-20 Beavers. The Korean War also proved the helicopter as a vital factor in modern warfare with its vertical take-off, landing, and hovering capabilities. However, it did not spell the end of the use of light fixed-wing aircraft for liaison duties.

7

The Years of Uncertainty and Redirection

After the defeat of Germany in May 1945, the American war effort concentrated on destroying the will of the Japanese to continue to fight. While the national focus was still on fighting, the aeronautical industry was looking toward a peaceful future. Aircraft manufacturers faced the postwar years with an exceptionally bright outlook. Although military contracts were gradually reduced and then canceled as the war was concluded in September 1945, most light plane builders already had designs on their drawing boards for new aircraft or improved versions of their wartime models for civilian buyers. Some manufacturers planned to make all-metal planes eventually, and the first one available in the post-war era was the Ercoupe. The Luscombe Silvaire followed with a metal fuselage, but still kept its fabric wings.

During the last weeks of the war, most aviation writers forecast an enormous post-war demand for small aircraft by the thousands of pilots who had learned to fly in the military services. A Civil Aeronautics Board report stated that the market for light aircraft would be ten times what it was before the war. Other government officials estimated that at the end of hostilities there would be approximately 350,000 Army and Navy pilots, 150,000 civilian pilots and students, plus some 2,500,000 men and women trained by the armed services in numerous aviation trades.

The year 1946 began with great promise at Lock Haven, as the company continued its strong commitment to sell planes in large numbers at low prices. The 20,000th Piper Cub, a Super Cruiser, was completed in May 1946 and bore the license number NC 20000. The current production then was in excess of 700 per month, and the elder Piper was jubilant. He told the press that:

"Fifteen years ago the light airplane was scoffed at and ridiculed by airport operators and private owners. After a brilliant war record, the light plane is today the backbone of the nation's non-scheduled aviation."

The statistics were impressive. No other aircraft manufacturer in the world had built so many non-military airplanes. The 20,000+ Cubs produced since production had begun in 1931 were officially totaled as follows:

In the uncertain years following World War II, Piper and private owners experimented with a number of modifications that received CAA/FAA approval. The owner of this J-5A, an aerial photographer, cut down the rear fuselage to improve the visibility toward the rear. Wing tip plates were added, but it is not known if this improved the plane's capability. (Leo J. Kohn Collection)

Model	No. Produced	Description and Years Built
E-2	553	1931-1936 37 horsepower
J-2	1,082	1936-1938 40 horsepower
J-3	9,782	1938-1946 (40, 50, 55, 60, 65-hp models with corresponding model improvements and revisions of the Cub Trainer)
J-4	1,233	1938-1941 (50, 65, 75-hp side-by-side Coupe)
J-5	1,430	1940-1946 (75-hp, 3-place Cruiser. Includes 100-hp PA-12 Super Cruiser)
L-4	5,673	1942-1945 (65-hp Army "Grasshopper")
NE-1	123	1942-1943 (65-hp Navy Trainer)
TG-8	253	1942-1943 (3-place Army Training Glider)
HE-1	100	1942-1943 (100-hp Navy Ambulance)
L-14	8	1945 (125-hp 4-place Army utility cargo-liaison type)
	24	Miscellaneous and experimental
Total:	20,261	

Piper's personal post-war sales philosophy was still focused heavily on teaching people to fly and promoting the construction of airport facilities. His approach to selling light aircraft was still to offer the best design and performance characteristics compatible with keeping a low price for the buyer. Consequently, the company continued its traditional practice of designing and producing the lowest-priced model of any major manufacturer in each segment of the light plane market it chose to enter. Its marketing strategy was based on the belief that flight instruction formed the basis for market growth—that new sales in the pleasure, sport, and recreation markets to those who learned to fly in Piper planes were likely to recommend the purchase of the next tier of higher-powered Piper planes for business flying.

Devon Francis, a long-time aviation journalist, summed up the euphoric time when the light plane manufacturers were looking forward to a peacetime bonanza:

"That market was waiting," he wrote in his best-selling *Mr. Piper and His Cubs.* "Everyone said so. To begin with, was anyone stupid enough to think that the several million men in the U.S. Army Air Forces and in the U.S. Navy and Marine Corps air arms would be satisfied to be shackled to surface transportation? Each would be in the market for his very own flying machine. And the general public—uncounted hundreds of thousands of good citizens introduced to air transport during the war—would be assembling at the gates of the light plane factories to purchase their own wings.

The first Piper Cub Special manufactured at Piper's plant in Ponca City, Oklahoma, was rolled out in August 1946. Shown left to right are: A. Hanford Heckman, general manager; Tom Smyer, Oklahoma distributor for Piper; and J. W. Miller, Piper's domestic sales manager. (Piper Aviation Museum)

This crop duster, a modified Piper PA-12 Super Cruiser, was made into a bi-wing model with a 220-hp Continental radial engine in 1947. The fuselage, tail assembly, and landing gear were also redesigned, and a landing light was added. (Peter M. Bowers Collection)

"A G.I. Bill was rumored, which would finance trade and professional training for the millions in the armed forces who would be coming back to civilian pursuits. Untold thousands of them would want to get into aviation. That would mean the establishment of hundreds of flying schools. These alone would need thousands of airplanes.

"The light plane industry's belief in its future was as sublime as a child's conviction that the doctor brought babies in his medicine satchel."

This optimism was enhanced by an anticipated victory over Japan after the German surrender in Europe, and the firm belief

Jack Yentzer poses beside his "Staggerwing" Cub that was intended for high altitude dusting and spraying. It was built from a mix of parts from a J-3 and a PA-18. A 200-hp Ranger engine from a Fairchild PT-19 trainer was installed, along with a Whittaker landing gear. (Leo J. Kohn Collection)

within the industry that a demand for thousands of planes would follow. Many young designers began to create all types and sizes of aircraft on their drawing boards, including "airmobiles" or "roadable planes" that could be stored in a buyer's garage and run on the highways. In fact, some writers have called the late 1930s and 1940s the Golden Age of the Flying Automobile.

Although interesting to consider the possibilities, none of this type of dual purpose private plane has yet gone beyond the prototypes that have sought acceptability by the public; however, the quest for a successful flying automobile goes on. The Experimental Aircraft Association (EAA) has conducted roadable aircraft forums, and continuing interest has been shown by the SAE/World Aviation Congress, as well.

In 1940 Henry Ford had said "Mark my word. A combination airplane and motor car is coming." However, Bill Piper, Sr., was not concerned that the flying automobile would ever replace the light plane and summed up his reasoning in his 1949 book *Private Flying: Today and Tomorrow* this way:

"Aerodynamics being what they are, the roadable plane is neither a good plane nor a good automobile. In the air, it is held back by an enormous amount of drag due to the ungainly sedan body and automobile wheels. On the ground, the light weight essential for flying works against its performance as an automobile, making it frail and flimsy in comparison with ordinary cars."

The initial success of the military helicopter during World War II encouraged some would-be manufacturers to forsake fixed wings for rotating wings, although maintenance and reliability problems had not yet been completely solved. Autogiros were tried in consonance with the roadable idea, and the Autogiro Company of America designed the Roadable Autogiro. It, too, failed to be acceptable for production. A few inventors briefly considered jet propulsion for light roadable planes, although the voracious fuel appetite of the jet engine had not yet been conquered.

***

On March 14, 1945, the first civilian Cub manufactured since the Pearl Harbor attack was rolled out at Lock Haven. Because of long range plans projected months before V-J Day, exactly 1,000 Piper Cub J-3 Specials (re-designated the PA-11) were produced between August 14 and December 27, 1945. It was the civilian version of the L-4 that had been updated to make it the outstanding liaison plane of World War II, noted for its characteristics of safety and maneuverability. Most of the Piper production effort in the following year was devoted to the production of the Specials. Their 65- and 90-hp Continental engines were fully cowled, and had been quieted with a new muffler; a one-piece plexiglass windshield contributed to increased visibility. Standard equipment included hydraulic brakes that could be operated by both occupants. It featured a cabin heater, compass, carburetor heater, steerable tail wheel, and wires and fixtures for navigation lights. Capable of carrying a useful load of 540 lbs, the Special cruised at 75 mph with a maximum speed of 83 mph. With a cruising range of 206 miles, the gas consumption was 4.4 gallons per hour. In addition, both seats had been moved backwards a few inches, and the front seat had been raised about two inches. The result was that a Cub could be flown solo from the front seat, which gave the pilot better forward visibility. The fly-away cost was $2,295.

While the Special was intended primarily for student instruction, it was successfully adapted to many other tasks. Farmers used them for a variety of purposes, including checking fence lines, coyote hunting, searching for stray cattle, and traveling to nearby towns for groceries and supplies. It proved to be adaptable to crop dusting and spraying because it could carry 500 lbs of insecticide; an estimated 1,000 Cubs were modified for that purpose. In Alaska and Canada, a cargo version of the Special, called the Cub Prospector, was widely adopted by bush pilots for short haul work. In other locations, it was widely used for pipeline and power line patrol. Another model, the Cub Sea Scout, was offered with the same equipment as the Cub Special, with the floats interchangeable with wheels.

A peak production of 50 Cubs per working day was projected for June 1946, including then-current models—the J-3 Cub Special, the PA-11S seaplane, and the PA-12 Super Cruiser (the postwar version of the three-place J-5C). The latter, furnished with 100-hp Lycoming engines, featured an electric starter, dual hydraulic brakes, a 12-volt electrical system, and a cabin heater. It was flown from the front seat only, but dual controls were optional. Its first flight was made in December 1945, and there were a reported 5,000 buyers waiting for it.

What helped the light plane industry considerably in the immediate post-war period was the passage of the Serviceman's Readjustment Act of 1944, better known as the GI Bill of Rights, which included a Veterans Administration program to provide education and training for World War II veterans. The original legislation provided for a maximum of $500 a year for tuition, books, fees, and other training costs, plus a subsistence allowance of up to $50 a month. Veterans were entitled to one year of full-time training plus

Piper president William T. Piper, Sr., and vice president Ted Weld check a trophy sent to approximately one thousand Piper dealers for conducting local safety contests in 1946. The award was given to Cub pilots on their fields for flying the greatest number of hours in six months' time without an accident. (Piper Aviation Museum)

Piper always publicized its production milestones, such as this rollout of the 10,000th Cub in 1946. The 100,000th Piper aircraft of all types was completed in 1976. (Piper Aviation Museum)

William Piper, Sr., liked to greet visitors at the Lock Haven factory. This happy new owner of a Piper Pacer shakes hands with the company's president. Piper was called "the Henry Ford of Aviation" for his innovations in mass producing light aircraft. (Piper Aviation Museum)

The Piper family attends a meeting of Piper dealers in Colorado in 1957. Counterclockwise from William T. Piper Sr. (center), is Mary Harford (daughter), Howard "Pug" Piper (son), Margo Piper (Tony's wife), Thomas "Tony" Piper (son), Helen Piper (Howard's wife), Bill Piper, Junior (son), "Pud" Piper (Bill Junior's wife), and Elizabeth Harford (daughter). (Fred Weick Collection)

a period equal to their time in the service up to a maximum of 48 months. This enabled many to get their private licenses in light aircraft and then upgrade to commercial and air transport licenses in larger aircraft and proceed into a professional flying career.

By the end of 1946 Piper had produced a record 7,780 various models of Cubs that year, more than twice the number it had produced in any prewar year. Piper enlarged its plant facilities at Lock Haven and opened a new mid-continent plant at Ponca City, Oklahoma. There were more than 3,000 employees on the Piper payroll by the end of December 1946.

The Piper PA-12 Super Cruiser went into full production during the latter part of 1946, which proved to be an instant success. It was one of the first planes to be licensed under "modernized" Civil Air Regulations issued in 1945 by the Civil Aeronautics Board, which allowed it to be licensed as a carrier and a trainer. As a carrier it was permitted to carry a gross load of 1,750 lbs, sufficient for a pilot, two passengers, baggage, and enough fuel for a six-hour flight, or more than 600 miles at a cruising speed of 103 mph.

The Super Cruiser was equipped with a direct-drive 100-h.p. engine and was flown from the front seat, where the pilot had excellent visibility; the two passengers sat in the rear bench seat. Standard equipment included dual hydraulic brakes, parking brake, one-piece plexiglass windshield, cabin heater, carburetor heater, mixture control, full-swivel tail wheel, 12-volt battery, navigation lights, motor-driven generator, provisions for a full-panel of navigation instruments, and two-way radio. The fly-away cost was $3,295.

The float-equipped Piper Super Sea Scout had the same equipment as the Super Cruiser. It was sold with interchangeable wheel

William T. Piper, Sr. (seated), and (left to right) sons Thomas, William, Jr., and Howard, were all pilots and officers of the company. William, Jr., eventually became president. This photograph was taken in January 1961. (Piper Aviation Museum)

Owners of Piper aircraft manufactured at Lock Haven flew in for an Open House in August 1957. Annual fly-ins, called Sentimental Journey, have been conducted each year since 1985. Winners of flying contests and best-restored Cubs are awarded prizes. (Piper Aviation Museum)

landing gear in addition to the floats, which could convert it from a seaplane to a land plane in about two hours. It could take off from a runway by means of dollies, and could be landed carefully on grass strips on reinforced floats.

Next was the PA-6 Sky Sedan, an experimental low-wing, cantilever, metal monoplane powered by a 165-h.p. engine that gave it a cruising speed of 125 mph. It was designed to carry four persons and had retractable gear, electric starter and generator, two-way radio, and easy-to-read navigation instruments. Its cruising speed was 140 mph, with a cruising range of 600 miles and a useful load of 1,050 lbs. The sale price was to be $2,995. Although it was a favorite of Howard Piper, Mr. Piper's youngest son, only two were produced, and the project was abandoned because of high production costs.

The Piper J-4 Sky Coupe followed, which was a two-place, low wing model that was a distinct departure from previous Piper models. It had a single pusher engine, tricycle landing gear, and twin booms that supported twin rudders. Performance tests were not encouraging and it was never produced.

Plane manufacturers were deluged with requests from active and former Army Air Force and Navy flying personnel who wanted information on owning and operating their own light planes. Sales

agencies geared up to handle queries from war veterans who were interested in setting up their own airport businesses as fixed base operators, flight schools, and aircraft distributors. Aircraft manufacturers began thinking in terms of a process called "elimination engineering," which referred to cutting down on the number of parts in their military designs to convert them to civilian needs and wants.

It was the major pre-war light plane companies—Piper, Aeronca, Taylorcraft, Stinson, Luscombe, Rearwin, Ercoupe—that began major advertising campaigns with the military returnees in mind. The movement was enhanced when the G.I. Bill included flight training and college courses in aviation administration. As early as May 1945, light plane manufacturers released information about their designs, experimental models, finished prototypes, or just concepts for personal planes. Seven light plane makers (Piper, Aeronca, Republic, Culver, Taylorcraft, Globe, and Stinson) estimated that their combined output would be from 22,300 to 24,500 personal planes in the first year of post-war production.

When the victory over Japan was concluded by the two atomic bombs, Piper had developed a backlog of orders that amounted to an estimated $11 million. Orders from distributors across the country had to be rationed, and they were placed on a priority list. Various models of the Cubs and their derivatives were being turned out

The Whittaker landing gear on this Cub makes landings on uneven ground safer. Some owners have replaced the standard small tires with larger "tundra" tires for even greater safety in landing on gravel strips and beaches. (Robert Kopitzke Collection)

This crop duster found that cutting back the fuselage of his J-3 Cub made it easier to load the pesticide. The upper wing has been shortened and a lower wing added. (A. L. Cleave Collection)

at the rate of 15 per day, and total production for the civilian market had reached nearly 1,000 by the end of 1945.

It was a euphoric time for the light plane industry, and even *Fortune* magazine, professing always to be unbiased and objective, editorialized in the February 1946 issue:

"The trend is in the right direction—toward cheaper, safer airplanes, many more air parks, and much less government red tape for pilots. The outlook is good."

Such optimism was contagious among the engineers at Piper. Anticipating the demand for a plane that might appeal to the ex-fighter pilot, Piper production engineer A. Hanford Eckman recommended the development of the single-place Skycycle, a sort of motor-bike for the light plane world. One writer reported that Piper engineers had actually taken a droppable fuel tank, mounted a light 40-hp engine in it, cut out a cockpit, added an extension boom for a rudder and elevators, added a pair of wings and made it fly. That may have been partially true, but it was eventually turned out as a single-place plane that could cruise at 90 mph and had a range of

350 to 400 miles. It weighed less than 450 lbs empty and could carry up to 250 lbs, although the small cockpit would barely accommodate a pilot weighing 180 lbs. It was to be offered for $900; however, it was canceled when the company's management decided they should put the emphasis on turning out other models that would carry more than one person.

Some predicted that small helicopters would play a large role in the postwar light aircraft picture, but a survey by the U.S. Aeronautical Chamber of Commerce anticipated only 2,500 customers paying $5,000 each would be willing to buy them. Thus, the helicopter industry's anticipated income of only $12.5 million would "surely be insufficient to support even a tenth of the would-be manufacturers."

Respected aviation authors Reginald M. Cleveland and Leslie E. Neville, in their 1944 book *The Coming Air Age*, concluded that:

"...there is no reason why planes looking only a little different from the Cubs of yesteryear cannot fulfill most of the public's demands. Furthermore, these demands are almost identical with the Army's specifications for liaison planes, specifications which the

A J-3 Cub modified for crop dusting speeds over a field in south Texas. Telephone lines bordering a field can be dangerous hazards. (A. L. Cleave Collection)

The duster pilot of this low-flying J-3 Cub noted his accident report on the back of this photograph, "Short field, heavy load, deep grass, fence, in that order." (A. L. Cleave Collection)

"big three" [Aeronca, Piper, and Stinson] of the light plane field have been fulfilling since early in 1942....Predictions are that we shall have between 300,000 and 500,000 private planes in the sky by 1950. This sounds like a great many airplanes—until we realize that it will represent the output of our factories for less than a year and will mean there is one airplane for every 260 people. And even this somewhat limited prophecy is based entirely on the questionable survival of a healthy national economy following the war. The technicians will do their part; the question is one of statesmanship, not of engineering."

With this kind of go-ahead prediction dominating those who were thinking about private aviation's future in 1944, Piper management was more confident than ever that they were on the right path by designing and marketing new planes to satisfy an American public that would be eager to satisfy the "air conditioning" program for a three-dimensional world that Robert H. Hinckley had advocated in 1938.

William T. Piper, Sr., congratulates Max Conrad after flying around the world in record time in a Piper twin-engine Aztec. Conrad's many long-distance flights kept the company's name in the news for more than a decade. (Piper Aviation Museum)

S. Paul Johnston, another prominent aviation journalist, published a book titled *Wings after War* in 1944 in which he thought:

"...few radically new designs will appear on U.S. airports. The Cubs, Stinsons and Fairchilds that have been serving in the Army or the Navy will appear again in their gay civilian hues. They will be a bit more rugged, a little bit more airworthy, somewhat more reliable in engine and accessories, but basically they will be the same airplanes that they were in 1938 and 1939. The same skill will be required to fly them. The need for airport and maintenance facilities will be the same as always."

Johnston also pointed out that there were uncertainties about what the post-war military requirements for aircraft would be:

"Until then," he said, "few plans could be made until manufacturers have some inkling of what Government intends to do with the huge quantities of surplus aircraft which will be on hand at war's end. [In addition,] there are no clear-cut indications of Government's attitude toward the disposition of the huge aircraft plants that have been built with Federal money. Fears have been expressed that Government may some day move into some of them as a competitor."

Johnston believed that the postwar type of light planes would be conventional in design, and that engines for the two, three, and four-place planes would range from 80- to 300-h.p. He also predicted that landing gear would shift to the tricycle type, and all wheels would be retractable, except for the light two-seat trainers.

Max Conrad, the "flying grandfather," poses at New York's LaGuardia Airport in December 1964 after one of his many record-setting, long distance flights in Piper aircraft. Father of 10 and grandfather of 15, he logged approximately 50,000 flying hours during his lifetime and delivered more than 200 single- and twin-engine Piper aircraft to Europe, Africa, Asia, and South America. (Piper Aviation Museum)

Johnston did not accept the forecast that returning servicemen would be buying new light planes in large numbers:

"Brightest spot of all in aviation's first post-war decade," he wrote, "is the outlook for our domestic airlines....Air transport is at last over the hump. After years of struggle, it has succeeded in shedding its glamour. It has achieved the commonplace."

There was no doubt in the mind of William T. Piper, Sr., by now widely referred to as the "Henry Ford of Aviation," that the company was going to participate impressively in a post-war boom, and he was quoted as saying:

"Visions of an airplane in most garages are unfounded. But light planes will be big business."

In an article prepared for *Flying* magazine in 1947 he recognized that:

"We must concentrate on roomier aircraft with better performance in all categories, and not go overboard on our dreams of

airplanes of the future. I would be the last to say that the day will never come when all aviation's dreams will be realized. But in the meantime we must recognize that, for the present, half-flying, half-auto contraptions, machines that can fly at good cruising speeds but will land on a dime, and planes with removable wings or jet power, are still in a highly experimental category."

Piper remembered the optimistic predictions that were presented by some aviation writers, who had prophesied during the World's Fair of 1939 that everyone would own and fly planes. Everyone seemed to agree that light planes had clearly proven their value to the military services during World War II. The fact that the nation had become truly air-minded as a result was considered irrefutable.

More than 3,100 of various models of Pipers had been produced during the first six months of 1946, with nearly 1,000 scheduled per month by the end of the year. The Piper ads in the aviation magazines during that period carried a quote from Mr. Piper, Sr., that showed his optimism:

"When you investigate today's airplane market, you will find Piper leads in sales because it leads in value, safety and economy."

The Aircraft Industries Association told its members that the thousands of military and civilian pilots trained between 1938 and 1948:

"...compose the largest ready-made market for personal planes and for airport facilities that has ever existed." However, its yearbook cautioned that "if enough of them do not continue flying to support the personal plane industry, their neglect should be an unmistakable sign to airplane designers that a new airplane is needed which will provide more utility at a lower operating cost."

In anticipation of ever-heavier sales, Piper opened a new assembly plant at Ponca City, OK, in July 1946 with A. Hanford Eckman in charge. It was expected that 70 to 80 Cubs would be produced during the first month of production, and a total of 700 by the end of the year. Total aircraft production for Piper during 1946 was more than one-fourth of the industry's total of 33,254—more than any other of the 16 manufacturers of light planes then in business.

Although the elder Piper was inclined to be overly optimistic about public demand, he was concerned rightly about a serious national limitation for light plane flying: airports. He gave talks and wrote articles about this weakness, which was that the country needed many times the number of landing fields that were then in existence. He preached that the airplane was the world's most versatile means of transportation, and that good airports are more necessary for aircraft than good harbors are for ships, since the latter could be anchored off-shore and their loads transferred to smaller ships. Trains, automobiles, and boats could only go where there

Vice President Hubert H. Humphrey awarded Max Conrad the Harmon International Trophy in 1965. The award was for setting a non-stop distance record of 7,878 miles in a Piper Twin Comanche from South Africa to St. Petersburg, Florida. (Piper Aviation Museum)

One way of solving a hangar storage problem was this method used at East Boston, Mass. Municipal Airport and elsewhere. Cubs were set on their noses with the propellers protected by a block of wood. Fifteen planes can be parked in the space ordinarily taken up by five or six. (Piper Aviation Museum)

were rails, roads, and water, but air was everywhere. He urged state officials to develop airports in their respective jurisdictions as the need arose, starting with a field to fit present needs, but providing facilities for expansion. He felt that every community should have a landing field of some type, and cautioned that "the little plane has no business on a big airport." He added that "an airport is like a telephone. It has little value by itself, but its usefulness increases rapidly as the number of airports grows."

Piper realized that some of what he said was an over-simplification, but he felt sincerely that airplanes could be useful only if there were airports to receive them. His eldest son recalled that his father also:

"...campaigned tirelessly for small landing sites called Air Parks and for emergency strips, easily carved out by a grading machine, every few miles alongside major highways."

Several twin-engine Cubs, certified by the FAA, have been modified by their owners. This one, with Nelson 45-hp engines, was converted by William D. Fuchs, a Piper test pilot, and Charles Rhoads at Lock Haven in 1966. (William D. Fuchs Collection)

But as the company's board chairman crusaded for airports, various finished and tested models of the Cubs were lining up on the field at Lock Haven unsold, and tie-down space was increasingly hard to find. Sales dropped off drastically beginning in March 1947. There were 85,000 private and executive planes certificated by the CAA by then, and an estimated 80,000 of them were operated by private owners, business owners, charter services, and schools.

According to the Aircraft Industries Association (AIA) there were more than 30 personal aircraft models for the private owner to consider for purchase, ranging from two to seven-place machines:

"No less than 17 companies were actively competing for sales in this field alone," the association's *Aircraft Year Book for 1947* stated, "and there were as many more companies, groups and individuals hard at work on experimental models, some conventional, others radical and dangerously so. It was much easier to buy a plane than a motor car, and one's purchase could be financed in precisely the same way."

Piper sold 7,773 planes in 1946 and planned to build 10,000 in 1947. In a 1946 year-end report, the Aircraft Industries Association stated that a total of 35,000 personal planes had been produced in the U.S., and added optimistically:

"Given a favorable business atmosphere; assuming a flow of materials for planes and for landing fields and hangars; adequate salesmanship and production sufficient to keep costs low, then personal plane sales in 1947 will at least equal those of 1946."

This opinion was typical of the general optimism propounded by the aircraft industry's official publication during the immediate post-war era. During the three-day All American Air Maneuvers at Miami in the winter of 1946, Cubs had captured the majority of the light plane prizes, with Bevo Howard winning the Costairs aerobatic trophy; Verna Burke of Miami took top honors in the Women's Handicap, and Tom Davis, Winston-Salem, NC, won the Piper Handicap.

The Gulf Oil Co. resumed its sponsorship of the Annual Gulf Air Tour to Florida in January 1947, and that year's National Air Races at Cleveland for the first time featured a light plane event, with $25,000 in prizes offered by the Goodyear Tire and Rubber Co.

The Cub Flier, the company magazine, reflected the Piper enthusiasm at this time in the March-April 1946 issue with an article titled "The Cubs are Rolling Again." The editor concluded:

"In its years of leadership in the personal aircraft industry, the Piper organization, faced with considerable competition, looks confidently to the future."

But the rosy future came to a sudden halt. Without much advance notice, the War Assets Administration (WAA) suddenly placed more than 100,000 surplus warplanes, including 35,000 trainers like the Piper L-4s, on the market at drastically reduced prices. It was the federal government's massive effort to recoup as much as possible from the billions of dollars that production for war had cost. In his 1949 book, Piper noted that;

"...planes originally costing $18,000 to $29,000 each were sold for as little as $800. The bargains proved irresistible. Only too late did the buyers realize that it cost a small fortune to operate these fast, high-powered planes, which consumed 30 gallons of gas per hour—six to seven times the gas consumption of the light plane."

The Piper Tri-Pacer was introduced in 1950 as an option for the Pacer, and represented a significant change in light plane aircraft design for the company. From that period on, tricycle gear began to become the conventional gear for light planes. The Tri-Pacer proved to be very popular and enjoyed a 14-year production run. (Piper Aviation Museum)

William T. Piper. Sr., greets the buyer of the 5000th Tri-Pacer at Lock Haven. Nearly 9,500 Tri-Pacers and the less-expensive Caribbeans and Colts were produced between 1950 and 1964. (William D. Strohmeier Collection)

"The WAA's contribution brought the total number of private planes to 90,000, an increase in a single year of more than 250 per cent. Although we didn't realize it immediately, the supply had suddenly caught up with demand. The post-war market for personal planes had been thoroughly glutted.

"All through January and February of 1947 Piper Aircraft still produced planes at the rate of 30 a day, apparently heading for a record-breaking 7,500 for the year, when almost without warning the market collapsed. Sales in March dropped to 3 or 4 a day. At first we told ourselves hopefully that it was only a 'bad weather' slowdown.

"When unsold airplanes began to pile up all over the place we knew that it was something more than a momentary slackening. Something had to be done. If we couldn't sell them, we had to stop making them."

Piper tried to appear optimistic about the industry and wrote a statesmanlike article for the August 1947 issue of *Flying* magazine. He said;

"We have, fortunately, passed the plane-in-every-lunch-box stage of post-war flying and are in a good position to cope with the pessimism or optimism, and assuming that we are willing to profit by the lessons we have been exposed to in the past 20 years, I think the industry is in the best shape in its history. Sales during the next 20 years should make those during the last 20 seem miniature by comparison.

"But this will be possible if we profit by our mistakes and recognize a few fundamentals which we must face before light plane prosperity can get under way in these air-minded times.

"Here are some of the most important facts:

"Aviation is not a mass-production industry, either from the manufacturing or the consumer viewpoint. It is a craft industry and probably will remain so for at least another 20 years.

"Our best potential customers are not the youth of the nation—if they ever were. They are important, but our best potential customers are middle-aged.

"We must concentrate on making roomier aircraft with better performance in all categories, and not go overboard on our dreams of airplanes of the future."

It had become painfully obvious when this article appeared that the company had to cut back production, but parts and supplies

Piper began a new venture in 1948 when it purchased the Stinson Division of Consolidated-Vultee Aircraft Corporation. The plan was to produce the four-place Piper Twin-Stinson PA-23, shown here with one engine shut down during a test flight. It was developed from a proposal found in the Stinson files and eventually was re-developed into the Piper PA-23 Apache. More than 2,000 Apaches were built through 1963. (Piper Aviation Museum)

kept coming in to Lock Haven. At one point there was over $300,000 worth of steel tubing, thousands of gallons of dope, and hundreds of yards of cotton fabric on hand, plus scores of engines in crates stacked up in the storerooms.

Meanwhile, Piper's banker-creditors took charge of the company, putting their own men on the board of directors, and hired William C. Shriver to run it. A professional industrial trouble-shooter, he did so, harshly and without empathy. He closed the plant down and fired most top executives, except Ted Weld, the two Wm. T. Pipers, Howard Piper, and two other board members, then formed a board of his own. Although the elder Piper was allowed to retain his title as president, he was relegated to a small room in the hangar, but did not complain. Bill Piper, Jr., was transferred to California as a factory representative and salesman. In July 1947 the Ponca City plant was abandoned, and the work force at Lock Haven was reduced from 2,700 to 250 as the company was reorganized.

Shriver's major task was to cut costs, dispose of unsold planes, and find a market for the raw materials that had reached such mountainous proportions. He also insisted that a cheaper plane be designed, and the result was the two-place, side-by-side Vagabond, which biographer Devon Francis called a "pretty sad airplane." It was the first Piper side-by-side model and had a landing gear without springs, or even a Cub's rubber shock cord to absorb landing impacts. Three feet had been clipped off both wing tips, but it had a 65-hp engine that gave it a respectable 90 mph top speed. It was the first of the "short wing" Pipers that would follow.

Shriver's hard-nosed attitude and severe cost-cutting tactics worked, and he left in December 1947 after a year on the job. Mr. Piper recalled later that Shriver had been "pretty hard to take when he was here, but if he hadn't been here, we wouldn't be here now." He still admitted 20 years later that Shriver had saved the company by his cost-cutting measures.

Money was borrowed from the Reconstruction Finance Corporation, and in January 1948 workers were rehired, and the stock of airplanes and parts was slowly reduced. Piper himself reminisced later that:

"...the greatest lesson we learned in the critical year of 1947 is that the personal plane industry must make haste slowly."

One would not know from Piper advertisements that there was a dark shadow lingering over Lock Haven at this time. All ads were upbeat, touting Piper's new planes while the future still looked very bleak. One newsworthy bright spot in the news for Piper was a new altitude record set for aircraft having a gross weight of less than 1,102.3 lbs. Mrs. Mildred Zimmerman of Reading, PA, on September 26, 1949, climbed her 90-hp Piper PA-11 Cub Special to 26,138 feet as certified by a sealed barograph provided by the National Bureau of Standards. It had eclipsed the record of 24,311 feet set in 1940 by Grace Huntington at Burbank, CA, in a Taylorcraft.

"But we managed to pull through," the elder Piper recalled. "We sold every plane we had made up to the shutdown in July (a little better than 4,000 in six months) and paid off the bulk of our debts by early 1948. When we reopened for business we set our production rate at between 2,500 and 3,000 planes for the year. By that time the market had absorbed the 70,000 planes of 1946, and the market was beginning to show signs of recovery."

What had seemed to be a rosy post-war future for all the light plane manufacturers was not to be. The market for their products was clearly saturated, as the industry experienced a Great Depression of its own. William T. Piper, Jr., who had been an officer in the company since his graduation from Harvard in 1934 and later be-

Piper and other light plane manufacturers continually sought new uses for their products. A New York radio station leased a Piper PA-12 Super Cruiser to cover special events in the fall of 1946. The rear seat area was large enough to carry the station's announcer, portable transmitter, batteries, and other heavy equipment used during that period. (Piper Aviation Museum)

Cubs prove useful as air taxis for short flights from rural areas to airline airports. This Piper "Taxicub" ferried visitors from Lock Haven to nearby destinations. (Jay Miller Collection)

came its president, gave an enlightening talk in 1970 to the Newcomen Society that summarized his views of what happened to the light plane industry during that critical two-year post-war period:

"The delusion that hit the light plane industry in 1945 was that now, at long last, a half-million good citizens would acquire their own personal wings. In terms of potential sales, the sky would be the limit. The Air Age was here, with a plane in every garage. The evidence was overwhelming. An industry-financed survey supported the conclusion.

"Hundreds of thousands of men trained to fly war planes would be returning to civilian life, and did anyone think that they were going to be happy with a car averaging only thirty miles an hour? Millions of soldiers, mustered out, would be schooled under a GI Bill, and a hearty proportion of them would elect to take courses in flying.

"Lessons learned by one generation seldom endure through the next. This same belief—that personal wings would become a

commonplace—had pervaded the aircraft manufacturing industry after the Lindbergh flight in 1927. That so-called flying boom had proved to be pure *ersatz*. The Great Depression was not the cause of that bust; economic conditions only hastened it. In 1945, W. T. Piper (Sr.) issued a word of warning now and then about excess optimism, but he was all too human. He, too, was caught up in the hysteria.

"The light plane industry, with Piper in the vanguard, enjoyed a frenzy of production and sales right up to the doorstep of spring 1947. Then the market collapsed. This was an anomaly. American industry at large still couldn't fill the orders for steel, rubber, wood products and household appliances that had been damming up during the war. Automobile dealers still would not sell a car unless it carried an outrageous load of expensive extras.

"The reasons for the collapse of the light plane market were several, but a main one was that the product was exactly what it had been before Pearl Harbor. The Piper type of machine was still confined, by and large, to flying in the vicinity of airports. Its utility was minimal. It could not be driven to the grocery store. It had neither the speed, range nor the instrumentation for reliable cross-country transportation.

"In the ensuing six months the shakeout among light plane manufacturers was pitiless. Those of us who survived look back now occasionally and wonder how we managed it.

"The disaster was good. It made us reassess ourselves. If the Air Age of personal flying that we had been trumpeting did not exist, then what was our market? Indeed, *was* there a market? There was, but we did a lot of backing and filling to find it. What finally came out of the soul-searching was recognition that our kind of airplanes had a sizable niche to fill in the spectrum of transportation, but these were not the machines we had been making. They would have to accommodate four persons and upward. They would have to have a lot more speed and that meant more power. In comparison with the airlines, they had to offer a personal transport alternative. No longer would a man buy an airplane if, against a brisk

The Piper PA-6 Sky Sedan was proposed as a four-place, all-metal low-wing monoplane in 1946. Only two were made. The first model was fabric-covered with metal framed fuselage and wings; the second one was all-metal. The project was canceled when the post-war aircraft market collapsed. (Piper Aviation Museum)

Molton B. Taylor's Aerocar shows its roadable qualities for reporters at the Temco plant in Dallas, Texas, in 1961. It was one of several flying automobiles that progressed from the design to the prototype stage. William Piper, Sr., did not believe that such hybrid vehicles would ever replace the light plane. (History of Aviation Collection, Univ. of Texas at Dallas)

to a sleek, beautiful four-place plane called the Bonanza just after the return of peace."

What the younger Bill Piper was referring to was the Piper Tri-Pacer, the company's first venture into the tricycle era. It was a follow-on improvement over the four-place PA-16 Clipper, a high-wing, tail-wheel model that performed well with its 115-hp engine, but it had a short fuselage and a narrow landing gear. After it was introduced in 1949, Pan American Airways objected to Piper using that name, claiming that the word "Clipper" had been trademarked for their ocean-hopping giant planes. Although the Piper lawyers thought the charge was ridiculous, rather than engage in an expensive lawsuit, the Piper Clipper became the Piper Pacer in 1950.

The Pacer, still of tube-and-fabric construction, had begun life as an updated four-place plane. It had wing flaps and two fuel tanks in the wings. The empennage was slightly changed, and the main gear was widened to improve handling on landings. It was considered a step up from the Clipper because it had a more comfortable cabin, a little more power, and dual wheel controls instead of two sticks. It was priced at $3,295. A total of 1,120 Pacers were produced before production ended in September 1954.

head wind, a Ford V-8 could outpace him on the highway below. The light plane no longer could be called a light plane. It could not be noisy and unheated. Its seats could not be wooden benches overlaid with imitation leather stuffed with cotton batting. It must have hours of range. It must take off with reasonable assurance of getting where it was going, the weather almost notwithstanding.

"We were on a voyage of rediscovery. One of the first adjuncts to a more useful vehicle that we hit upon was the tricycle landing gear. It didn't matter that the Wright brothers had introduced the idea. It was new to us, if not to General Aviation. A two-place Ercoupe had employed it before the war, and Beech had applied it

The Pacer did not sell well when it was first introduced, and Max Conrad, a Piper dealer, instructor, and fixed-base operator, as well as chief pilot for Minneapolis Honeywell Corporation, had an idea. Max had fallen on bad times and had to sell the Cubs he used for instruction. At the same time the corporation favored their plush DC-3 for executive transportation over his slow-flying Cubs. His wife had become unhappy, and Max had suggested she go to Switzerland with their 10 children while he stayed in Winona, Minnesota, until he could bring them back when things were better financially.

One day in early 1950, while over-flying Lock Haven on a flight to the East Coast, he looked down and saw several rows of

To prove that the Taylor Aerocar could fly, a test pilot makes a demonstration flight for the cameraman in March 1961. It cruised at 100 mph and had a range of 300 miles. On the highway it had a "practical" speed of 60 mph. The Aerocar received full FAA certification in 1958, and one model was presented to the National Air and Space Museum. (History of Aviation Collection, University of Texas, Dallas)

unsold Piper Pacers lined up beside the factory. He landed and contacted Bill Strohmeier with an idea to help out with sales. Strohmeier, now working for a New York public relations firm as advertising representative for Piper, thought the idea had merit and contacted Jake Miller, assistant sales manager, who agreed, but suggested that Max should discuss it personally with Mr. Piper.

Max's idea was to fly a Pacer across the Atlantic Ocean and on to Switzerland alone. Piper could reap the publicity benefits from such a flight, and Conrad would be able to visit his wife and children, whom he had not seen for over a year. The senior Bill Piper liked the idea, but fully realized the risk both of them would be taking with such a venture. Conrad's biographer, Sally Buegeleisen, describes what happened:

"Here's what I'll do, Max," William Piper said. 'As a dealer, you get twenty-five percent off the top. If you make it to Europe, I'll take another twenty-five percent off. And if you return it to Minneapolis, I'll deduct another twenty-five. That leaves only twenty-five percent, and we'll talk about that when you get back.'"

It was a fair deal as far as Max was concerned, and he took delivery of a new Pacer. The one he chose was a stock model with a 135-hp engine. The only modification he asked for was a constant-speed propeller and the addition of two extra gas tanks of 130 gallons total capacity, which gave it a range of about 2,500 miles. He persuaded his friend Bill Lear, manufacturer of aviation radio equipment, to furnish a low frequency radio, two ADFs (automatic direction finders), and a VHF radio for communication and navigation. He devised his own system to ensure oil pressure to the engine when adding oil to the tank in flight.

Many different types of experimental landing gear were installed on Cubs to ease landings on rough terrain. This Bonmartini eight-wheel tubular track landing gear, developed for a Swiss firm, was one of several similar types that did not prove successful. The large, low-pressure tundra tires used today are judged the most satisfactory. (Smithsonian Institution)

When the word was released about what Conrad expected to do he was the focus of the aviation press, many of whom seriously doubted he would succeed. In August 1950, already late for such a trip across the north Atlantic in good weather, he flew to Teterboro, New Jersey, and was besieged by radio, TV, and newspaper reporters. If he were successful, he would be the first pilot to make a solo round trip across the Atlantic in such a small plane.

Max planned to fly the standard route of other transatlantic fliers from the United States to Labrador, Greenland, Iceland, and

This is the second prototype of the L-14 (designated as L-4X), a more powerful Army liaison plane than the L-4. This one is shown in 1945 before the installation of a long-stroke landing gear. The rear structure was hinged to admit a stretcher patient, as in the Navy's HE-1/AE-1. (Peter M. Bowers Collection)

Scotland, and then proceed to France and Geneva. As could be expected in late August in the far northern latitudes, he battled icing and thunderstorms that ran him off his course. He was uncertain of his position at times, but made it to Switzerland for a happy reunion with his family. He returned to his base at Winona, Minnesota, the following month even though winter had descended over the route and he again encountered icing on almost every leg.

Conrad flew the Atlantic two more times to win further acclaim for himself and Piper. In 1951, flying the same Pacer, he flew non-stop from Winona to Mexico City and returned across the Gulf of Mexico to Washington, D.C. Shortly afterward he flew non-stop from Minneapolis to Miami with a cargo of frozen Minnesota snowballs for delivery to the queen of the Miami Air Races.

"The Flying Grandfather," now 68, set an official world and U.S. non-stop distance record in the Pacer to capture the speed record for Class 2 aircraft from Los Angeles to New York, a mark that was not broken until 1959. To help celebrate the 50th anniversary year of the Wright brothers' 1903 first flights, he made a 14-day, 17,000-mile trip in which he visited each of the 48 contiguous state capitals with greetings for each of the governors. On the return trip he set an unofficial speed record from San Francisco to New York. Looking back on this fortnight of transcontinental peregrinations, he said, "It was the toughest job I ever tackled."

These flights brought exceptional publicity to Piper, but this was not new for Max. He had been front page news a decade before when he participated in one of the most dramatic experiences of a long flying career that had begun in 1927. In 1941, duck hunters had gone hunting in the Mississippi River bottoms early on a warm November morning became trapped in a howling blizzard a few hours later. The temperature dropped to 7 degrees below zero, the lowest ever recorded in that area's history.

When Max heard about their plight, he took off in a Cub the next day and flew from daybreak until midnight, dropping messages, food, and matches, and guiding ground rescuers to the stranded hunters. In the role of aerial "pointer" he flew gradually tightening figure 8s until the hunters and their rescuers were within hailing distance.

During his lifetime and more than 50,000 hours of flying, Max Conrad made more than 140 ocean crossings in single- and twin-engine Pipers, including non-stop flights from New York to Palermo, Italy, and from Chicago to Rome. For several years he averaged over one flight a month to the British Isles, Europe, and Africa, and also made deliveries throughout Latin America. He was indisputably Piper's best advertisement for their single- and twin-engine aircraft.

***

One of the significant aeronautical changes in aircraft design during the 1930s was the introduction of the tricycle landing gear. Fred E. Weick, inventor of the two-control Ercoupe, had proven the capability of the tricycle landing gear in 1934 with his W-1A. A tri-gear aircraft named the Stearman-Hammond Model Y was the winner of the safe aircraft competition in 1936 sponsored by the aviation section of the Department of Commerce. Only a few were produced at a cost of $3,500 each, far in excess of the low cost of

Alaskan bush pilots use the various models of Piper aircraft to carry unusual loads. This J-3C pilot has attached his canoe to one of the floats to ferry it to his favorite fishing locations. (Alaska Pictorial Services)

William T. Piper, Sr., after check-out in an early model of the twin-engine Apache. (Piper Aviation Museum)

$700 that was recommended as the ideal to encourage production of light planes at the time.

It was World War II that saw the introduction of aircraft in large quantities with tricycle landing gear, i.e. the B-25, B-24, P-38, P-39, and C-54. A castoring nose gear enables an airplane to withstand crosswind and gust conditions during taxiing, takeoff, and landing, giving it a wider margin of safety than one with a tail wheel.

Ray Testerman of Tulsa, Oklahoma, and Tom Smyer, owner of Smyer Aircraft Corp. of Ponca City, Oklahoma, experimented in 1947 to see if a tricycle gear could be installed on their Cub trainers. The standard gear of a tail-wheel Cub was exchanged, right gear for left side, left gear for right side. By reversing this fitting, complete with shock cords, a change in the center of gravity was accomplished. By adding a wheel under the nose, the Cub was in level attitude, thus giving greater visibility in taxiing. A tail skid was added in place of the tail wheel. The changeover from a tail-wheel Cub took only about four hours, and very little modification was required in the structure under the cockpit. Smyer planned to produce the gear in kits that would retail for about $200 and applied for CAA certification.

It is not known if the Testerman-Smyer modification had any influence on Piper's engineers, but Bill Piper, Sr., gave Fred Weick credit for his company following the characteristics of the Ercoupe when the Tri-Pacer PA-22 with tricycle gear was introduced in 1950 as an option for the Pacer. It was promptly accepted by Piper enthusiasts. The Tri-Pacer had the ailerons and rudder connected, and the nose gear configuration made the Pacer a safer plane for light plane pilots.

Mr. Piper finally had what he called a "businessman's airplane," and it enjoyed a production run of nearly 14 years, as 7,670 of them were turned out between 1951 and 1960. Shortly thereafter, Cessna began to equip its light planes with tricycle gear, which became the conventional rather than the unconventional gear for most light planes.

Joe Halsmer of Lafayette, Indiana, an airline captain, wanted to improve the Tri-Pacer even further. He installed two 90-hp Continental engines in the nose and tied them together into a single nose shaft that mounted two fixed-pitch propellers, one behind the other, and one for each engine. Howard Piper described it as one of "a number of research projects" and emphasized that the Tri-Pacer was used only as a test bed. The advantage that was hoped for was that such an engine installation would eliminate the mounting of power plants, and thus prevent control and performance problems if power was lost on one engine. Testing did not support the theory and it was not successful.

A follow-on model to the Tri-Pacer was the PA-22-108 Colt, a two-seat, tandem trainer without flaps. A total of 1,820 Colts were built between 1961 and 1963. It was the last tube-and-fabric model that Piper built.

Although considered very successful, Bill Piper, Jr., said the Tri-Pacer was a "makeshift" idea as far as the company was concerned, because to be more stable, the main gear on a tricycle plane should be spread wide enough to give the plane stability on the ground. The only way to achieve the needed stability was to design a low-winged aircraft, which permits the main landing gear to be placed as far apart as needed. And so the idea for the Piper Apache was born—an all-metal, twin-engine plane that appealed to businessmen for corporate travel, air taxi operators, and private owners. The Apache PA-23 was the lowest-priced light twin on the market.

"Our first thought was to make a twin-engine version of the four-place Tri-Pacer with its fabric skin, relatively low horsepower,

A U.S. 40-cent stamp honored William T. Piper, Sr., in 1991.

A U.S. 32-cent stamp honored the Piper Cub in 1997, along with other world famous aircraft.

agers and Station Wagons. All of the jigs and tools for them were shipped to Lock Haven by the spring of 1949.

Chief engineer Walter Jamouneau and Designer Fred Strickland unveiled the Piper Twin-Stinson, and Bill Piper, Sr., said it represented a big step forward in providing a moderately-priced plane for around-the-clock transportation. He said, confidently:

"We feel that this type of airplane will do a great deal to give the businessman even more utility, since it will permit him to complete more of his trips after dark and over weather."

The deal included the Stinson plant in Wayne, Michigan, and about 200 Stinson Station Wagons, incomplete airframes, and parts. The Piper company soon found itself trying to sell planes that were in competition with its own four-place Family Cruisers. As a result, the smaller Stinsons were eventually disposed of at bargain prices.

The design studies for a twin-engine aircraft had been acquired as part of the purchase, and the Piper Twin-Stinson prototype flew on March 4, 1952. It was of tube, metal, and fabric construction, with retractable tri-cycle landing gear and twin vertical fins and rudders. The wheels were slightly exposed when retracted (similar to the venerable DC-3 transport); this position served to minimize structural damage in case of a wheels-up landing. All but the aft section of the fuselage was metal-covered, and the fuselage construction was of welded steel. It was to carry four people and cruise at 150 mph with an absolute ceiling of 21,000 feet. The subsequent history of this aircraft has faded from the company's records, and little is known about the reasoning for the decision to abandon it.

Another attempt to build a multi-engine plane was the purchase of a Bauman B250 Brigadier in 1949. It was a pusher design; Piper engineers considered redesigning it to a tractor engine configuration, but the expense was deemed not worth the effort and it, too, was abandoned.

***

a fixed-pitch propeller, and a fixed landing gear," Bill Piper, Jr., said. "But time, engineering, and test flying proved this would not be practical from an appearance or performance standpoint, and the airplane developed into a low-wing, all-metal machine with controllable propellers and a retractable landing gear.

"Originally, this was to be a $17,000 machine, an unheard of low price for a twin, and remember, we are now talking about the dollar ...when a cup of coffee was still a nickel. Yet even that figure gave all of us a feeling of discomfort. We were abandoning our birthright.

"The Apache was the only all-metal airplane on the market with a tubular steel framework completely enclosing the passenger compartment. That was because we started out with the concept of a fabric machine. The Aztec, a later airplane and a lineal descendant of the Apache, has the same type of construction; in fact, some of the same tools are used in its manufacture. Going to metal caused us some trauma. Workmen had to be re-schooled. A fabric-covered airplane could be turned out with as few as 250-500 tools, such as drill fixtures, milling and welding fixtures, router and drill templates, and dies for forming and stretching metal. One of our all-metal airplanes, such as the Navajo, requires 10,000 tools, and the pressurized version required 6,795 *additional* tools."

Meanwhile, Piper began another venture into twin-engine production in early 1952 with the announcement that it was going to produce the Piper-Stinson, a twin-engine successor to the single-engine Piper Stinson Station Wagon, after it had purchased the Stinson Division of Consolidated-Vultee Aircraft Corporation in December 1948. Piper purchased Stinson on his own terms and calculated that his factory and dealers would also make money selling Stinson Station Wagons, and by servicing more than 5,000 Voy-

It had been clear since 1947 that the day of the fabric-covered, tandem-seat, high-wing airplane as its principal product was coming to a close for Piper. Credit is given by historians to Thomas F. "Pug" Piper as the guiding force behind the company's introduction of modern aircraft designs into production. He was not an engineer, but was vice president of engineering, and was responsible for coming up with a concept which he then had turned into design and production. By 1950 he realized that companies looking for transportation of executives and individuals were looking for low-priced aircraft that could carry at least four persons and were powered by two engines for safety and reliability.

It was the Apache PA-23 that filled these specifications. After 17 years of building tube and fabric-covered aircraft, Piper proudly advertised the Apache PA-23 as its first all-metal plane. The first production plane came off the line on December 31, 1953; a certifi-

It was a Piper milestone event when the 20,000th Cub, a PA-12 Super Cruiser, was turned out in the spring of 1946. It is shown face-to-face with an E-2. (Peter M. Bowers Collection)

cate of airworthiness was presented to Mr. Piper on February 2, 1954. It was also Piper's first twin-engine model, and the first named after an American Indian tribe. In November 1959 an Apache was the 50,000th Piper plane produced at Lock Haven.

The production of the Apache marked the beginning of an entirely new era and a distinct turning point in Piper's history. It had to sell for about $40,000, a considerable sum above what a cost analysis had first shown, and there was great concern among the sales distributors and dealers that they would have no customers. In fact, one dealer gave up his distributorship when he was asked to take one on consignment.

Bill Piper, Sr., felt that, since his company had made the Apache and it had his name on it, he was determined to show how easy it was to fly. On the morning of July 21, 1954, at age 73, Alfred M. Munroe, a CAA pilot examiner, gave him a thorough flight check and issued his twin-engine rating. As he climbed off the wing, the elder Piper grinned and said, "Anybody can fly that thing." He was said at the time to be the oldest person ever to earn a multi-engine rating. Piper sons Bill, Jr., and Howard delivered an Apache from Lock Haven to South Africa by way of the South Atlantic Ocean in March 1955.

"But the Apache did sell," Bill Piper, Jr., said. "For its type and price, the airplane had the market all to itself, and continued to have for several years. In the nine years that it was produced we marketed over 2,000 of these planes."

Properly priced for the time period, Piper had produced the world's least expensive twin-engine aircraft, and it provided a profit—enough to build a research center and manufacturing plant at a former naval base at Vero Beach, Florida, in 1957. This led to the manufacture of more sophisticated aircraft far beyond what was envisioned when the company began so many years before. In addition to the Apache was the single-place Pawnee PA-25, built in Lock Haven, for use as a crop duster and sprayer. Next was the Cherokee PA-28, certified in October 1960—actually the first model built entirely at Vero Beach. The subsequent models, several of which are derivatives and upgrades that were built there, are the Aztec, Papoose, Warrior, Archer, Dakota, Arrow, Seneca, Saratoga, Navajo, Chieftain, Mojave, Cheyenne, Seminole, and Tomahawk.

It was in this period of development that William T. Piper, Jr., took over the presidency of the corporation from his father in 1967, while his father retained the position of Chairman of the Board. Howard Piper, his next oldest brother, was Executive Vice President, and Thomas Piper was Vice President. A 1969 study by the Harvard Business School summarized the company situation this way:

"With about 30% stock ownership in Piper Aircraft, the Piper family retained complete operating control, even though the family lacked the 51% ownership necessary for formal control. This combination of family ownership and management gave the Piper family the opportunity to set an informal work atmosphere and to determine corporate policy.

Rather than mount twin engines on a Cub, Harold Wagner of Portland, Oregon, decided to mate the fuselage of a PA-11 Cub Special on the right with a J-3 fuselage in 1949. He installed a spacer on the J-3's propeller so it could spin behind the PA-11's without touching. (Peter M. Bowers Collection)

"A great deal of family pride existed in having managed a pioneering light aircraft company to a sales level of nearly $100 million by the end of 1968. However, an extended period of future growth more rapid than could be financed by retained earnings was a serious threat to Piper family control. The new expansion of the product line, combined with a recent decline in profit margins, was beginning to put a strain on the financial resources of the company, and in 1967 Piper sold $10 million in long-term debt. This represented the first long-term debt since 1945."

The possible need for additional capital to finance a further expansion led Piper's top management in 1968 to a re-evaluation of the company's position in the light plane industry. The history of the original Piper Aircraft Corporation changed rapidly at this point. Chris Craft Corporation purchased 200,000 shares of Piper stock on the open market and announced that it was going to take over in January 1969. Piper rallied with a proposed sale of stock to the Grumman Aircraft Co., but the Securities and Exchange Commission (SEC) rejected the sale.

Piper next found a possible buyer in the U.S. Concrete Pipe Co., but again the SEC disapproved. In desperation, the company contacted the Bangor Punta Corporation, which agreed to battle Chris Craft. The Piper family held roughly one-third of the outstanding shares and agreed to sell them to Bangor Punta. By late summer Bangor Punta and Chris Craft both purchased enough shares to gain equal seats on the board of directors and removed William Piper, Jr., and his brother, Thomas, from their board seats. However, they remained with the company until 1973, when Thomas left to join Beechcraft and Bill, Jr., retired.

In a series of lawsuits, Chris Craft sued Bangor Punta and the Piper family for damages for alleged violations of the SEC rules. The suits were finally settled in 1976 when the U.S. Supreme Court ruled against Chris Craft. The Piper family sold their shares to Bangor Punta, giving that company complete control of Piper.

Bangor Punta sold Piper to Lear Siegler in 1984; the operations were moved to Vero Beach, Florida, and the Lock Haven plant

was closed. In 1987 the company was bought by M. Stuart Millar of California, who intended to resume production of the Super Cub and several other Piper models. Millar also planned to offer the Super Cub in kit form for about half the cost of the fully-completed factory-built plane. However, his plans did not work out, and the company went bankrupt in July 1991, although the court allowed several Piper models to be built at Vero Beach, including a few Piper Super Cubs.

As a result of the bankruptcy, the New Piper Aircraft Corporation was formed in July 1995, with the new company acquiring the remaining assets of the former. At one time Piper operated six manufacturing facilities. Today, the new Piper organization is still one of the leaders in production of general aviation aircraft. The only plant operating at present is located at Vero Beach, Florida.

***

The last of 22,206 civil Cubs and 8,197 military Piper Cubs had long ago rolled out of the Lock Haven facility, but the memories of those original fabric-covered, single-engine Cubs and their successors linger on at the airport, with the Piper Aviation Museum as their focal point. Each year, usually in June, hundreds of Cub fans, their families, and flying enthusiasts, along with their various models of the original Cubs and their progeny, congregate on the airport for a nostalgic "Sentimental Journey." There is found proof that the legendary Cubs in all their many shapes, models, and forms are still flying and in great numbers.

In 1996 the Piper Foundation purchased the former Engineering Center building at the airport for permanent occupancy by the Piper Aviation Museum, along with contributions from the state's historical commission, the Clinton County Community Foundation, former dealers and distributors, owners of the present company, and aviation organizations, such as the Aircraft Owners and Pilots Association and the Experimental Aircraft Association. Previously, a room in the rear of Hangar 1 and a large mobile van provided the only displays featuring the history of the company. The improved

This rear quarter photo shows that a vertical stabilizer and elevator were added between the PA-11 and the J-3. (Peter M. Bowers Collection)

facility now includes several Piper models in the attached hangar and historical displays, memorabilia, and equipment, including a Link trainer, in a museum on the second floor.

Thus, the spirit of William T. Piper, Sr., who died on January 15, 1970, at the age of 89, lives on at the Lock Haven Airport named in his memory. He was revered by his employees and respected by all who knew him. This admiration was expressed by many pilots, including Robert N. Buck, retired Trans World Airlines pilot, who set a junior transcontinental speed record in a Piper Cub at age 16. In a *Reader's Digest* article in 1965 he wrote:

"Why was this airplane so successful? There's no doubt about it—Mr. Piper. If you look at a Cub, how it's made, how it flies, you see the character of the man. Mr. Piper makes you think of the men who built this country, the tough, true, unfancy pioneers who believed in principles and stuck to them. Actually he is a simple man with a simple formula: no frills and hard work."

Fred E. Weick, noted aeronautical engineer who designed the Ercoupe and was chief engineer at the Piper Engineering Center in Vero Beach, agreed. He expressed his praise in his memoir *From the Ground Up*:

"I had known Bill Piper ever since 1945, when we both served on the CAA's Non-Scheduled Flying Advisory Committee. We had called each other by our first names, but when I referred to him as Bill within the Piper organization, I was looked at as if I had taken an undue liberty. Within the company, everyone referred to him as 'Mr. Piper.' Out in the field, however, people usually called him 'Bill,' and I think he liked it. Piper was a forthright and honest man with an open countenance. His build was husky, and he was of medium height. His tastes were simple, but he had an astute business sense. In sum, William T. Piper was a man of outstanding character."

This Piper J-3 was the first aircraft moved from storage at the National Air and Space Museum for display at the giant Steven F. Udvar-Hazy Center, near Dulles International Airport, Virginia, in March 2003. (National Air and Space Museum photo by Carolyn Russo)

The elder Piper had received many accolades and awards during his lifetime from the aircraft manufacturing industry and aviation organizations for his pioneering. Airplanes bearing the family name were literally distributed all over the globe. His adult life had been a story of successful American free enterprise through his wise and efficient management. The family he raised had stuck together to build a profitable business based on a simple formula: Build good airplanes at a price people were willing to pay. It was for all these characteristics and accomplishments that the airport at Lock Haven was named the William T. Piper Memorial Airport in his honor. He was paid a national tribute by having a 40-cent United States air mail postage stamp issued in 1991 with his image in full color and a Cub in the background. The Cub itself was featured on a 32-cent stamp issued in 1997. Mr. Piper was enshrined in the Army Aviation Hall of Fame in 1976 and the National Aviation Hall of Fame in 1980.

Perhaps a final tribute to the man and his plane took place quietly on March 17, 2003, when the National Air and Space Museum's Steven F. Udvar-Hazy Center, a 300,000 square-foot hangar at Dulles International Airport in Virginia, was ready to receive the initial group of more than 300 planes that would follow for public display. The first artifact aircraft trucked to the site from the museum's storage facility in Suitland, Maryland, was a Piper J-3 Cub in mint condition, resplendent in its traditional "Cub Yellow" paint. Built in 1941, it had been hanging in the rafters of the Paul E. Garber Restoration Facility for many years until the new museum became a reality. It had accumulated more than 6,000 hours of flying time before being accurately restored in 1975. Today it is poised as if in flight above the larger aircraft on the floor below.

One of the senior Piper's personal legacies was *Private Flying: Today and Tomorrow*, the book he wrote in 1949 that was a declaration of the state of the industry and the future of light plane aviation as he saw it at that time. He included "Ten Commandments for Safe Flying" for young pilots:

1. THOU SHALT NOT BECOME AIRBORNE WITHOUT CHECKING THY FUEL SUPPLY.
2. THOU SHALT NOT TAXI WITH CARELESSNESS.
3. THOU SHALT EVER TAKE HEED UNTO AIR TRAFFIC RULES.
4. THAT SHALT NOT MAKE FLAT TURNS.
5. THOU SHALT MAINTAIN THY SPEED LEST THE EARTH ARISE AND SMITE THEE.
6. THOU SHALT NOT LET THY CONFIDENCE EXCEED THY ABILITY.
7. THOU SHALT MAKE USE OF THY CARBURETOR HEATER.
8. THOU SHALT NOT PERFORM AEROBATICS AT LOW ALTITUDES.
9. THOU SHALT NOT ALLOW INDECISION IN THY JUDGMENT.
10. *THOU SHALT KNOW ALWAYS – THE GOOD PILOT IS THE SAFE PILOT.*

The final paragraph in his book reflected the firm belief that:

"...a healthy personal plane industry is of great material and social value to the United States. The private pilot serves as one of the most effective instruments of goodwill."

8

Cubs Circumnavigate the World

It was probably inevitable that someone would want to try to fly around the world in a Piper Cub. The reliability and ease of maintenance of the L-4 model of the Cub had been proven during the war, and the new derivative models available after World War II had even more powerful engines, increased range, and the capability to carry heavier loads.

The idea of possibly circling the globe in a Cub came to Clifford V. Evans, 26, and George Truman, 39, in 1946. Both had been Air Force pilots during World War II and were then flight instructors for the Brinckerhoff Flying Service at the College Park Airport, near Washington, D.C. Their students were mostly pursuing flight training under the GI Bill of Rights.

One day, as Evans watched idly out the hangar window, a student pilot taxied a Piper PA-12 Super Cruiser to a stop outside and switched off the engine. As it coughed to a stop, Evans said to Truman, standing nearby, "You know, I'll bet one of those Cubs could be modified to fly around the world." Joining Evans at the window, Truman nodded. "If you put a tank in that back seat," he mused, "and the stops for fuel were close enough together, maybe you *could* do it."

Significant achievements have often had such small beginnings. Within 24 hours Evans and Truman were pouring over world aeronautical charts and plotting a route around the world that included hops of 850 to 1,000 miles each. The more they talked, the more such a flight seemed possible.

As the weeks went by and the men quietly carried out their calculations, they became obsessed with the possibility. Their wives encouraged them, reluctantly at first, then eagerly.

They received no encouragement, however, from the aircraft engine and instrument component manufacturers they contacted for financial backing in return for endorsing their products. An offer might be made, they were told by several, but only "after you've completed the flight."

Evans and Truman did not give up, though. After studying the capabilities of several light aircraft, including some government-surplus planes, they settled on the Piper Super Cruiser that had sparked the idea originally. A three-seat craft with a 100-hp engine, it had enough space in the cabin for two extra gas tanks of 50 gallons each and could cruise at about 100 mph. If they couldn't get permission to land and refuel at a Russian airport nearest the Aleutian Islands, they anticipated the longest flight would be the approximately 1,800 miles across the North Pacific, but wanted enough fuel on board for an additional 500 miles' range as a safety margin.

They decided to fly solo in two similar planes for mutual assistance and follow an easterly route to take advantage of the general west-to-east flow of air in the northern hemisphere. Both planes had to have a sufficient cluster of instruments in order to fly under instrument flight rules when they encountered weather restrictions. They wanted to obtain an instrument panel "such as no light plane

Clifford V. Evans, Jr., of Washington, D.C. (left), and George Truman of Los Angeles, California, are photographed after completing their plans for a round-the-world flight in two Piper Super Cruisers. Both were flight instructors at an airport in Maryland when they decided to attempt the flight. (William D. Strohmeier Collection)

had ever seen before," according to Evans in a June 1986 article in *Esso Air World* magazine. In addition, they wanted:

"...a drift meter of a special type, and radio equipment capable of receiving range signals far enough away from the transmitting station to give us a sizeable target to hit."

Evans and Truman were convinced that the flight was feasible technically; they were also certain that secrecy was essential to avoid being upstaged by someone with better financial backing. Therefore, between giving flight lessons they huddled furtively in a corner of the main hangar, discussing plans and assessing the latest developments. During this time Evans, who was studying mechanical engineering at the University of Maryland while also serving as a flight instructor, averaged less than six hours' sleep a night. Truman was trying to amass enough flying time to become an inspector for the Civil Aeronautics Authority. He had no other income, so he spent as much time instructing as he could. Meanwhile, both men added children to their families during this period of preparation.

What was significant about this proposed flight of two light planes was not that they intended to try to set a round-the-world speed record. If the flight were successful it would be the first world-circling flight in a class of aircraft powered by less than a 575-hp engine. What they hoped to prove was that the globe could be circled by small planes, and thereby demonstrate the capabilities, efficiency, dependability, and safety of American-built light aircraft.

"We were just two pilots left over from the war," Evans said. "We were two pieces of surplus property that the War Assets Administration was not trying to sell. Consequently, we had to attempt to sell ourselves. Everyone was willing to sell us items at a more or less reduced price, but unless we could print our own money we were in no position to buy anything more expensive than a quart of oil."

Once most of the details of the flight were established, financing it and modifying the planes became the major, almost insurmountable obstacle. Evans and Truman, thinking the publicity would help sell planes worldwide, approached officials at the Piper plant in Lock Haven. All they asked Piper to do was:

"...give or lend us two planes and enough cash to cover our expenses, plus something for ourselves afterward."

Piper's reply, while not a turn-down, was typically cautious:

"Check with the Lycoming people to see about furnishing the engines."

Lycoming, on the other hand, while not very hopeful, but also wasn't altogether negative. Evans and Truman presented more precise details about the flight, and it looked as though Piper and Lycoming might both support the flight when they saw how well the two pilots had planned it.

Meanwhile, Evans and Truman scraped together what cash they could. Evans sold his pre-war car, borrowed money from relatives, and cleaned out his savings account. Truman cashed in the defense bonds he had accumulated during the war and mortgaged his mobile home.

The two world fliers are greeted upon their arrival in Los Angeles after crossing the Pacific (left to right): Clarence Bessemyer, president of the Los Angeles Chamber of Commerce; George Truman; Los Angeles Mayor Fletcher Bowron; and Clifford Evans. They completed the world flight without mishap and were the first light plane pilots to successfully complete a round-the-world flight.. (Don Downie Collection)

The two happy pilots pose beside George Truman's *The City of the Angels*, named for Los Angeles, Truman's adopted home town. The planes were modified with a 100-gallon auxiliary fuel tank in the rear seat of each Super Cruiser to give them a 2,600-mile range. (Don Downie Collection)

Los Angeles Mayor Fletcher Bowron looks on as Clifford Evans points out the signature of Pope Pius VII made on each of the Cubs when they passed through Rome on their 1947 world flight. The flags and logos of the nations and cities visited were painted on the left side of each fuselage. (Don Downie Collection)

Then, just when it seemed that Piper and Lycoming might support the flight, both reneged. Postwar cutbacks and other economic factors had severely affected the aircraft industry by 1947, and the predicted sales of light planes did not materialize.

"We were tempted to quit," Evans and Truman said later. "We made a list of every company that made parts for the Cub and besieged them with letters, telegrams, phone calls, and personal visits, appealing for funds in return for publicity for their products.

"It finally became evident to the Piper Corporation, the Lycoming Division, Sperry, and Bendix that we would remain camped on their respective doorsteps until they broke down. Just to get rid of us, as much as anything else, one after the other they acquiesced."

Piper's management, impressed by their sincerity and planning, agreed to let the fliers have two secondhand but nearly new Piper PA-12 Super Cruisers. William T. Piper, Sr., had his engineers design and install two 52-gallon tanks in the rear seat area to give each plane enough fuel for about 24 hours of flight. One of the Piper engineers asked facetiously:

"Why not make the cabin leak-proof, put the pilot in a diving suit, and fill the whole thing with gas?"

As soon as they realized that they would be sitting in front of more than 100 gallons of aviation fuel they asked if ways of dumping the fuel could be included in the event of an emergency. A young Piper engineer designed a system that vented the fuel from the bottom of the tanks to the outside of the aircraft. The pilots could then reach outside the side window, unscrew the caps, and release the fuel into the atmosphere. In the event of a water landing they could dump the fuel, replace the watertight caps, and the buoyancy of the tanks would be enough to keep the entire plane afloat for a while if there were no other damage. Truman tested the system and found that fuel could be dumped from both tanks in 90 seconds.

The instrument panel that the two proposed "was the kind that private pilots dream about," Evans said:

"Besides the best of rate instruments that Kollsman makes—sensitive altimeters, rate of climb, air speed, and the usual engine gauges—they had installed two Sperry instruments, a small electrically-driven, non-tumbling gyro horizon, and a Gyrosyn compass. By the time this equipment had been crowded into the cabin it had taken on the appearance of a child's toy box. Everything was there; it was a question of finding anything. There were valves, gas lines, an extra oil tank, converters and inverters for the electrical instruments, a Grimes panel light, and switches strewn over every available space."

They then took the planes to a radio shop in New Jersey and asked to have a receiver, high-frequency transmitter, a VHF transmitter, a spot-tuner on the receiver, a loop antenna, and a trailing antenna. The shop supervisor took one look, thought a moment, and said, "It can't be done—but we'll do it."

They also wanted a small drift meter, but none was available, so Evans designed one that was "small, easy to install, and weighs very much less than one pound." He hoped to have it patented after the flight.

The U.S. Coast Guard helped them by providing dinghies, lifevests, flares, and survival provisions, "plus a few things that we did not know existed." With the extra gas and borrowed radio equipment, as well as winter clothing, the planes were 430 pounds over normal gross weight, and therefore had to be licensed as Experimental.

One of their final requirements was to find an oil company that would either furnish them with fuel or extend credit. The ESSO petroleum company would not give them gas and oil gratis, but did provide domestic and international credit cards to use and pay later if they refueled at ESSO facilities.

"We had so many bills then we felt a few more could not worry us," Evans said. "We accepted the cards and received, in turn, more than fuel and lubrication—service and courtesy in greater quantities than our expenditure warranted."

Lycoming, when learning of Piper's acquiescence, warmed to the project, and sold Evans and Truman two new engines for a token payment of one dollar each. It now appeared as though they could start by the early summer of 1947.

The fuselage on the right side of both world-girdling Piper Super Cruisers lists the major cities visited during the world flight. (Photo by the author)

Since the two planes were identical, Truman took his plane to Dayton, Ohio, for load and pitch tests on the plane's aluminum propeller. During the last test flight the engine failed in the traffic pattern, and he had to set the Cub down in a wheat field. It nosed over on its back, briefly knocking Truman out; otherwise, he was unhurt. It was later found that the cause of the failure was water in the fuel line and the carburetor, not an engine malfunction.

Repairs were quickly made, and the propeller tests were passed. Truman and Evans then flew their planes to Washington National Airport, where public relations personnel from Piper and Lycoming had arranged a departure ceremony. The well-wishers included embassy representatives of countries in which Evans and Truman planned to touch down. The fliers were given a party, and the planes were christened. Evans gave his Cub the name *The City of Washington* for his hometown, and had water from the Atlantic Ocean splashed on the nose of the plane. Truman christened his plane *The City of the Angels* for his adopted hometown, Los Angeles, California.

During the press interviews they stressed that they were not going to try for a speed record, and figured it would take six weeks to make the trip. "We're going to take our time and see the sights like regular tourists," Evans told a *New York Times* reporter. After the ceremonies they flew to Teterboro, New Jersey, their official starting point. It was now early August, and later than they had originally planned to start. They would probably have to fly at least the final one-third of the route under winter conditions. With no deicing equipment, flying at the far northern latitudes could be dangerous and even fatal.

The threat of freezing weather, though, was not as worrisome to them as running out of money. Until just before the flight they did not know how they would pay cash if required for fuel en route, or cover such expenses as spare parts, landing fees, meals, and lodging; no oil company or parts manufacturer would agree to underwrite these expenses for the possible publicity.

Evans managed to persuade a relative to put up some unidentified security, thus enabling them to get international charge cards and obtain $850 in traveler's checks. With this money in hand they kissed their wives and daughters goodbye, posed for newsreel photographers "until we felt like puppets," and taxied out for the adventure of their lives. At 11 o'clock in the morning of August 9, 1947, they lifted their Cubs into the haze above the Teterboro Airport in New Jersey and headed northeast. Within minutes, however, they lost sight of each other and the horizon, and had to fly mostly on instruments. They had filed a flight plan for Presque Isle, Maine, but in the confusion of the takeoff, Truman had gotten mixed up and headed for Bangor.

"We weren't too familiar with our radios yet, and we couldn't raise each other," he said. "An exchange of messages between Bangor and Presque Isle got us back together, and we were never separated again for more than a few minutes."

But that first tense day of flying gave them forewarnings that the flight would not be an easy venture.

Weather was to be a constant worry that was to plague them throughout the world flight. Arriving at Presque Isle they rested, and on August 10 flew to Goose Bay, Labrador, where they were delayed for three days by a report of rain and fog over the next leg of the flight. On the thirteenth, in Arctic blackness, they flew the 750 miles to Bluie West One, a U.S. Air Force base on a fjord in southern Greenland, for refueling. Truman called it a "nightmarish flight," as they picked their way cautiously through the ever-twisting fjord in semi-darkness with mountains towering above them on both sides. The flight took nearly nine hours due to headwinds.

A six-day delay on Bluie West One occurred that they had not counted on: both contracted influenza. They were confined in the

The two Cubs are shown landing at Teterboro Airport, New Jersey, their official departure/arrival point. Since George Truman landed first in *The City of the Angels*, his aircraft was entered in the record books as the first light plane to circumnavigate the earth. (William D. Strohmeier Collection)

base hospital, which delayed their departure until August 24. On that day they took off in marginal weather and flew east above the overcast to Meeks Field, at Reykjavik, Iceland, 950 miles away. Flying by dead reckoning in the haze, they overshot the field but realized their error, identified their position in time, and turned back. Within an hour after they landed, heavy fog developed and the field was closed.

On August 28 Evans and Truman climbed into their Cubs and took a heading for Prestwick, Scotland. They found it fogbound and landed instead at Newtownards, Ireland, for refueling. Two hours later they took off for Croydon Airport, near London, where they were surprised when reporters acclaimed them as pilots of the smallest planes ever to fly the Atlantic. They had flown the 3,602 miles from New York to London in 42 flying hours.

Two days later they flew to Ypenburg in the Netherlands by way of Brussels. This detour was made so Evans could visit the Van der Bogaerts family, who lived on the outskirts of Hedel. Evans, his family, and their church had been sending food and clothing to the needy family since the end of the war.

On September 3 Evans and Truman arrived at Orly Field, near Paris. From there they flew to Marseilles, and were unable to proceed immediately because of severe rainstorms. On September 7 they reached Rome's Ciampino Air Field, where Pope Pius XII added his signature to the fuselages of both Cruisers.

The next leg—1,350 miles to Cairo and Baghdad—included a thousand miles over water. Then they headed southeast and made an originally unplanned stop at Dhahrain, Saudi Arabia, which they had been persuaded to make by U.S. Embassy officials in order to visit American employees of Aramco, the Arabian-American Oil Company. However, they were detained there for six days by Saudi airport officials, who had procedures for handling foreign commercial and military aircraft, but not private civilian planes. The officials were in no hurry to check the fliers' visas and flight permits before finally releasing them for departure.

"It seemed that the rule book, which the Customs officials depend on entirely for their decisions, had a place in it for the disposition of military and commercial aircraft and crews," Evans reported later, "but in no place did it mention Piper Cubs. We were told that we would just have to wait until a new book was written. We wondered if we might not have to take out Arabian citizenship papers, embrace the Mohammedan religion, and visit Mecca before we would be allowed to leave. Luckily, King Ibn Saud came to our rescue and cut the knot in the red tape."

Early on the morning of September 19 Evans and Truman took off for Karachi, Pakistan, covering the 1,100 miles in 9 1/2 hours. They flew to Jodhpur, India, the next day, where they were guests of the Maharaja. Impressed by the palace, Evans described it in a letter to his wife as an "amazing place to be stuck out here in the middle of the desert." Truman recalled the Maharaja as:

"...something right out of *Arabian Nights*. He was just 23 years old, but weighted 300 pounds and had 125 automobiles."

He also had a large gun collection, and was surprised that neither Evans nor Truman carried any weapons with them for protection.

On September 22 they continued flying across India and into Burma through heavy rain to a landing at Akyab, a small village on the Bay of Bengal, before going on to Rangoon. By the 27th, seven weeks after departing from the United States, they were halfway around the globe. Ten days later, after a stop at Hanoi (then French Indo-China), they landed at Hong Kong's Kai Tak Airport, where they were grounded for six days while a typhoon raged off the coast of southeastern China.

Finally, on October 6, they left Hong Kong and headed north to Shanghai. Three hundred miles into the flight, however, they encountered 80-mph headwinds and decided to land at Amoy (now Xiamen), China. When they did not arrive at Shanghai on schedule, radio messages were sent to stations along the route, asking for information about them. The winds held them at Amoy for four days; when they subsided, Evans and Truman still had to contend with 40-mph headwinds all the way to Shanghai, where they stayed for five days. They used the time to have their planes inspected. They met Major General Claire L. Chennault, famous leader of the Flying Tigers, and then president of China's Civil Air Transport airline. Chennault offered them jobs as pilots after they completed their flight; Evans accepted the offer a year later.

The next leg was to Fukuoka, on Kyushu Island, Japan. There, a ham radio operator in New Jersey patched through a call from the pilots to their wives, the first conversations they had with them since leaving the United States. Subsequent landings were made at

The *City of Washington* was purchased after the flight by William T. Piper, Sr., and presented to the Smithsonian Institution's National Air and Space Museum in 1949. The *City of the Angels* was eventually sold to different owners and was restored to its original condition by the current owner, Harry P. Mutter, historian for the Piper Aviation Museum in Lock Haven, PA. (Photo by the author)

Nagoya, Tokyo, and Nemuro, the latter a small airfield at the northern tip of Hokkaido.

On October 28, unable to obtain permission from the Russian government to land in the Kuriles, which would have been a relatively short hop from there to the Aleutians, they had no choice but to fly the risky 1,680-mile non-stop flight across the northern Pacific from northern Japan to the U.S. Air Force base at Shemya, located almost at the end of the Aleutian Islands. The weather broke for them, and with a two-plane B-17 escort they took off in bright moonlight on what turned out to be the most nerve-wracking experience they would have. Evans explained what happened:

"The night was clear as spring water. Tail winds pushed our ground speed to 150 mph. All went well. A minor cold front was forecast to be in our path, and that was what we thought we had run into after about five hours of flying. We realized that, far from being minor, it was a major, well-developed warm front after we had been in it for over six hours. During that time everything that we had dreaded occurred. We could not see past our instrument panels for hours at a time. George picked up wing ice that forced him from 4,500 ft. down to 500 ft. before a warm rain column melted the clinging stuff. My engine quit, leaving me in a clammy sweat. It was cockpit trouble, of course, and the engine caught right up again when I switched tanks. We came out of the overcast at dawn, only to discover that we had picked up an unprophesied wind that was drifting us 22 degrees to the left—right for the shore of Russian territory.

"The most cheerful sight of the trip was Shemya Island, dismal mist-shrouded little rock that it is. We broke through the cloud cover, and the two-mile runway seemed to smile at us."

The two tired pilots landed their Cubs at Shemya on the afternoon of October 28, 13 hours and 35 minutes after leaving Japan. Their safe arrival marked the first time a light aircraft had crossed both the Atlantic and the Pacific.

The going had not been easy because of the almost constant poor visibility and high winds that rocked the Cubs mercilessly. They agreed that the Aleutians were rightly considered "the home of the worst weather in the world." The U.S. Air Force had helped by providing the two B-17 Flying Fortresses from the 3rd Air Rescue Squadron to "mother" them on shifts during much of the flight to Shemya. On October 31, accompanied by one B-17 and a Navy PBY flying boat, Evans and Truman left Shemya and arrived at Adak Island, farther up the Aleutian chain, 3 hours and 30 minutes later.

The weather showed no improvement as Evans and Truman progressed slowly up the string of island bases toward the Alaska mainland. On November 2 they flew to Cold Bay, then toward Naknek, turning back when visibility deteriorated and icing developed.

"Treacherous as they [the Aleutians] were," Evans commented, "they seemed anti-climatic after that Pacific crossing. We still played the game cautiously, however, knowing very well that we could be killed as dead in the home stretch as in the Himalayas."

Two days later they made it to Elmendorf Air Force Base, near Anchorage, where, grounded by snowstorms and zero cold, they had to spend a week. They next followed the Alaska Highway to Fort St. John, stopped at Edmonton and Lethbridge, Alberta, then on November 26 flew 1,275 miles nonstop to Van Nuys, California, their first landing in the United States.

After receiving welcoming congratulations from the city for which Truman had named his airplane they proceeded east, making nine stops for fuel and visits to Piper dealers at Phoenix, El Paso, Amarillo, Oklahoma City, Dayton, and Harrisburg before setting down at Teterboro on December 10, 1947. Truman landed a few seconds before Evans, so his aircraft was entered in the record books as the first light plane to circumnavigate the earth. They had covered 25,162 miles in 122 days, 23 hours, 4 minutes, and had been in the air for 275 hours.

Broke when they started and still broke when they landed, they were satisfied that they had accomplished what they set out to do. "There had to be somebody who was the first to circumnavigate the world in a 'flivver," Evans said afterward, referring to the Model T Ford of bygone years, the automobile that helped put the nation on wheels, just as Mr. Piper had put the nation in the air. Truman added:

"There are probably thousands of pilots in the country who could do what we have done if they were careful. That's about all we were trying to prove."

In an article in *Esso Air World* magazine, Evans summarized their flight:

"Weather, sickness, officialdom's petty displays of authority, and more weather, accounted for 74 days of the 123 total. We flew on 44 days and the five-day remainder we just wasted, frittered away, with resting and the very minimum of sight-seeing.

"Undoubtedly, the most amazing aspect of the trip is not that we made it without mishap, but that the equipment functioned perfectly throughout the entire 275 hours. We had to rely on our instruments in whole or part for nearly half of that time. We ran the engines at nearly full throttle practically every hour. We encountered temperatures of from 130 F to -25 F. The planes sat on the ground, virtually unprotected, in a two-day sand storm and through a three-day typhoon. Yet, unbelievably, the maintenance would have cost us not over $50 apiece if we had had to pay for it ourselves.

"I believe that although chance played a large part in the rate at which our trip progressed, the eventual success of the flight had nothing to do with luck. I attribute this outcome to three factors. In the order of their importance they are: the smooth performance of our equipment, George's determination to keep going in the face of discouragement, and our knowledge of our own abilities or lack thereof. We took no chances that were not absolutely necessary."

Truman and Evans were asked many times what they thought their flight had proved. Evans provided a reply in his article: "Beyond proving that George and I were capable of flying 25,162 miles round the world in a Piper Cub, we firmly believe that it has proved that light planes, as well as all planes, can go anywhere provided they are handled with care. We hope that we provided a stimulus to aviation in general."

After the welcoming activities had run their course, Evans and Truman made short flights to air shows in the eastern part of the country. They visited the White House and met President Truman. Before the meeting, George Truman was warned by an aide that he should not claim that he was a distant relative of the president. He didn't. A few months afterward the borrowed radio and navigation equipment in both planes was returned to their owners, and the pilots went their separate ways.

Evans died in 1975 and Truman in 1986. Although they had not claimed any point-to-point records for speed between cities or an around-the-world speed mark for light aircraft, they achieved

something no one can take away: they had circumnavigated the earth in two very small, single-engine aircraft without mishap, and were the first to do so. They had been able to take advantage of advances in communications and navigation equipment and a worldwide network of ground-based radio stations that had been developed under the stimulus of World War II.

In tribute to the flight's success, the Piper PA-12 Super Cruiser *The City of Washington*, flown by Cliff Evans, was purchased by William T. Piper, Sr., and presented to the National Air and Space Museum in Washington, D.C., in September 1949. The museum preferred Truman's *The City of the Angels* because it was credited with being the first of the two to land upon completion of the flight, but he decided to keep it for barnstorming and appearances at air shows. It was sold to a Piper dealer in Virginia in the early 1950s and restored to a standard three-place PA-12. It was then bought by pilots Ray Ellison and John Cornish of Fredericksburg, VA, in 1957, who kept it until January 1997, when they sold it to Harry P. Mutter, historian for the Piper Aviation Museum in Lock Haven. Corporate and private sponsors donated materials and equipment to restore it back to the condition it was in during the historic flight. David M. Liebegott donated 1,500 hours of his time to do the work; he was honored by being first to fly it after the restoration. Mutter makes promotional tours in it to benefit the museum, and displays

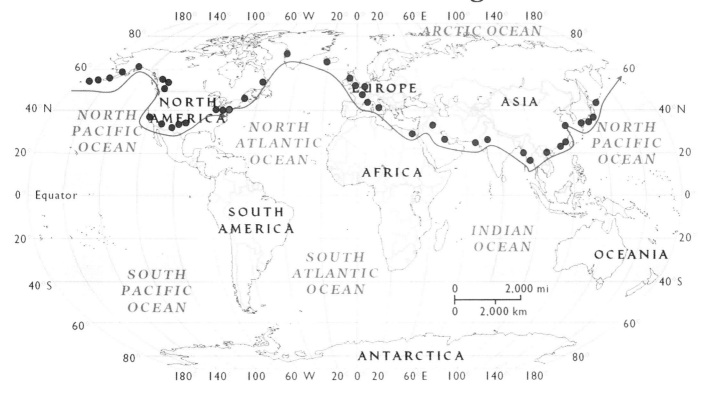

Map of the world flight route that Clifford Evans and George Truman planned in 1947. They made 53 takeoffs and landings and spent 275 hours, 25 minutes in the air. The total distance flown was 25,162 statute miles. (Illustration by Kevin K. Hudson)

it at the "Sentimental Journey" fly-in held at the William T. Piper Memorial Airport at Lock Haven airport each year.

***

It was nearly 30 years later that two more pilots seriously considered making a world flight in Cubs with the objective of establishing a globe-circling speed record for light aircraft weighing 1,000 kilos (about 2,200 lbs) or less. Paul D. Nanney, 29, of El Cajon, California, and Robert L. "Bob" Ambler, also 29, of San Diego, who were employed as aerial fish spotters off the California coast, decided they would try it in 1976 when fishing season was over. Both owned Piper PA-12 Super Cruisers and began their research and flight planning. They studied a copy of the International Flight Manual issued by the Government Printing Office and obtained maps and a booklet about flying the Atlantic and crossing Europe from the Aircraft Owners and Pilots Association (AOPA).

They decided early that they would fly eastbound, as most other world-circlers have done, to take advantage of the prevailing west-to-east winds in the northern hemisphere. The route of flight was planned from their home base at Gillespie Field, near San Diego, to Moncton, Canada, across the North Atlantic to Greenland, Iceland, and Scotland, and then through Europe to Italy, Greece, Turkey, Iran, Pakistan, India, Burma, Malaysia, Singapore, Philippines, Okinawa, and Japan. Because over-flight restrictions by the Russians would not be waived, they had no choice but to plan the rest of their flight across the North Pacific to the Aleutians, then proceed southward through western Canada and home to San Diego.

Nanney and Ambler prepared their 30-year-old Super Cruisers by adding fuel capacity in the wings instead of installing tanks in the back seats.

"In order to stay in the normal category," Nanney reported in an *Air Progress* magazine article, "we had to go through the agony of getting STC approval for our added wing tanks. This, in itself, was a major undertaking. We now had 74 gallons in the wings, which would give us plenty of range for all parts of the trip except the North Pacific crossing, for which we would add extra fuselage tanks."

They installed a full panel for instrument flight and, for communication and navigation, crammed in each plane two ADF heads, two VORs, two VHF radios, a high frequency radio, transponder, and what they considered "most important," an eight-track stereo to listen to music during long legs of the flight. They "dressed up" their Cubs with new tires, brakes, and props, and overhauled both engines; Ambler had his plane's wings recovered.

Unlike Evans and Truman, Nanney and Ambler filed for an official sanction by the National Aeronautic Association to establish a world speed record for the flight that had to be flown during the period May 1 through July 31, 1976. Although they hoped to

depart on May 1, they were delayed by radio problems, then weather interfered, and they could not leave until May 13. Weather plagued them all the way to Goose Bay, Newfoundland, and Narssarssuaq, Greenland, where they arrived on May 25.

The duo took off from Greenland headed for Iceland, but had to return because of wing icing. They could not get off until six days later, but because of having to battle 60- to 80-knot headwinds, they had to refuel at Kulusuk, Greenland, before taking off again for Iceland. Both had to fly on instruments when they experienced "white-out" conditions where "you can't tell up from down nor even if you're in a cloud or not," Nanney said. "You can't tell if the ground is ten or ten thousand feet below you."

Ambler radioed Nanney that he was picking up ice and was returning to Narssarssuaq to refuel; he said he would meet Nanney later in Iceland. Ambler arrived at Kulusuk safely, but was unable to notify Nanney of his status because of communication difficulties. Nanney waited in Iceland for his friend for several days and decided to push on when he had not arrived and didn't have any word from or about him. It was the last Nanney knew about his friend until later, and didn't see him again until he returned home.

Ambler arrived in Iceland eleven days later and decided not to try to catch up with Nanney. He spent the next several weeks flying around Europe and returned to California via the reverse route.

When Nanney finally heard that his friend was all right and would not join him, he continued through Europe easily until he ran into the international political rivalry between Greece and Turkey. Not knowing that the two nations were then at odds, he was informed that he could not fly over the Greek border to Ankara, Turkey, and that if he tried, he would be shot down either by the anti-aircraft guns of one country or the other. He solved the problem by flying to the island of Cypress, then to Ankara.

From there to Malaysia, Nanney said, "it was my last contact with civilization" meaning that he thought the conditions for flyers were much more primitive than he had imagined. While he had no problems in the air, it was on the ground that he met with bureaucratic and logistical resistance. Fuel was difficult to purchase, and oil was almost impossible to find. He spent an entire day in India going to an oil refinery to get a mere two liters of engine oil.

And India "has to be the world's capital of paperwork," according to Nanney. He had to collect signatures from what seemed to him to be hundreds of officials in Ahmedabad, where he found that he could not get fuel until he cleared customs, and he could not clear customs until he had purchased fuel. He put on such a loud harangue with workers on the ramp that he attracted attention from someone in authority and was finally refueled and allowed to take off for Rangoon. There he ran into overtime charges for a customs inspector and found that a bottle of whiskey, which he had been advised to bring from Cypress for bribe purposes, should have been two bottles. He purchased the second bottle from the duty free store at the airport terminal, gave it to the airport official, and was then allowed to go on his way.

It was on the 800-mile flight from Rangoon to Penang where Nanney encountered the most vicious weather he and his Cub had ever experienced. The hard rain and severe turbulence "became savage," and he thought the strong down- and up-drafts were going to rip the fabric off the plane and smash it down into the Bay of Bengal. All he could do was cling to the controls, try to maintain level flight, and hope for the best.

He landed safely at Penang after ten and a half hours of punishment that the faithful Cub managed to survive during the thrashing it received. When he checked the plane over, he found that the paint had been stripped from all its leading edges—wings, struts, and tail feathers. It took a week for the inside to dry out.

Nanney's next clearance problem came when he tried to file a flight plan from the island of Borneo into the Philippines, which required a 10-day advance notice. He had applied from Cypress well in advance, but there was no clearance from the islands waiting for him upon his arrival. He tried for eleven days by telephone to get help from the American Embassy, and finally got a diplomatic note that allowed him to go on his way. When he arrived in Manila there were more difficulties, such as a complete lack of ramp tie-downs for the Cub, and he was not allowed to move the plane to a safer location on the field. There was also a requirement to pay for a 24-hour guard. The crowning blow came when he was getting ready to leave. A DC-10 airliner, with its four engines roaring to taxi its multi-ton load out for takeoff, flipped the Cub over on its top. Fortunately, the only damage was torn fabric, which was repaired by the apologetic airline manager.

To Nanney's surprise, he had no problem getting clearance into Japan. In Tokyo, he fitted extra gas tanks into the fuselage during a leisurely week there and got daily weather reports on the Aleutians from the U.S. Air Force base at Misawa. When satisfied, he flew to Kushiro to clear customs and filed a clearance on July 17, 1976, for Cold Bay, a base midway up the Aleutian chain. However, he later admitted he actually planned to land at Shemya, a military base on a small island 1,525 miles from Kushiro near the end of the Aleutian chain, which was then closed to civilian aircraft during the Cold War years. He was confident that he would be allowed to land there if he declared he had an emergency because he was out of fuel.

He flew all night in and out of the clouds and gave estimated position reports as required, all the time monitoring weather reports from Shemya, which reported a ceiling of 300 feet and visibility of one-eighth of a mile in fog. To complicate matters, the VOR, precision approach radar, approach lights, and localizer there were all reported out of commission. When he flew out of communication range of the Shemya station a Flying Tiger cargo jet relayed in-flight weather information to him, which indicated a stiff crosswind on his route of flight. He tried to correct for it, but by 10 AM the next morning he was unsure of his position, and called the FAA air traffic control center in Anchorage, Alaska, to ask for assistance. A Navy Lockheed P-3 Orion patrol plane on a routine ocean

surveillance mission out of Shemya was diverted to try to locate the slow-flying Cub.

Nanney activated his Emergency Locator Transmitter and set the transponder to help the patrol plane find him, but to no avail. As the minutes ticked away and only a few minutes of fuel remained in the Cub's tank, Nanney realized he would have to ditch. Suddenly, he was located by a ground radar station and vectored toward the nearest land 85 miles away, which was identified as Amchitka Island. He headed toward it, but realized his world flight was over. He knew he had to ditch while the engine was running so he could still control the Cub to the moment of splash-down. He descended slowly for an estimated 15 minutes under reduced power and made a smooth landing in an unusually calm sea.

Fortunately, the patrol plane crew soon found the Cub. A Japanese fishing trawler, the *Jinyo Maru*, was located on the Navy plane's radar and was directed toward the Cub, now slowly filling with water. Nanney climbed out on top of the wing and managed to yank the life raft out of the back seat of the cabin by ripping a hole in the overhead fabric. He inflated it and sat in it on top of the wing to wait for rescue or for the plane to sink. A crew member in the Navy plane took a photograph showing Nanney sitting on top of the wing.

The crew of the *Jinyo Maru* had seen the plane go into the water and had already reported it to its mother ship, the *Yuiho Maru No. 15*, but took no action immediately, probably because the captain was advised by the Navy that a U.S. Coast Guard cutter was already on the way. However, the trawler crew hauled up their nets and sent a raft to the Cub. The Japanese sailors pulled Nanney aboard after he had been in his own raft on top of the wing about two and a half hours. The crew members gave him blankets, dry clothes, and a drink of whiskey.

Nanney was transferred to the U.S. Coast Guard cutter *Rush* when it arrived on the scene. The cutter crew found the Cub, which was still floating because of its empty fuel tanks, and approached it carefully to avoid damaging it. If possible, they intended to lift it aboard. The log of the cutter states tersely:

"*Rush* alongside downed aircraft. 1803 — *Rush* has hooked up a line to the tail of the aircraft and to *Rush*.

"1815 – Aircraft hookup to the starboard cargo boom to attempt to bring the aircraft aboard *Rush*.

"1850 – *Rush* cut loose aircraft from the cargo boom. Aircraft sank in position 52 degrees, 25.5N, 179 degrees, 38.5E."

There was no explanation in the ship's log for cutting the Cub loose. Apparently, the captain decided that either the plane was too damaged, or was not worth further effort to bring it aboard.

Nanney was taken on the cutter to the Naval Air Station on Adak Island, where he was interviewed by the Search and Rescue Coordinator. He admitted he had no prior permission to land at Shemya, but thought he would be permitted to do so if he declared an emergency. He reported in his magazine article that the Federal Aviation Administration later charged him with operating his aircraft in a careless or reckless manner.

In a newspaper interview after his return to San Diego, Nanney blamed the Air Force, Navy, and Coast Guard for events that led to his ditching, waiting for 2 1/2 hours in 40-degree waters for rescue, and losing his aircraft. He said the Air Force had given him an inaccurate weather forecast for Shemya, which caused him to alter his course in the wrong direction, ultimately leading to his running out of fuel.

Paul Nanney's attempt to fly a Cub around the world in 1976 ended in the loss of the Cub and near disaster for himself. Since that time, no other pilot of any of Piper's fabric-covered, high-winged, single-engine Cubs have succeeded in circling the globe alone. That fact makes the successful world flight by Evans and Truman in their separate Piper Super Cruisers in 1947 even more significant in the continuing saga of the legendary Piper Cub.

It can be said with certainty that Nanney's sturdy 30-year old Super Cruiser deserves no responsibility or blame for his flight's failure.

Paul D. Nanney is shown sitting in a life raft on top of his Piper Super Cruiser after ditching it out of fuel in the North Pacific. He was rescued by a Japanese fishing boat and a Coast Guard cutter. The plane was allowed to sink when it could not be hauled aboard the cutter. (U. S. Navy photo)

9

The Era of the Super Cub

The final production model of the legendary Piper J-3 Cub was rolled out of the Piper factory at Lock Haven on March 4, 1947, and was sold to the Klamath Indian tribe in Oregon to use for forest patrol. Mrs. Pearle T. Robinson, head of academic flight instruction in the Washington, D.C., school system, flew the plane from Lock Haven across the Rockies to Oregon. As far as was known at that time, she was the first woman pilot to fly a light plane from the East Coast over the northwestern Rockies. She made the trip without a radio.

More than 20,000 Cubs, including the various military versions, had been produced at Lock Haven in the decade after December 1937, more than any other single type of aircraft in history. When the single-engine, high-wing, fabric-covered derivatives are counted, the total is over 48,000. During that period and ever since, Cubs have been modified, customized, adapted to special uses, tailored for unusual purposes, personalized in various ways by their owners, converted with non-standard landing gear, had many different engines installed, and have even been sold as kits to be assembled by the buyers. They established altitude and distance records, performed "impossible" aerobatic stunts, and made many heroic flights to save lives. They put the common man and woman in the air, and proved that almost anyone, even many of the physically handicapped, could fly safely with proper training.

But was the Cub era really over when the last yellow J-3 was put out in the sun to await a ferry flight from the factory to its new owner?

As noted previously, it was the PA-11 Cub Special that was offered to replace the grand old J-3. It was an updated J-3 with an improved design, such as a fully-covered engine cowling, a raised front seat to improve visibility, and was made available with Continental 65-, 85-, and 90-hp engines. As the power increased, so did the capability to carry increased loads, have a higher rate of climb, and cruise at an increased speed. The Special, first flown in August 1946, was the first post-World War II model to get past the proto-

type stage, and the first Cub that could be flown solo from the front seat.

Some Specials were developed into agricultural aircraft for dusting and spraying; most were marketed as trainers, and many

Super Cub advertisement

A Super Cub crop duster is put through many tests to show its prowess for steep takeoffs over obstacles from short strips. This one took off with a full load in much less than 200 feet. (Peter M. Bowers Collection)

were exported; a few were outfitted with tri-cycle gear. Seventeen PA-11s were shipped to France in 1949 as aerial crop dusters to increase the productivity of post-war French farms. By this time there were over 700 crop-dusting Cubs in Argentina and 300 in Brazil, and they could also be found doing this work in Uruguay, French West Africa, and Morocco. Nearly 1,500 had been sold by November 1949 when production ceased.

When World War II was ending, W. T. Piper, Sr., did not want to see the two-seat Cub concept phase out completely, because he felt it was necessary to continue to lure the younger age groups into learning to fly at the least possible cost. Walter Jamouneau improved the J-5C Cub by having 75- and 90-hp Lycoming engines installed. This required that the designation to be changed to the PA-12 Super Cruiser. After a first flight in December 1945 it was reported that nearly 5,000 orders were received. However, only a total of 3,760 were turned out at Lock Haven and Ponca City by 1948, when the market for light planes collapsed. It was this model that had encouraged Clifford Evans and George Truman to make their epic round-the-world flight in 1947.

It was clear when the light plane industry nose-dived in the 1947-49 period that the public wanted something more appealing that would enable the company to recover from a wilting market. The production of the two-place, side-by-side PA-15 Vagabond, which William Shriver had insisted be built and project engineer David Long had designed, marked a turning point in the Cub's on-going evolution. Powered by a 65-hp Lycoming and marketed for $1,995, the Vagabond's first flight took place in October 1947, and 585 PA-12/PA-17 Vagabonds were built in 1948-1950; however, only 214 of the PA-17 Vagabond Trainers with dual controls were produced.

Meanwhile, there was a perceived notion that those who had already learned to fly would want a low-priced model in which a family could enjoy making trips together. The answer was the four-place PA-14 Family Cruiser in 1948, a further development from the PA-12 Super Cruiser. It featured wing flaps, a co-pilot position, widened fuselage, and a 155-hp Lycoming engine. It was first of-

fered at $3,825, but was under-priced, and the company had to call a production halt. Only 238 Family Cruisers were sold in 1948 and 1949.

Piper still believed there was a market for a four-place model, and it was the Clipper's turn next. Designated the PA-16, Jamouneau actually redesigned the side-by-side, two-seat Vagabond by adding two passenger seats behind the two pilot seats and having it powered by a 115-hp Lycoming engine. There were wide doors on both sides for easier entrance, and it was equipped with a starter and generator. It was offered at a relatively low-priced $2,995, which was considerably less than any competitors' two-place models! Its first flight was in January 1948 but, again, the post-war down market allowed only 736 to be built.

The production of the PA-18 Super Cub was authorized in the fall of 1949; it would also be a tandem seat model similar to the PA-11 Cub Special, but with increased power that would give it even more short field takeoff, climbing, and lifting prowess—so

A Super Cub, modified as a duster/sprayer, is shown with the tank in the rear seat and baggage area. It is this ability to carry such special loads that the agricultural model PA-18 is so popular with crop dusters. (Peter M. Bowers Collection)

The Super Cub has been used by farmers for more than five decades to give them the ability to check on their fields personally at harvest time. (Piper Aviation Museum)

much that some would call it the "Poor Man's Helicopter." When engines were gradually upgraded from 90 to 125, 150, and higher horsepower, it could carry heavier loads and fly farther than anyone ever could in a stock model J-3. Its short takeoff and landing (STOL) capability was the magic quality that made it one of the outstanding aircraft for a new era of the Cub, and was the basic reason for its versatility and popularity. The first flight was made in mid-1949, and it was certified on November 18, 1949. The first Super Cub marketing efforts were aimed toward flying clubs and flight schools as the initial trainer for those wanting to enter the world of flight as pilots, and subsequently advancing to larger aircraft.

There were three versions offered initially. One was the bare minimum standard model without any extras, and intended to be used primarily for training; another was the deluxe model, with starter, battery, generator, and other extras. The third was the agricultural model, intended for spraying and dusting crops.

One of the first government agencies to purchase the Super Cub was the Atomic Energy Commission. A fleet of 10 aircraft was used in the western United States during the 1950s to carry out a uranium exploration program. They made radiometric surveys of the terrain, including Isorad mapping, for about three years in the search for additional sources of uranium-rich deposits for the rapidly developing nuclear energy industry. The flying was hazardous, as the planes flew their survey altitudes at 25 to 100 feet and required a high degree of low-speed maneuverability near cliffs and in box canyons. However, the Super Cubs had only two accidents during the entire program, neither one with serious injury. The first

of these aircraft was acquired after flying nearly 1,500 hours by the National Air & Space Museum in 1976.

To improve the Super Cub's capabilities beyond having more powerful engines it had other improvements: manually-operated wing flaps; slightly shorter wings; dual-mounted fuel tanks in the wings; and metal propellers. Numerous small airframe changes were offered in the 1950s to handle the increased weights of the heavier engines that were requested by buyers. As a result, the Super Cub became a faster-flying workhorse, beginning with modifications for crop spraying and dusting work. These were produced with special equipment additions, such as wire cutters on the landing gear

The oversized tundra tires have been popular with pilots in arctic areas for landings on rough and unprepared fields. John Bennett is shown en route to Point Barrow, Alaska, in 1967 in "Bud" Helmericks' Super Cub with the tires. (Harmon "Bud" Helmericks Collection, courtesy Bruce McAllister)

These Piper Super Cubs are parked in the Pakistan desert to assist in eradicating locusts during the 1950s. Almost complete eradication was reported. Six Super Cubs sent to Iran at the same time noted results better than 90 percent. (William D. Strohmeier Collection)

struts to slice through telephone wires and extra dust or spray tanks for agricultural work. Outfitted with tandem gear or larger, low pressure tires, the Super Cub was capable of safe landings on rough and soft surfaces, such as arctic tundra, rough glacier ice, and deep mud. They have also been outfitted with combination ski/wheels. A Swiss manufacturer produced a caterpillar gear for Cubs that consisted of an endless rubber belt and four lightweight wheels that absorbed shocks on rough ground like an army tank. It was ideal for farmers, ranchers, and others who wanted it for hauling light loads, patrolling fences, or hunting coyotes.

Since its introduction, the Super Cub has become one of the most popular aircraft in the arctic regions of Canada and Alaska. In fact, at this writing, more Super Cubs are registered in Alaska than any of the other 49 states. The additional power enabled Anna Louise Branger to set an altitude record of 26,800 feet in April 1951 flying a PA-18 Super Cub. Her record was broken by Caro Bayley in September that year, also with a Super Cub. A former WASP and aerobatic champion, she reached 30,203 feet during an all-women air show in Miami. Bayley described the flight in *Woman Pilot* magazine:

"I took off from the blimp base on the causeway at Miami....I took off, had oxygen and a barograph, was up for about four hours, came down, did my aerobatic act. The temperature was ninety on

A Super Cub PA-18-105 was a special militarized version that was used to train U.S. Air Force pilots at civilian contract schools in the early 1950s. It is shown on the field at Lock Haven, PA, with civil markings. (Piper Aviation Museum)

A Super Cub shown here has one of several modifications made for spraying various types of crops. Note the small propeller under the engine nacelle that helps disperse the chemicals. (Piper Aviation Museum)

the ground and thirty-four degrees below zero at altitude. The Cub went up to fifteen thousand feet nicely, but up to twenty it was a bit draggy. By the time I hit thirty, I stayed at one altitude for a long time.

"There was no wind that day. If there'd been any wind I would have had to fight to keep on the peninsula. I made a huge circle— Palm Beach, West Palm Beach, Naples, down almost to the Florida Keys and back up. And you look down and you can't see any people. You can see the road but nothing on them. The only thing you can see is the trail (wake) behind the boats (but) you can't see the boats."

Bayley landed the Cub and then flew her Pitts Special aerobatic plane, following a routine that enabled her to win the 1951 aerobatic championship that same day. Her Super Cub record was unbroken for that class of aircraft until it was eclipsed by a Mooney light plane that reached 33,732 feet in 1984. The current light plane record in that weight class is 36,188 feet, held by A. Hoffman of Austria.

The capability of the Super Cub came to the attention of farmers when Piper began marketing the PA-18A. During three years of development work, it was modified and reinforced to accommo-

To meet requirements for high volume application of agricultural chemicals, Piper engineers developed equipment that could cover a 33-foot swath with 15 gallons per acre, or a 50-foot swath with 10 gallons per acre. This proved especially useful to defoliate cotton crops and allow more sunlight to reach the lower bolls, thus facilitating harvesting by mechanical cotton pickers. (William D. Strohmeier Collection)

This rough terrain tread-type landing gear is shown on a PA-18 Super Cub of Italian registry. It is one of several types of landing gear to improve safety when landing on rough terrain areas. Most tandem gears did not work satisfactorily for very long. (Peter M. Bowers Collection)

Cubs have been towing gliders for many years. Many glider pilots first obtain private pilot licenses in light aircraft before taking glider lessons. (Piper Aviation Museum)

date a large 110-gallon tank suited to hold either liquid or dust, making it capable of spraying up to 220 acres of crops in 45 minutes. The tank could be removed through the turtle neck of the plane, leaving a large area behind the pilot's seat for freight or cargo. Civil Air Regulations allowed it to carry a 2,000-lb. gross load for all such special purposes. The 125-hp model could take off and land in less than five lengths of its own fuselage, and fly safely at a speed as slow as 35 mph.

The Super Cubs also had other work capabilities that attracted the attention of the farming industry: fertilizing, seeding, defoliating, weed and insect control, and land reclamation. The insect control potential received international praise and gratitude when it was learned that a small group of Super Cubs successfully carried

out spraying operations against locusts in Pakistan in late 1951 when the area was experiencing the worst infestation of the pests in more than 80 years.

In the first month the Super Cubs sprayed 20,000 gallons of liquid poison, concentrating on breeding areas favored by the destructive insects. From 12 to 19 trips per day were made, often over hilly areas that required application at some points in a 60-degree bank. The locust mortality rate varied from 20 to 90 percent, and gradually increased to nearly 100 percent. Pakistan's Food and Agriculture Minister, Abdus Sattar Pirzada, commended the pilots for exhibiting "very great enthusiasm, perseverance, and capacity for hardship and facing danger in extremely difficult circumstances." At that time, locust-killing Super Cub crop dusters were also being used in Uruguay, French West Africa, and Morocco.

The Super Cub is one of the most-used aircraft for glider towing in the United States. This one is towing a Schweizer 1-26 sailplane at Tehachapi, California. (Peter M. Bowers Collection)

Agricultural pilots must do their dusting at extremely low altitudes. With power on and flaps down, a Super Cub will fly as slow as 33 mph. One is shown here at the working level, just a few inches above the crops. (Peter M. Bowers Collection)

The initial price for a Super Cub was $3,595, but this has escalated over time, as some customers requested models with extras and ever-more sophisticated electronic navigation and communications equipment. The armed forces were interested in the increased performance of the Super Cub, and Piper produced several variants. The prototype was the PA-19, a variant of the PA-18C. The Air Force ordered 243 PA-18Ts for training purposes. About 70 were produced under the Mutual Defense Aid Pact for Turkey and Greece; thirty were sold to the U.S. Army.

Between 1952 and 1957 the U.S. Army and Air Force procured additional versions of the Super Cub that were designated L-21A and 21-B. The L-21A, powered by a Lycoming 125-hp engine, was accepted for short-range liaison work, and 150 were delivered. 584 L-21-Bs followed with 135-hp Lycoming engines.

In time, nearly 1,700 L-18s and L-21s were built for the Army, and the latter were used extensively overseas, especially in the Far East. A few L-21Bs remained in the Army inventory in the early 1960s for use by the Reserves and were re-designated U-7As.

As might be expected, some Super Cub owners experimented with modifications that the Piper engineers had not envisioned. One was a stagger-wing Cub that N.P. "Jack" Yentzer of Sheridan, Wyoming, built for agricultural use. It had a J-3 fuselage with a Super Cub top cabin structure, wings, and tail; a 200-hp Ranger engine from a Fairchild PT-19 trainer; Whitaker tandem landing gear, and doped glass fabric skin. With the capability to carry a useful load of 1,800 lbs, Yentzer had designed the craft for work on crops and ranches located at high altitudes.

Sprayers do their work at slightly higher altitudes than dusters to get the best dispersal. Here a Super Cub demonstrates its capability over a Pennsylvania field. (Peter M. Bowers Collection)

Seaplane models of the Cub have been produced since the Taylor E-2. The amphibian shown here gives owners more choices for destinations when planning flights. (Aircraft Owners and Pilots Association)

Another use of the hard-working Super Cub is fish-spotting off American coasts. This fishing boat crew takes a Super Cub seaplane along and launches it over the side for a water takeoff and retrieval. (San Diego Aerospace Museum)

Claude Holbert of Stuttgart, Arkansas, was another pilot in the agricultural business who modified his Super Cub into a biplane. He and his mechanic, Bill Dorstch, added a 21-foot metal wing and a spring steel landing gear, and called the conversion a "Loadmaster." By adding this wing area, they found that the Cub could lift a gross load of 2,300 lbs and consistently operate safely off a quarter-mile strip.

The Super Cub was improved during the 1950s for agricultural work as a result of suggestions from the field. One significant development was a quick dump valve for emergency use in which a pull of a lever in the cockpit would dump a full 110-gallon load of chemicals in seven seconds. Different mountings of spray booms and nozzles were installed with high capacity, wind-driven pumps.

Various applicators were used as required for dispersion of various dust, spray, seed, and fertilizing chemicals. Changeover from dust to liquid could be accomplished in about an hour. The slow-flight characteristics of the Super Cub enabled better foliage penetration.

The Super Cub and most other production Pipers were easily adapted to water operations on EDO floats. A universal landing gear—a ski-like attachment—was developed by All-American Engineering Co. that enabled Cubs to operate from any type of surface—land, water, snow, ice, or mud. An eight-wheel tubular track landing gear was developed for the Swiss by Giovanni Bonmartini, an Italian inventor, to decrease takeoff distance in rough terrain and allow landings to be made in three-fifths of the normal distance necessary.

The Super Cub has proven its versatility as a seaplane. Although the airframes are similar to the J-3 and PA-11, the heavier Super Cub has longer, stronger float struts, and has seen extensive use with EDO metal floats and as an amphibian. (Peter M. Bowers Collection)

A three-wheeled dolly is used for takeoff from a paved runway by this Wag-Aero CubY on pneumatic floats. A Cub look-alike, it is manufactured with government-approved parts. (Peter M. Bowers Collection)

Above: A Super Cub with a J-3/PA-11 rudder tests a combined wheel-ski landing gear in Alaska. Small wheels are attached to each ski to prevent them from scraping on the ice or paved runway. (Alaska Aviation Heritage Museum)

Above: A typical Super Cub instrument panel. Many owners have had their panels customized differently, as new instruments are available. The Super Cub flies very well under instrument conditions. (Arthur H. Sanfelici Collection) Right: Alaska State Troopers fly Super Cubs with extra police equipment, including a video camera in the cockpit. Alaska has more registered Super Cub owners than any other state. (State Trooper Sgt. Mike Kincaid Collection)

Super Cubs were used by the Israeli Air Force during the Six-day War with Egypt in 1967. Machine guns and rockets were attached to the wings and fired by the pilots. (Jay Miller Collection)

Concrete fencing posts are attached to bomb racks under the wing of a 150-hp Super Cub in New Zealand to be dropped from the air at the site of a construction project. (W. G. Fuller Collection)

Cubs had been towing sailplanes to get them aloft for many years, but 46-year-old Robert Fisher of Moses Lake, Washington, wanted to be first to fly in a sailplane from coast to coast, and did so in the summer of 1961 with the help of a Super Cub as a tow plane.

Fisher was towed aloft from Seattle in *Miss Columbia Basin*, a Schweizer 1-23 model glider, and hop-scotched his way across the country with a series of aero tows and releases for 2, 813 miles, to Amityville, Long Island, New York. The Cub would release him to a point about 10 miles short of each intended destination, so most of his 59-day flight was a free ride.

Fisher made 31 stops across the continent, and his longest tow flight was 345 miles from Minidoka, Idaho, to Rawlins, Wyoming. His highest altitude on this leg was 16,200 feet. The Super Cub had been furnished by the Ellenburg, Washington, Civil Air Patrol.

***

During the years of production of the Super Cub it underwent several engine power increases. It was available with power ratings from 90 to 150 hp between 1949 and 1994, while the standard model

was equipped with a 150-hp engine. This remained so until production ceased. While production was geared for civilian consumption, the U.S. Army procured Super Cubs as L-18s and L-21s with 135-hp Lycomings and 150-hp Continentals. Several were used in Southeast Asia during the Vietnam War.

Many temporary or experimental changes were proposed over the years on the military models, including Whitaker tandem wheels, extra fuel tanks, and at least one with a nose wheel. In 1977 Piper proposed using metal wing flaps on the Super Cub originally, but none were produced. However, the fabric ailerons were eventually replaced with metal in 1978.

The story of the Super Cub in the northern latitudes is a history of adaptation of an airplane to the worst environment that an airplane is asked to work in. Alaskan and Canadian pilots have proven to be the most creative Super Cub modifiers. Many of the dozens of modifications that have been developed for the Super Cub include 36-inch low pressure tires, enlarged baggage compartments, constant-speed propellers, and the 180-hp engine. They operate their planes where the air below freezing stings like needles, and a man and his plane are intruders in this harsh environment. Oil defies

Owners and aircraft service facilities for light planes have modified Cubs in many ways to satisfy an expected demand. Robert N. Decker of Rhinebeck, New York, marketed this modification to turn a float plane into an amphibian. The landing gear rotates on pivots at the point of suspension on the floats and is locked down by a drag link with a snap lock. (Arthur H. Sanfelici Collection)

circulation, hoses and metal become brittle, wheels do not want to turn, and skis can weld a plane tight to the ice.

The Super Cub's simplicity and short take-off capabilities have made it a favorite for bush pilots who make a living braving the extremes of the arctic. Welland W. "Weldy" Phipps, a Canadian pilot famous for his flying and rescue operations above the Arctic Circle, was awarded the McKee Trophy in 1961 "for meritorious service in the advancement of aviation in Canada." He won it partly for the development, testing, and certification work required to produce large balloon tires bearing 5 lbs. pressure that became a standard part of Alaskan and Arctic flying. The Phipps wheels and tires make it possible to land anything from a Super Cub to a large deHavilland Caribou on just about any snow or rough ground that a person could walk on without sinking in.

Phipps was inducted into the Canadian Aviation Hall of Fame in 1993, where he joined other aviators so honored for their:

"stubborn struggles against impossible odds...for unfailing courage...that have stood the test of time." His citation also commended him for "the application of his aeronautical abilities in designing and perfecting the use of super-balloon tires, and his numerous flights into the high Arctic (that) have been of outstanding benefit to Canadian aviation."

Phipps was also known for his innovations when he was far away from sources of replacement parts. On one occasion in the High Arctic when he broke a Super Cub's tail wheel, he found a shovel, cut the handle down, and fixed the blade at a trailing attitude where the wheel was normally located. He was able to taxi,

albeit with a loud scraping noise, when he had to land on a cement runway. On another flight, he repaired a Cub's fractured vertical stabilizer with two ski poles, and in another instance used a small piece of plywood to repair a gash in the same area.

Weldy Phipps is recalled for his sideslip stall landings of the Super Cub into limited areas under perilous wind conditions. One story, unconfirmed, is that while fighting an extremely high wind, he made a safe landing right inside a hangar.

***

April 1976 was a historic milestone for Piper. That month it delivered its 100,000th airplane, which happened to be a PA-31 Cheyenne. However, the company decided that a proper symbol to celebrate the occasion was to paint a Super Cub with the famous "Cub Yellow" paint job and J-3 markings and label it "100,000 Pipers" on the nose.

The history of the Super Cub came to a decision point in August 1981 when Piper sold the marketing rights for it to Wes-Tex Aircraft Corp. (WTA) of Lubbock, Texas. The deal included over a dozen unsold 1981 models, and the last Super Cub was rolled out at Lock Haven on November 22, 1982.

Production tooling and the type certificate for the PA-18 was retained by Piper in the WTA agreement. As noted in Chapter 7, the company went through several changes of ownership and was eventually acquired and reorganized by the Cyrus Eaton Group International in 1992, who reorganized the company as New Piper Aircraft, Inc.

It was found that public interest in the Super Cub did not diminish, and production was started again at Vero Beach in 1988 after a six-year hiatus. The first Super Cub flight there took place on July 26, 1988, and production continued until December 1994. Of the total of 10,326 Super Cubs built, only 102 were made at Vero Beach.

***

The future did not look promising for the Super Cub when New Piper Aircraft, Inc., decided not to resume building the plane that had evolved from that 37-hp Taylor E-2 so many years before. Many Cub lovers felt that the light plane era, during which many thousands had learned to fly, was over. But Jim Richmond, CEO of Cub Crafters, Inc, of Yakima, Washington, and his son Nathan developed a clone that they call Top Cub, and have made a substantial number of sales to law enforcement agencies, bush operators, and weekend flyers. They are hand-built airplanes that take advantage of better engines, tougher landing gear, and stronger frames, and can be provided with the latest in avionics and instrumentation. The result is a Super Cub that sells for upward of $150,000, compared with the original Super Cub's price of about $3,000.

A Super Cub lands on a "postage stamp" field on top of a mountain near the John Day River in Oregon. It is this short field landing and takeoff capability that appeals especially to pilots operating in the far north. (Alaska Bush Wheels photo)

Two Super Cubs with tundra tires on watch near a nuclear power site. Light planes are favored for security patrols. (Alaska Bush Wheels photo)

"Super Cubs, like Harley-Davidson motorcycles, have a cult-like following and are dearly loved," according to Richmond. "Everyone who owns a Super Cub dreams of flying it to Alaska. And all of our customers always want all of the Alaska 'mods.'"

Another entrepreneur who specializes in modifying the Super Cub is F. Atlee Dodge of Anchorage, Alaska, known as "the Guru of the Super Cub." He designs special equipment for it, such as extra-strong landing gear, lumber racks, engine cowlings, exhaust systems, folding seats, expanded fuel tanks, float fittings, skis, and an enclosed baggage compartment. Dodge ships his Super Cub modification products as far away as Borneo and South Africa.

Two others who make a living with the Super Cub in Alaska are Vernon and Lura Kingsford, owners of Scenic Mountain Aircraft Co. at Moose Pass. They offer a three-day float plane instruction course for those who want to gain that certification. Many pilots fly to Alaska for a summer vacation and take the course so they can do their own bush flying. One of their graduates is Catherine G. "Cady" Coleman, a NASA astronaut.

Dick Wagner is president of Wag-Aero in Lyons, Wisconsin, one of the nation's largest aircraft homebuilders' supply companies. He saw a demand for a kit version of the J-3, which he called the CUBy. It weighs just under 700 lbs. empty and can carry a load of 648 lbs. with an 85-hp engine. With a gross weight of 1,340 lbs. allowed, the top speed is said to be 90 mph.

It is the 90-, 125-, and 135-hp engines that were originally designed for installation in the Super Cub; the 150-hp engines then became standard until production stopped. The light airframe and a low-speed wing makes it desirable for flying in the back country, where air strips are short and the altitudes are high. The Super Cub does not complain when tundra tires and skis are mounted. And it is well-liked when floats are attached; however, adding wheels to the floats does result in a weight and drag penalty, but is worth the advantage that amphibians have by giving pilots more choice about places to land.

Bush pilots have found that the Super Cubs they fly into remote areas need some special modifications for safer operation. For example, a longer propeller is recommended by some operators, such as that manufactured by Roger M. Borer, to give them better takeoff and climb capabilities. Safety cables, stronger axles, and large tires are also suggested for landings on rough terrain, gravel bars, pack ice, and for surviving unseen potholes. A windshield defroster, a heavy-duty tail spring, and increased baggage space are other modifications that are available and recommended for those who choose to operate into remote areas, especially in the northern latitudes.

The Super Cub clones that Richmond and the others produce have not gone unnoticed by the New Piper Corporation at Vero Beach, Florida. Possibly fearing law suits, the concept has not met with their approval. What Cub Crafters do is build the same steel-tube fuselage covered with fabric, but use a stronger landing gear, a more powerful engine, and a baggage compartment that can be used as a sleeping berth. The plane is built of parts from FAA-approved vendors across the country, which is not against federal regulations. Each Cub Crafter Super Cub is equipped with the latest avionics as the buyer may desire, and other cockpit modifications can be ordered as long as they meet FAA certification. Cub Crafters is also considering the possibility of offering the PA-11 Cub Special, which was the intermediate two-seat "tail-dragger" model between the J-3 Cub and the Super Cub.

Lee Budde, with his wife, Jennifer, own Airframes, Inc., at Big Lake, Alaska, which repairs, refurbishes, and makes new metal fuselages and other parts for Super Cubs. The fuselages they build are four inches wider than the factory-made models and are welcomed by those wearing heavy parkas for winter flying. Cub Crafters is one of the regular customers for their air frames. According to Budde, Alaska has three highly marketable items besides oil: "seafood, scenery, and Super Cubs."

Another spin-off of the Super Cub is produced by Aviat Aircraft, Inc., of Afton, Wyoming. They call it the Husky, which features a 180-hp engine and is slightly larger and stronger than the

Two Super CUBys stand by for delivery to a buyer at the Wag-Aero facility in Lyons, Wisconsin. (Jay Miller Collection)

original Super Cub. It has a five-hour, 800-mile range, a top speed of 145 mph, and can be flown solo from the front seat. It also features semi-Fowler flaps, vortex generators, constant-speed propeller, and an updated airfoil. A stripped down model called the Pup was being tested at press time.

Alaskans and Canadians are innovators when it comes to bush flying. They solve their aircraft maintenance problems to meet their immediate needs in ways that the aviation authorities may not approve of if they know about them. But they also know how to modify their planes to get them certified to improve their performance. Take the North Star, for example. Morgan D. Williams, Jr., owner of Custom Flight Components, Ltd., at Perkinsfield, Ontario, Canada, a long-time restorer of old planes, specializes in rebuilding them and improving them in the process. He wanted a Super Cub seaplane and could not find one that suited him, so he designed and built a kit plane—the North Star. The Super Cub design was the basis for it. He used the same USA 35B airfoil, but squared off the wingtips, strengthened the wing, made wider flaps, and added a door. He simplified the fuel system, raised the gear slightly, changed the belly contour, added a baggage door, extended the floor, widened the cockpit area, added a powerful landing light, changed the cockpit instrument locations for better accessibility with mittens on, and installed an electric heater for the oil sump for all-season operation.

Pilots who have flown a kit-built North Star with all its improvements claim that it picks up where the Super Cub left off.

Piper Cubs have been honored by placement in many aviation museums around the world. This Super Cub is displayed in the Deutsche Air Museum in Munich, Germany. (Bob Kovalchik Collection)

Williams says that, although the North Star may look like a Super Cub, it is a new airplane, not a rebuild or modification.

And so the story of the amazing Piper Cub continues, albeit with many modern enhancements. The original, seemingly fragile fabric-covered, high-winged, single-engine Cubs and their progeny were in active production for two generations of pilots, and were the most widely-produced non-military planes in U.S. history. Like their ubiquitous larger brothers, the renowned Douglas DC-3s, the Cubs fly on and on. There is no doubt that hundreds will still be flying many years from now.

10

The Cub Adventurers

The lure and pleasure of flying has encouraged many owners of the original Cubs and their offspring models to consider shaking the cares and worries of an earthbound existence and flying where they have never been before. Many have flown entirely across the United States, but none may have made the flight more times than Dr. Barney Rottschaefer and his wife, Susan. They made 14 round trips to the west coast from Pennsylvania in their PA-22 Tri-Pacer between 1964 and 1974 to visit their daughter Susan in California.

But there are the true adventurers who deliberately seek destinations they have dreamed about just for the thrill and fun of flying their Cubs there at low altitudes. Four stories of such adventurers—two teenagers, a dentist, an airline pilot with five other pilots, and a business man and his wife—have been chosen to show that it is still possible to fly one of Mr. Piper's light single-engine aircraft almost anywhere they choose for modern-day, wistful, unforgettable flight experiences.

Kernahan ("Kern") Buck, 17, had that urge during his early high school years in the 1960s. He and his brother Rinker ("Rink") Buck, 15, are sons of Thomas F. Buck, a headstrong, eccentric former 1930s era barnstorming pilot and World War II flight instructor who had lost a leg in a crash. He delighted telling about the risky flights he made as a young pilot and instilled a love of flying adventure, especially in these two of his 11 children. He taught them elementary flying maneuvers before they could drive, and insisted they learn how to repair and maintain his planes.

It was the older Kern who came up with the idea of flying with his younger brother across the country to the west coast after he passed his test for a private license. Kern had about 140 hours of flying time and wanted to build up his experience to qualify for a commercial license. Rink was too young at the time to qualify for a private license, but was able to keep a plane straight and level and could read maps.

In the fall of 1965 their father allowed them to buy a tattered 1946 Piper Cub Special (PA-11) with a 90-hp Continental engine for $300. He agreed to let them put it into flying condition and plan

a cross-country flight from their Basking Ridge, New Jersey, flight strip to California. Rinker was caught up in his older brother's enthusiasm and agreed to work with him, recognizing that his brother always looked on the bright side of life, but sometimes had a "brood-

Rinker Buck, 15 (left), and his brother Kernahan, 17, pose for news photographers with their restored Piper J-3 Cub in the summer of 1966 during their coast-to-coast flight. They were the youngest on record to fly across America. The westward flight was made in six days without a radio. (Carmine Photo with copyright permission of Rinker Buck)

ing, dreamy side," as he later wrote in *Flight of Passage*, a best-selling book about their adventure. Rink admitted that he had a rebellious nature, a "rotten attitude" toward authority, and was at constant odds with his father. It appeared at first the two male siblings would never be able to get along on such a long trip in a slow Piper Cub. However, getting away from home might be what Rink needed to solve his problems about himself.

The brothers spent many hours over the next six months getting the Cub ready for their adventure. They stripped the old fabric off, sanded the rust off the tubular steel framing, covered the fuselage and wings with new fabric, painted it, replaced a few parts, and reassembled everything for flight. To make their own money to cover these expenses, they used the family's old Willys Jeep that was equipped with a snow plow and hitch. They earned $600 after a month of plowing, enough to pay for the fabric and new parts.

On a bright spring day in 1966 they rolled the Cub out into the sunshine. It was in mint condition, and they received the finest praise the old barnstormer could bestow, "It's a damn fine airplane, boys. I'm proud as the blazes of you two."

The work was completed by the end of May, and the two brothers figured that they would need $300 for fuel, meals, and motel rooms only on rainy nights. Rinker took a job exercising trotter horses at a horse farm nearby. Kern found work at a grocery store.

Rinker would be the navigator, and became intensely interested in maps for the flight. Their father and a friend who was a pilot for a corporation warned them that the trip would be difficult crossing the Rocky Mountains, especially since they were flying without a radio to get advance weather or traffic information. The southern route through a pass between the towering Guadalupe Peaks east of El Paso, the least difficult leg for their Cub, was recommended. That pass "was a highly mysterious and emotional place for me," said Rinker:

"I had always been captivated by the early airmail era in aviation, when brave men flew open cockpit in any weather to get their cargo through, and many of them died doing it.... Now Kern and I, in a plane no better than the Mailwings and Fairchilds that the airmail pilots flew, would follow the same narrow opening through the great continental wall."

Rink said he was "passionate" about going through the pass because his father had never fulfilled his own dream of flying across the Rockies. His brother wanted to fly coast-to-coast:

"...to discover himself and find a way to stand out," Rinker explained. "I wanted to beat my father at something, and beat him good...I was fixated on the mountains and the pass as a way to measure myself against my father."

Kern test-flew the Cub, and they were ready to go on the Fourth of July, 1966. They had saved $326, "a comfortable margin over the $300 we had budgeted for the flight." Their father had given each of them watches and sunglasses, and they set out on the first day's flight from their grass strip at Basking Ridge, New Jersey, to Indiana, Kern flying in the front seat, Rinker in back with the maps. It was not an easy trip. They battled low clouds, poor visibility, and turbulence, and followed the railroads and highways with a gas stop at Carlisle, Pennsylvania. They learned there that the weather ahead was ominous, but might be avoided if they veered south and landed at Washington, Pennsylvania, instead of heading for Pittsburgh. Rinker described this leg of the flight:

"It was the most murderous corridor of turbulence I have ever experienced. For the next hour and a half I detested my brother. I hated him for catapulting so hard over the mountains, hated my father for letting us make this trip, hated that society of hard, cynical pilots into which we were born, and which obligated me, more or less, to earn my manhood by proving that I could take this abuse. After an hour my knees and shins, hammered by the turbulence and the shuddering stick against the cockpit walls, ached like scavenged meat."

But Rinker felt differently after Kern landed the Cub successfully in a rainstorm. It had been the longest cross-country flight so far in their lives. Now that they had flown across the Allegheny Mountains, Kern was confident that there could be nothing worse on the rest of the trip. They departed for Indiana in the late afternoon, landed at Columbus, Ohio, made a fast refueling, and continued to East Richmond, Indiana, home airport for a crop duster company. It was dark when they landed, and the Cub had no lights. They slept that night on the ground under the wing in their sleeping bags.

The flight on the second day of flying proceeded southwest under low skies and fierce headwinds to a duster strip at Brinkley, Arkansas, mostly following a rail line, with gas stops at Indianapolis and Blytheville, Arkansas. The duster pilots were unfriendly and did not take kindly to the Cub sharing the parking ramp with their Stearmans. Kern and Rink spent that night in a cheap motel where they found, to their amazement, that the rooms were rarely occupied for more than an hour at a time.

They left the next day for Texas, where Rink said:

"Geography became spiritual. The panorama of cloud, prairie, and river was transcendent, and it seemed to me that we had entered entirely new light. Horizons as open as this were a visual baptism for an eastern boy...Texas *was* different. Unshackled from the fence lines and confining horizons of the east, we were free, completely free, perpetually united and animated in an element of sky that seemed to stretch forever."

It was not long before the two teenagers found out why old pilots advised them while flying low over desert and mountainous areas: *Never take off in the middle of the day*, especially in a feather-like Piper Cub. The turbulence was cruel, and both found they developed bruises on their legs and knees from the control stick banging back and forth, and around their bellies, where they had tightly cinched their seat belts. They landed at Albany, Texas, and stayed overnight in a hotel after buying typical Texas hamburgers with a sauce "thick as swamp mud" that contained mustard, pickle relish, jalapeno peppers, chopped onions, Tabasco sauce, and something that looked like "week-old refried beans." They each took one bite, flushed them down the toilet, and sought a restaurant that served chicken-fried steak.

The next leg took them up the long incline from the 2,000-foot elevation of Albany to 4,000 feet, as they continued along the fabled "southern route" of the air mail pilots over the rocky desert and serrated hills to Sweetwater, Texas, and then on to Wink, where they experienced their first plane malfunction. On the approach to land Kern found that the elevator refused to respond, and they made a hard landing. A friendly mechanic found the trouble was a broken elevator spring, probably caused by the turbulence, and quickly replaced it with a new one that he happened to have on hand. It was from him they learned that they were the subjects of nationwide radio newscasts as the youngest aviators ever to attempt to fly coast to coast, something that had not occurred to either of them.

They planned to make a stop at Carlsbad, New Mexico, before taking on the fearsome Guadalupe Pass. En route they had another emergency, when there was a heart-stopping noise and the engine cowling began to shake violently. The entire plane began to tremble, and it looked as if a forced landing in the rocky desert was inevitable. But Kern persisted by reducing the throttle and flying a nose-high attitude to maintain his altitude. Both were afraid the engine was doomed and their flight was soon to end. Somehow, Kern nursed the Cub into the Carlsbad airport.

Both jumped out to see what damage had been done and found that the problem was the failure of a cowling gasket. The banging noise and vibrations were caused by the metal fittings repeatedly striking the landing gear and underside of the fuselage. The only damage was to some fabric under the fuselage.

A crusty old crop duster came to their rescue. A licensed mechanic, he was in charge of dusting operations and wandered over to see the Cub with the broken gasket dragging underneath. He had heard of their flight on the radio and, to their pleasant surprise, quickly replaced the gasket, made a hot patch repair of the fabric, and touched it up with white paint. He then gave the engine a complete check and adjusted the mixture and timing in preparation for the higher altitudes they would be flying. He refused to take anything for his work, and they launched in mid-afternoon for the assault on the pass, which would require them to coax the 90-hp of the Cub up to at least 9,000 feet, but they knew they needed more than that to get through the Guadalupe Pass safely.

The wind, turbulence, thin air, and the threat of hypoxia were their enemies as the Cub inched up the east face of the mountains. Kern was able to full-throttle the Continental to reach 11,600 feet, and they could see the immense V of the pass ahead. The Cub was now on the edge of a stall and began to lose precious feet, but Kern was not to be discouraged, even though they were proceeding only by inches forward into the pass. He managed to regain footage slowly between downdrafts and forged onward, with the mountain sides seeming so dangerously close that he could not turn around.

Rink was scared when he realized they couldn't turn back. He vividly described his feelings:

The Coast-to-Coast Route of the Buck Brothers, 1966. (Illustration by Kevin K. Hudson)

"That final entry into the pass was a hallucinogenic blur for me. There was so much heat and noise in the cockpit, the glare shield above my head looked too hot to touch, and now the walls on either side of the pass tumbled up, quite close. There were moments when I looked out and the twin peaks were more or less level with us, and other moments when we were in a downdraft and they disappeared above the top of the wing. I felt exhausted, wanting to cry, but not wanting to, overwhelmed by a desire to escape into sleep."

The gallant Cub made it through the pass, and the two young pilots were overjoyed as they gradually descended into thicker air and headed for El Paso seventy miles away. The fuel cork was showing nearly empty as the city rose ahead out of the desert, the largest habitation they had seen since leaving Pittsburgh. They had to land at the general aviation airport because they had no radio, and were met with a number of television, radio, and newspaper reporters, shouting questions and elbowing their way into position around the plane as they shut the engine down. Neither could understand why they were being given such attention.

"As far as we were concerned," Rink wrote later, "we were just two kids from New Jersey pursuing our own private dream."

The reporters liked this "Aw, shucks" pair and associated them with the Kennedy brothers. They showed them wire service reports and the write-up in the local El Paso paper, and asked for different poses by their Cub. When asked where they were headed next, Kern looked at their sectional map, checked the approximate mileage, and answered, "Tucks-on." The reporters laughed and made notes furiously. Here were two innocent kids from New Jersey who had never heard the correct pronunciation for Tucson.

This question was followed with another, "Where are you going after that?" Kern was on a roll and answered quickly, "Yumma. After Tucks-on, we'll land at Yumma for gas." The reporters obviously felt that here were two plucky kids who had never been far from their New Jersey home. They were on a long trip clear across the country in a flimsy airplane that only one of them was licensed to fly. They obviously had never heard the correct pronunciations of these two Arizona cities before.

That night at a motel in El Paso they saw themselves on television, in color no less, which was still relatively new in 1966. They were ready to leave the next day when their father called to tell them to fly over to the El Paso International Airport to meet with a television crew that was coming in from Dallas to interview them. He had personally phoned the tower operator on duty to ask that he give his boys landing clearance by using a light gun. However, the tower operator went off duty and did not relay the information to his replacement that a Cub without radio would be landing soon.

Kern entered the landing pattern and turned on the approach. He was very busy looking out for other aircraft and depended on Rink to look for a green light from the tower. Rink saw a green light, but it was flashing, which meant "stand by," not clearance to land. Rink did not know the difference and told Kern he saw the green light. Just as Rink landed, a large cargo plane roared over their heads and had to make a go-around for another approach, which meant an inconvenience and an expense to the airline in fuel consumption that no pilot likes to incur for his company.

Kern was furious when he found out that Rink had misinterpreted the signal, and was sure their trip had ended there in El Paso. He knew he was in trouble. The FAA tower supervisor threatened to pull Kern's license, but was interrupted by a pilot who had befriended them and confronted the supervisor brusquely until Kern could not stand it. He said the supervisor was only doing his duty and he was guilty as charged. The supervisor took no action, but said he had to file an incident report to FAA headquarters in Washington, which Kern would have to answer when he got back home.

The boys had their television interview, mad at their father for having arranged it, and that evening went over to Mexico with the pilot who had interceded for them, along with his wife and sister-in-law. They took off the next day at daybreak and followed Highway 10 west to Deming and Tucson for gas, then Highway 8 to Gila Bend and Yuma.

They were admittedly two bored, tired teenagers by this time, grinding along at about 75 miles an hour at a very low altitude. They saw a Greyhound bus coming down the highway straight at them, and Kern decided to play "chicken" with it. He lowered the Cub to about five feet above the highway and headed toward it. The bus driver shined his high beams on, but Kern was not to be turned aside. The bus driver careened off the highway into the gravel and was last seen by Rink trying to get the vehicle back on the road. They imagined what his fellow drivers would say when he got to Tucson and tried to convince them that he had been run off Highway 8 by a Piper Cub. Their teenage rationale was, therefore, that they would not be reported to any authorities, and they weren't, as far as they ever knew.

Their stop in Yuma led to a confrontation with several U.S. Border Patrol officers who demanded that they strip the airplane for inspection, because there had been an illegal crossing by an aircraft from Mexico the night before. Both boys tried to tell them they had landed the afternoon of the day before, but the ranking officer did not want to listen. Rinker recalled some of his Dad's stories about how he had talked himself out of arrests for alleged flying violations. His self-admitted "rotten attitude" toward authority surfaced, and he demanded that the officer show a search warrant. Not sure that he had to have one, the officer backed off, especially as a crowd gathered and supported the lads' story. A newspaper reporter said loudly that he would have a good story if these two boys from New Jersey, about to set a record and getting a lot of favorable press coverage for their trip, were ordered unnecessarily to strip out the Cub's seats, floorboards, engine covers, and open the inspection plates. Rinker reported in his memoir that "the Border Patrol pickups flashed their lights and spun gravel and dust all over the airport" as they hurried out of sight.

The trip from Yuma to Brown Field, San Diego, was one of the longest they made, but an easy one. They were caught on top of the clouds as they neared the coast, but Kern found a hole and spiraled down to a soft landing. As they taxied in, a sea breeze was blowing and they could smell the salt air of the Pacific Ocean. It was proof to them that they had indeed flown coast-to-coast, and had done it in six days.

They were met by a horde of reporters, all shouting questions, and left as soon after refueling as they could. They flew through smog to the San Juan Capistrano Airport; en route, intercepting helicopters with movie cameras dangling out the windows gave them a problem and caused them to make three passes before landing on the small runway. They were met by another horde of reporters, and people who just wanted to see and touch the two teenagers who had completed such a grueling trip. Rinker described his feelings:

"Everyone there was thrilled about our flight, their imagination of what a transcontinental crossing in a Piper Cub must have been like. But I was exhausted, tired of flying, and all I could remember was five days of nonstop turbulence and a blurry scramble through a mountain pass. I was stunned by the spectacle of it all, the queer logic of what excited people. Kern and I were oddballs, aviation nerds, sons of an eccentric, one-legged ex-barnstormer. One Saturday we took off and flew west for the mountains, and the Saturday after that we hit the next ocean, and now we had this personal monkey off our backs."

They did not realize it, but they were the youngest persons ever to fly coast-to-coast in a light plane.

The brothers were pleased that they had completed their personal rite of passage. Their father was proud of both of them, and that mattered. They returned home following the same route and had no problems flying east through Guadalupe Pass. When they got to Junction, Texas, Kern got in the back seat and let Rink fly the leg to Austin, where he made a smooth, unaided landing. It was a crowning moment for the younger brother that his older sibling trusted him enough to let him do it. Instead of retracing the route from Texas through Arkansas, they flew south to Florida and up the coast to their home airport, and a rousing welcome from press and friends.

For the first time in history, two teenagers had made a round-trip, coast-to-coast flight in a Piper Cub without a radio, and had experienced only two minor aircraft malfunctions. In the dedication to *Flight of Passage*, Rinker writes:

"This book is for my brother, Kernahan Buck, who got us there, and for my father, Thomas Francis Buck, who taught us to dream and then had the sense to let us go."

It was not only a memorable adventure for two gutsy lads, but also a tribute to the Cub and its engine. The airplane, Rinker said later in an interview:

"...symbolizes the American desire to seek meaning and caring relationships through adventure and challenge. That's what flying is."

***

Anyone who has dreamed of flying where others have rarely been might consider taking a Piper PA-11 Cub Special seaplane alone to the northwestern provinces of Canada, to Alaska and the Yukon, and roughing it. Dr. George Erickson, a retired Minnesota dentist, author, and lecturer, did just that in what he calls the Tundra Cub that he had bought in the late 1980s. He landed on rarely explored lakes and rivers, dared the weather, and set up camp where he pleased. He chronicled his solo flight in a delightful memoir titled *True North: Exploring the Great Wilderness by Bush Plane*.

Erickson trusts his Cub that can fly a thousand miles, likes its lack of complexity, and describes it in a satisfying fashion:

"The Tundra Cub is a simple aircraft. Move the stick or push rudder pedal and cables convey each input to ailerons, elevators and rudder. Designed to take off and land around forty mph, the Cub can almost promise that emergency landings will be injury free.

"Like the Wright Flyer that skimmed the dunes of Kill Devil Hill, the Cub's fabric skin enfolds a framework of wood and steel. Given proper care, her Dacron sheath will stay supple for more than thirty years.

"The Cub's chrome-molybdenum tubing is a rust-resistant alloy of iron, the metal of meteorites, our only source of iron until we

George Erickson poses beside a previously-owned Cessna 172 seaplane. He preferred the PA-11 Cub Special on floats for his solo adventure to the far north, which he relates in *True North: Exploring the Great Wilderness by Bush Plane*. (George Erickson Collection)

learned how to process ore. Her cowling, propeller and the spars of her wings are made of aluminum, a metal once so precious that the Washington monument originally wore an aluminum cap, and the kings once preferred it to silverware. Her propeller, like that of the Flyer, is simplicity itself; two rotating airfoils with wing-like cross sections that pull the Cub along. The Wrights' hand-carved prototype had a remarkable efficiency of 66 percent, but modern aluminum props like the Cub's have raised it to 88.

"The Cub's spark plugs are fired by two magneto-driven ignition systems derived from the work of Michael Faraday, the English genius who discovered the relationship between electricity and magnetism in the early nineteenth century. Using his insights, the Cub's magnetos create pulses of electricity by whirling wires within a magnetic field. Were it not for people like Faraday, we'd still be riding horse-drawn buggies and dirty steam-driven trains; we'd be lighting coal oil lanterns and sweating through long summer nights.

"With no hydraulics to leak, no starter, generator or battery to fail, the Cub's a Spartan but practical machine. Engine, propeller, airframe and a few instruments—that's all."

Erickson's Cub has no navigation radio, no Loran, no gyro horizon or gyro compass.

"I navigate by pilotage," he says, "using a compass (when it works), common sense and a map, employing the same basic flight skills that led Lindbergh to Paris. Were I to plop one of my friends whose aircraft brims with electronic gadgets into my primitive Cub, he'd surely pop a stroke."

Erickson calls the plane a Tundra Cub because it:

"...has traversed the Yukon and measured the tides of Nome. Skimming the margins of Hudson Bay, it has dipped a wing to polar bears and delivered me to the banks of the Thelon River, where fifty yards into the bush I performed a nervous pirouette, surrounded by the shaggy descendants of worlds long past—musk oxen."

In the third week of July 1995, he decided:

"...to seek renewal in the sights and sounds and scents of the North, in its people, stories and myths."

With long-range gas tanks and extra gas in five-gallon plastic bags stashed in the back seat of the 1947 Cub that he had flown north many times before, he set out unhurriedly from Lake Vermillion, near his Minnesota home at Eveleth:

"...buoyed by my freedom to choose destination and course without consultation, with only myself to please."

His first landing was to clear Canadian customs at Sand Point Lake, which is a required stop for transiting seaplanes and boats. From there his itinerary took him to such watery landing places as Moosenose Lake at Ilford, York Factory and Churchill in Manitoba, and on Ennadai, Baker, and Garry Lakes in Nunavut, homeland of the Inuit, which became a separate territory in 1999 and a homeland for the original inhabitants of the region. At these stops he fished with homemade lures, occasionally pitched a tent for an over-

Erickson's Tundra Cub sports a novel engine cowling ornament at Glacier Lake, Northwest Territories, Canada. He found the antlers at his camp site, but could not fit them into his Cub to bring home. (George Erickson photo)

night stay on a beach, fought the blood-thirsty mosquitoes, black flies, and relentless arctic winds, observed the musk oxen and caribou herds, made friends with the gentle, modest Inuit natives, and listened to the wild tales of the white inhabitants. At times, he would tie the floating Cub to a tree and wander around the area to observe the animals.

From Garry Lake, Erickson headed southwest to Reliance, past Snowdrift, and on to Fort Smith, on the border of the Northwest Territories and Alberta. He reminded himself that the farther west he traveled, the larger the compass "error" became. He noted that:

"...although compasses point to the more southerly *magnetic* pole, the *geographic* pole is the navigator's constant, and from my westerly perspective the two now lie 25 degrees apart. Consequently, to fly south, I need a compass heading of 155 degrees. Were I to fly a 180-degree heading, I'd miss Fort Smith by almost a hundred miles."

The next stop was on a small lake between the Peace River and Fort St. John, where the temperature reached 80 degrees—"just right for laundry and a swim." He decided to fly to Fort St. John in British Columbia and ran into a squall line. The wind stiffened, and the Cub:

"...like a just-roped stallion, begins to leap and dive. I throttle back to reduce the stress on the Cub, then counter with stick and rudder as we struggle through turbulent air."

He made a landing in rough waves on Charlie Lake and was able to taxi to a small seaplane base, where he met the caretaker, who took him to a local inn. For the first time in many days he slept in a bed without "hidden pine cones, knuckled roots, or unseen stones" to jab his back and hips.

From Fort St. John, Erickson headed for Juneau, the capital city of Alaska, via Fort Ware and Telegraph Creek in British Columbia. He had a radio problem on this leg and was unable to transmit or receive. He would be entering the United States, which meant he should have a clearance to land and would have to clear customs. As he crossed the Alaskan Coastal Range, the engine suddenly lost power and he added carburetor heat. That worked, but he reviewed what he should do if he had to go down. He had flown into warm maritime air from the dry inland air mass and, instead of being surprised, "I should have expected [carburetor] ice." He was confident, however, and said:

"If I had to, I could land almost anywhere, as it's not much different from landing a seaplane on grass, which I've done many times. Once down, I'd flip on my Emergency Locator Transmitter and wait for a chopper or ski plane to fly in a mechanic. For the takeoff, it's aim downhill, keep the nose up a tad, and pour on the power."

Erickson toured the small city and the nearby Mendenhall Glacier, took photographs, and witnessed the spawning of the sockeye salmon. He took off and photographed the mass of blue-green crevasses and fishing trawlers as he headed to Skagway (a Tlingit word for "windy place."). As he cruised serenely along, a hammering sound interrupted his reverie. The rubber strip between the cowling and the nose bowl had come loose and was banging against the cowl. He landed on the Lynn Canal and made repairs with duct tape. Just as he closed the cowl, a loud whoosh surprised him. He saw several four-foot dorsal fins heading straight for the Cub. It was a pod of orca whales, but they veered off and did not come close enough to upset the Cub.

High waves at Skagway cautioned Erickson not to try a landing there, so he proceeded to a landing on the Taiya Inlet at Dyea, a ghost town farther north. He explored the area on foot, including the cemetery, where many men and women were buried who had died attempting to cross the Chilkoot Pass during the Gold Rush days of 1898.

Erickson flew to Fraser to clear customs, and on to the next stop at Whitehorse, capital of the Yukon Territory, with a landing on Schwatka Lake. Then it was on to Ross River, and then Virginia Falls, the latter in the Northwest Territories. He landed on Glacier Lake, coasted to a stop on a nearby stream, and pitched his tent. He saw an odd-looking object sticking out of the reeds on the shore and found that it was a set of moose antlers. He wanted to take them home, but knew they would never fit in the Cub, so he lifted them onto the cowling like a hood ornament and snapped a picture. He fished, stayed overnight, slipped the Cub out of the valley the next morning with his camcorder attached to a wing strut, and flew to Rabbit Kettle Hotsprings and the nearby Nahanni Falls to film the area. Then it was on to a landing and a rainy campout at Little Doctor Lake, followed by a short flight to Fort Simpson, at the junction of the Mackenzie and Liard Rivers. He followed the Mackenzie River north toward Wrigley. Along the way, admittedly bored, he made a near fatal decision. He lowered the nose and flew a few feet above the waves, "seeking the thrill of low-level seaplane flying." He put in a little nose-high trim and countered it with a little forward pressure, so that if he got distracted and released the stick, the Cub would climb.

"For twenty miles, the Cub roars along in ground effect just above Mackenzie's face," he recalled. "Then, as the village of Wrigley appears on the horizon, my chart slips off my lap and disappears between the rudder pedals.

"After climbing ten to fifteen feet, I duck my head beneath the panel and reach for the map, taking care not to push forward on the stick. It's quite a stretch, but within a few seconds my fingers close on the map. Just then, I spot a candy wrapper lying against the firewall and, in spite of warning myself to look around before I retrieve it, take a few extra seconds to get it within my grasp.

"The Cub is a *light* airplane. Fully loaded, it weighs only thirteen hundred pounds. Shift just fifty pounds a few inches forward and her nose will begin to drop. And though I'm certain that I've cranked in enough trim to keep the nose up as I reach beneath the panel, I'm about to learn that I'm wrong.

"As my head comes back above the panel and my hand returns to the stick, the Cub receives two almost simultaneous, staggering jolts as the keels of her floats slice into the Mackenzie at ninety miles per hour. Fortunately, I've just begun to pull back on the stick, and the Cub staggers skyward as I gasp in disbelief."

Erickson cursed himself for being so foolish and promised himself never to fly again within fifty feet of *anything*, except when landing.

Erickson proceeded next via Norman Wells and over Great Bear Lake, the world's seventh largest, and across the Arctic Circle to Coppermine. It was the most northern stop he would make, and marked a return to the new Nunavut province that would be officially established afterward in 1999. He fished there for char, as he had done many times so far in his journey, and then departed for the 150-mile flight to Port Radium, on the northeast shore of Great Bear Lake, where pitch blend, from which uranium and its close relative radium, is derived. He fished there for grayling, where they were so plentiful that "you can hang a hook on a bowling ball and still catch plenty of fish."

Yellowknife, capital of the Northwest Territories and located on Great Slave Lake, followed, where diamond fields have been found, supplementing the gold-bearing quartz that had been exploited previously. The flight to Stony Rapids, Saskatchewan, was through fire-blackened clouds of acrid smoke that sickened him from fires that had been caused by summer lightning and had destroyed the forests below. He stopped en route at Uranium City, a modern-day ghost town that had formerly boomed when there was a demand to make atomic bombs and fuel power plants, and was now almost empty.

It was at this stop that Erickson realized he had lost the Cub's gas cap because he had left it on top of the wing after refueling at Yellowknife. Fortunately, he was able to cover the tank entry with duct tape and had not lost much fuel, since he had flown on only one tank. He beached the Cub and set up his tent, started a fire, and fixed himself a meal. Looking west, he saw an advancing line of thunderstorms that could spell trouble for the Cub. He quickly doubled the tie lines on it and heaped sand around the tent to keep the wind from underneath. The storm's fury of wind and rain hit his tent and the Cub viciously, followed by hail the size of marbles:

"Fortunately, my springy tent can tolerate marble-size hail," he said, "as can the drum-like skin of the Cub, but golf-ball-size hail or larger could reduce the tent and the Cub to rags, and larger hail can kill. Were the Cub to be trashed and I survive, having hidden beneath my foam mattress and sleeping bag, I'd be forced to wait for Search and Rescue planes to find me when I failed to reach Stony Rapids."

The worst did not happen. The hail stopped suddenly, and the storm moved on. He took off without difficulty and landed on the Fond du Lac River at Stony Rapids, Saskatchewan, where he bought a gas cap from a wrecked truck for $15—"the penalty for being careless in a sellers' market."

Erickson's flight path continued southward to Cree Lake, Southend, The Pas, Norway House, and Red Lake, filming the scenery as he went and fishing at the latter from the door of the Cub. He cleared customs at Crane Lake and finally landed on Lake Vermillion, home of the Tundra Cub. It had been flown about 7,000 miles

George Erickson's 1947 PA-11 Piper Cub Special is beached on a lake near the Nahanni Range at Little Doctor Lake, Northwest Territories, during his solo seaplane adventure in the mid-1990s. (George Erickson photo)

in 17 days and 85 flying hours with only two minor problems with the aircraft, both of which had been solved with duct tape. Its pilot had flown a course "determined by weather and whim" and renewed his "long standing love affair with the North."

When asked if he was apprehensive about flying a seaplane alone at low altitudes over large land areas where there were often no lakes or rivers in case of a forced landing, he says that such flying doesn't worry him because:

"I trust my equipment, my training, and common sense, and though some solo travel has its hazards, what good are our dreams if we lack the courage to follow?"

His advice to other pilots:

"Take care of your equipment, don't take chances with the weather, and stay cool in a crisis."

***

A group of Piper Cub J-3 pilots calling themselves the Cub Six-Pack decided they would take nostalgic flying excursions into the past and fly as a group where their whims took them. They agreed that they wanted to revisit "...the lost art of low and slow long-distance flight in an old airplane using nothing but a sectional chart, plotter, compass, and a watch," said Lyle Wheeler, former Pan American Airways captain, in a book titled *Cubs on the Loose: Old Airplanes – New Adventures* that is written by Wheeler from NC-87881, his airplane's point of view. He and five other pilots, all owners of J-3 Cubs, had been flying from a small airstrip at Frostproof, Florida, since 1993. The oldest was 55 at the time, and the youngest was 47. Their piloting experience ranged from 700 hours to Wheeler's 42,600 hours.

"Each knew and understood," Wheeler writes, "that there is always something new to be learned about flying an airplane and

Two of the Six-Pack Cubs are parked for an overnight stay during an annual fly-in at Quincy, Florida. Lyle Wheeler's book *Cubs on the Loose: Old Airplanes - New Adventures*, tells of the joy of leisurely flying in groups at low altitudes. (Leighton Hunter photo)

that a J-3 Cub could be a very tough teacher as is very subtly demonstrated on occasion."

It was in June 1966 that the Cub Six-Pack departed Crystal River, Florida, on a typical relaxed, unscheduled journey "to see as many airports as we could and still cover a reasonable distance each day." The first landing of the group was at Live Oak, Florida, and then on to Moultrie and Plains, Georgia, for the first overnight stay. The latter, Peterson Field, was one of the few remaining grass commercial airports in the United States.

Their itinerary concluded the second day with an encampment on a private airport on Ware Island, Georgia. Over the next few days the six planes proceeded to enjoy a Cub Fly-in at Gadsden, Wetumpka, and Eufala, Alabama, before drifting back to Georgia at Camilla and returning to Thomasville, some camping near their aircraft, and others seeking the nearest motel. The Six-Pack group split up and returned home, vowing to continue to take a similar trip the next year.

Only four of the former half dozen Cubs made their two-week jaunt the following year. They took off in their usual loose formation and headed for St. Simons Island via several other Georgian stops through an area of low ceilings and visibility. The next day the group proceeded to join friends for a cookout in their honor at Rock Hill, South Carolina, with refueling stops at Hilton Head and Orangeburg, South Carolina.

NC-87881 tells the story of what happened to the "humanoids" as they planned to fly on to the First Flight Airport at Kitty Hawk, famous test area used by the Wright brothers:

"As you know, we Cubs were made to be flown by our pilot who watches landmarks on the ground 99 percent of the time. The other one percent we expected him to use our compass if there were few landmarks to follow or if visibility should go bad to the point where it is difficult to see those landmarks any distance away. This latter situation was where we were at this time and due to complacency on the part of my humanoid, my compass was at least twenty degrees out of calibration. Furthermore, he had not recognized this fact and would not do so until four days later when things really turned sour."

Wheeler, leading the formation, guided them to Albemarle, North Carolina, through rain showers, low clouds, and fog. One of the Cubs had a "breathing problem" which called for a replacement engine fitting and an unplanned night for the group at the "No-Tell-Motel" nearby. Their plan was to proceed to the Kitty Hawk landing site the next day, and they made several landings en route. When they landed at Manteo, only ten miles short of Kitty Hawk, they learned that no overnight camping was allowed at the First Flight Airport, although they could land for a visit but not leave planes parked there longer than 24 hours.

While they were deciding what to do, the friendly airport operator named Tim offered a proposition. Would the pilots consider making a formation pass by the Wright brothers' memorial monument so a professional photographer could take pictures to be used in a publication to advertise a future antique/classic fly-in? They would and did. The Cubs made two passes in formation and landed with a nasty crosswind at the First Flight Airport. Unfortunately, Wheeler's Cub broke a tail wheel steering spring, which he quickly replaced with a spring from a local hardware store.

The "humanoids" proceeded southwest in an attempt to reach Plains, Georgia, again, but were hampered by low visibility and rain and landed at Orangeburg, South Carolina. They never made it to Peterson Field, their destination airport, and detoured south to escape the stalled weather conditions. Giving up, they eventually headed home.

The following year, two Cubs of the Six-Pack decided to visit Plains again, followed by stops on grass fields at Pensacola and Quincy, Florida. The crews slept in their individual canvas tent "igloos" beside their planes, but went in town to a motel where they persuaded the owner to let them shower. From there they "played it by ear" and proceeded to other Florida air strips. That October they again took off for a three-day adventure to a fly-in at Thomasville, Georgia, where Wheeler participated in a "poker run," whereby pilots paid $5 each and drew cards at four stops and a final card at Thomasville. The best poker hand at the end won the pot.

It was another year when two of the Six-Pack Cub members decided to attend the annual "Sentimental Journey" at Lock Haven, more than 1,100 miles from the home airport at Venice, Florida. Lyle Wheeler and Leighton Hunter made their way north, with stops in each state. The nearer they got to Lock Haven the worse the weather, and they had to return to land at Bellefonte after being only five miles from their destination. They landed the next day at Piper Memorial Airport, the birthplace of the Cubs, where Wheeler's

Cub had rolled out on January 14, 1946; Hunter's had been "born" there in 1938. They logged 19 hours, 30 minutes flying time getting there.

Both pilots made local sight-seeing flights during the four-day fly-in and headed south via different landing sites "in the interest of exploring grass runways whenever possible." Wheeler's fondest memory that year at Lock Haven was the sight of so many fabric-covered Cubs returning to the nest, the forums and seminars, the many vendors with reasonable prices, and the opportunity to meet former Piper officials, like William T. Piper, Jr., former CEO, Max Booke, former treasurer, and test pilots like William and Alice Fuchs, a husband and wife team who had been production test pilots. The Piper Museum, still growing in its quarters, is an attraction by itself, but was made all the more enjoyable by being able to talk with docents who were former Piper employees.

Wheeler again joined a brother pilot in May 1997 and departed the Sun Coast of Florida for the series of flights to small grass fields along a route that would take the two Cubs to Lake Itasca in northern Minnesota, a two-mile square body of water where the mighty Mississippi River officially begins. After reaching this destination, their plan was to follow the river southward along its 2,340 miles that mark the boundaries for ten states before reaching the Gulf of Mexico.

This time, it was agreed that one of the pilots would take along a handheld Global Positioning System (GPS) in order to take the worry out of navigating through hazy conditions to locate small airfields and avoid any Class B airspace along their route. As they cruised farther north the temperatures dropped, ceilings lowered, and the winds increased, so that camping out in the cold did not seem appealing. When they arrived in Minnesota they were pleased to find that many of the state's airports had established well-maintained turf runways for light aircraft beside the runways with all-weather surfaces.

Three of the Six-Pack Cubs fly by the Wright National Memorial at Kitty Hawk, North Carolina, as a tribute to the brothers who started it all in 1903. The pilots landed at the First Flight Airport and received a tour of the monument and grounds. (Jim's Camera House photo)

Lyle Wheeler and the other members of the Six-Pack of vintage Cubs pause at Ware Island, Alabama, during one of their many nostalgic flights, which are made without navigation aids. (Leighton Hunter photo)

They arrived at the goal of their long journey in the northern part of the state and circled Lake Itasca. They landed and set up their tents at Nary National Shefland Airport, a small field near Bemidji, and motored to the Itasca State Park, where they walked across the stones marking the beginning of the river, where it is only about 20 feet wide. After a night's stay at the airport they flew to Grand Rapids for fuel and followed the river via Brainerd, Little Falls, and St. Paul to Red Wing, where the landing was actually made in Wisconsin, across the river from Minnesota.

The next destination was Max Conrad Field at Winona, where they slept in their sleeping bags inside the airport's administration building. They then drifted southward following the Mississippi River on the succeeding flights, with fuel stops and three layovers during the next few days. They landed in Iowa, Illinois, Missouri, Tennessee, Kentucky, Arkansas, and Louisiana, where the giant river emptied into the Gulf of Mexico. They proceeded to fields at Wiggins, Mississippi, and Atmore, Alabama, which were headquarters for many hard-working agricultural planes. They returned home to Venice on June 5, 1997, after flying 4,200 miles. They had been in the air for 64 hours, 50 minutes, and had set their Cubs down at 55 different landing sites.

Without radios, but with the GPS, their only navigation problems were caused by having to make detours to avoid controlled airspace. However, refueling had been an occasional hassle when they landed at small airports, where local officials did not insist on pump maintenance and, according to Wheeler:

"...were too dumb to understand the value of a full-service airport and were content to let it die or kill it off themselves if it would not die."

At De Funiak Springs, Florida, they had to use automobile fuel from a local service station for the first time.

Their only navigational problem on the trip had occurred when they tried to gain permission to enter Class B airspace at Minneapolis without a radio or proper navigation instruments. After much negotiation, the FAA controller allowed them to be escorted by a

pilot whose plane was properly equipped. Wheeler commented in the final pages of his book:

"Hearing of our plans to go through Class B airspace, many skeptics have told us that it is impossible to do in Cubs that do not have communication radios or navigational electronics in them. We have also been told that it is foolhardy and a little bit stupid to even think of such extended trips in these old unequipped airplanes. True, this trip with the involvement of Class B airspace does present some problems, but anything can be solved with a little clear thinking, common sense, and planning."

These Cub pilots had shown that there is still enjoyment in flying to distant places "low and slow" in a light plane. As Wheeler notes:

"Most Johnny-come-lately aviators do not understand that even though most of the Cubs do not carry, nor wish to carry, all of the modern-day avionics equipment, which they feel is unnecessary for traversing the world's airspace, we are still able to cross great distances with no problems."

***

Proof of Lyle Wheeler's statement can be found in the adventures of Charles W. "Cully" Culwell and his wife, Marilyn, of Dallas, Texas, who have visited many out-of-the-way places in the world in their Piper PA-18 Super Cub, but without flying it across the oceans to get there. Their flying odyssey covers a period of 16 years—from 1987 to 2002, during which they visited 49 countries and flew nearly 78,500 statute (68,300 nautical) miles, at an average estimated speed of 98 mph (85 knots). This equates to more than three times around the world at the equator.

Marilyn Culwell makes a minor repair on the wing fabric of *Yellow Bird* in Africa. She has a private pilot license, and flew with her husband on all of their flights in foreign countries. (Culwell Collection)

The Culwell Super Cub rests somewhere in Germany during a European visit. It was flown 842 hours during trips to Africa, Australia, New Zealand, and Europe. (Culwell Collection)

Cully received his private license in 1949 while in high school, but with limited resources flew very little. However, while stationed at Elmendorf Air Force Base in Alaska during the Korean War he got additional ratings, did some part-time flying for the Alaska Float Plane Service, and developed a love of the outdoors, friendly people, and "the need to experience the unknown." Since then he has also flown gliders, aerobatic biplanes, and ultra-lights, and over the years has owned a total of 16 aircraft. He married Marilyn Karen Krebs in 1955, also an adventurer at heart who soloed in 1961, and together raised a family who shared his love of flying.

The world sight-seeing saga of the Culwells dates from 1971, when Cully bought a wrecked Super Cub and rebuilt it as a father-son project with Michael, then 15 years old, and then taught him how to fly it. It was not the first time Cully had brought home a derelict to be reconstructed. He had been married only a month when he towed a tattered Taylorcraft behind his car to his garage and gave it a total rebuild.

After many years of flying the Super Cub's cotton covering had deteriorated, and it was relegated to the back of the hangar. In 1986, when Cully was in "a retirement mode," the plane was rebuilt with the help of several top-notch mechanics—Bob Geron, Joe Cragin, and Darryl Shock. Cully's contribution was the custom instrument panel, which accommodates radio and navigation equipment for instrument flight, while Marilyn helped with the fabric rework. The only parts used from the original aircraft were the control sticks, the seats, and the fuselage frame, which was beefed up in several places for extra strength. The engine chosen was a 160-hp Lycoming and a high performance propeller. New wings were manufactured by Wag-Aero, which in turn had the main spars beefed up at the strut attachment points. To accommodate the longer propeller, a taller and stronger landing gear was bought from F. Atlee Dodge of Anchorage, Alaska, along with his extended baggage compartment kit. New wheels, brakes, and tundra tires were added so

landings could be made on unimproved fields and beaches. The original 18-gallon gas tanks were replaced with long-range tanks, also from Dodge, that held a total of 65 gallons, enough for nearly ten hours of flying. The new baggage compartment extended about one-third of the way back in the tail; additional srorage space was added under the rear seat. Improved seat cushions were obtained from Cub Crafters, with the rear one being modified to accommodate a tent and air mattress. Reel type shoulder straps were installed for safety.

Since Marilyn always flew from the rear seat and frequently relieved Cully, an altimeter was built into the wing root that enabled her to hold altitude, since she could not see the altimeter over Cully's shoulders. Headsets were worn to combat the engine noise, and they communicated through an intercom. Later noise-canceling Bose headsets were used, and a GPS was added when it became available.

The first extended trip in the Super Cub, christened *Yellow Bird*, took place in the summer of 1987. When the plane work was finished Cully flew it to Aspen, Colorado, where he picked up a friend who flew with him to Whitehorse, in the Yukon Territory of Canada.

CULLY and MARILYN CULWELL

UNITED STATES- Alaska . Arkansas . Colorado Idaho . Kansas . Louisiana . Montana New Mexico . Oklahoma . Texas . Utah

CANADA- Alberta . British Columbia Northwest Territory (Tuktoyaktuk-Arctic Ocean) Yukon Territory

AFRICA-Kenya · Rwanda · Tanzania

AUSTRALIA - New South Wales Northern Territory · South Australia Tasmania · Victoria

NEW ZEALAND - Great Barrier Island Stewart Island · Waiheke Island North Island · South Island

The list of the many places the Culwells have visited with *Yellow Bird* is recorded on its fuselage. The plane has been placed in the new Frontiers of Flight Museum at Love Field, Dallas, that opened in the spring of 2004. (Culwell Collection)

His friend returned, and Marilyn flew in by the airlines to join him. They entered Alaska at Northway, but bad weather forced them to fly back into Canada, clearing in at Dawson. From there they flew to Inuvik, then to the village of Tuktoyaktuk, where the Mackenzie River flows into the Arctic Ocean. When the weather improved they flew back into Alaska, making entry at Fort Yukon.

The two spent much of the rest of the summer flying down through Alaska as far south as the Gulf of Alaska. They landed on every type of strip, including beaches and gravel bars. They returned to Dallas after 119 hours of flying and 48 landings. Marilyn tells what they decided to do next:

"Later that summer we saw the movie *Out of Africa* at a local Dallas theater. As we left, Cully announced, 'We're going to ship the Cub to Africa!'

'Of course,' I said, 'You're crazy!'

The next day he was on the phone trying to find a shipping container, calling embassies, missionaries, and just about anyone he could think of to see how we could accomplish this 'miracle.' One year later, after unbelievable red tape, we met this special little plane in Nairobi, Kenya."

Cully had spent many hours working on the modification of the inside of the 20-foot shipping container in which the Super Cub just barely fits. He explains how the loading was done:

"The wings went in first and were hung leading edge down. The tail wheel was removed, and the spring bolted to the floor, while the main gear was held down with cables. With the help of a hoist installed in the container, the engine was laid on its end with the prop shaft pointing up and bolted to the floor on a platform that matched up with the motor mount fittings."

The basic plan for their trips was that the container would be sent to Houston from Dallas and loaded on a freighter for transport to Africa, their first planned country. They would make their flying tour, and after that, the plane would be returned to its container and sent to the next planned tour destination. Upon arrival, the container would be trans-shipped by train or truck to a pre-arranged airport, where the plane would be assembled. Local helpers would be recruited to hold the wings in place while Cully inserted and secured the bolts. Cully and Marilyn would do the rest of the assembly by themselves.

Beforehand they obtained visas and studied the flying regulations and maps of the countries to be visited provided by the Aircraft Owners and Pilots Association (AOPA) and government sources. Cully wrote numerous letters to the members of the Experimental Aircraft association (EAA) in each country telling of their plans and asking for advice.

The first trip abroad from July to September 1988 was to nearly 30 bush camps and safari lodges in Kenya and Tanzania. When they arrived in Nairobi, Kenya's capital, they found the container with the Cub in excellent condition and assembled it. Cully summarized the difficulties they encountered:

"The inefficiencies and corruption that exist in Africa (with the exception of South Africa at that time) created a real challenge for someone trying to accomplish what we were trying to do. It took almost a year to get permission to bring the aircraft into the country. When we arrived, they would not let us have the plane. It took some real ingenuity to solve the problem. Each time before taking off from Nairobi, we had to go to three different offices to fill out forms and pay fees. Then we would have to go to the control tower to file a flight plan. However, there was no way to close it after arrival. It was clear that all the authorities wanted at each of these offices was our U.S. dollars.

"There was no weather information of any kind available from the government. If a plane came in, we would ask the pilot where he had come from, and if it were where we were going, what the weather had been like on his flight. In flight, pilots monitored the same frequency for safety and to share weather information.

"There were no navigation aids, except for a VOR at Nairobi, which was down in a valley and useless once you got away from the area. This would be like Texas having only one nav/aid for the entire state. Streams with water and road systems almost do not exist, and there is only one railroad track that runs from Mombassa on the coast through Nairobi into what is once again called the Congo. So it's definitely not like the rest of the world, where you can correlate your position by looking at highways, rivers, and towns to determine where you are. However, with the global positioning system (GPS) available today, the navigation problems have gone away."

Despite the difficulties from Cully's point of view, Marilyn found some surprises: Delightful climate; friendly, helpful, smiling

Fuel for the Culwell Cub is strained through a chamois cloth to remove impurities during refueling stops at most foreign airports. (Culwell Collection)

members of the Kikuyu tribe, who worked in the bush camps and lodges; and excellent food and clean accommodations at most of the bush camps. In the air, it was easy flying most of the time. They met many English-speaking tourists and employees, and saw the African wildlife up close on their flights. In addition to their own Cub flights with a video camera mounted on the struts, they made sight-seeing game drives with other tourists, and at one point took a balloon ride. They carried caps and small pins they designed to give away as "thank-yous" to those who helped them.

They visited 19 different bush camps in Kenya with names not found in world atlases, like Kilaguni, Sambura, Lake Baringo, Musiara, Kichwa Tembe, and Mweiga. Landings were made at six locations in Tanzania, including Mount Kilimanjaro, Tarangire, Lake Manyara, and the Ngorangora Crater before returning to Nairobi in August. The final tally of flight time in the Cub was 34 hours, 10 minutes, with the longest flight being 3 hours, 30 minutes.

The Cub was disassembled and placed in the container and designated for shipment to Melbourne, Australia, the destination of their next trip. It was not to be returned to the States. Cully explains:

"We always planned for the next year's trip in advance. Before we left Kenya we saw the container loaded on a truck that was to take it to the rail yard. It arrived in Melbourne, Australia, some weeks later and was placed at the Tyabb Flying Club Airport by the man who, at that time, was head of the AOPA in Australia."

True to their plan, Cully and Marilyn arrived in Melbourne, Australia, on April 15, 1989, where they greeted the container, re-assembled *Yellow Bird*, and began their first adventure flights "down under." Over the next six weeks they visited the major modern cities of Canberra, Sydney, and Brisbane, and made a flight across the Bass Strait to the island of Tasmania, a dangerous three-hour flight. With no life raft aboard they could not have survived long if they had to ditch.

A video camera on the Super Cub's wing strut documents flights of *Yellow Bird* to colorful destinations. One of the sites filmed because of its extraordinary beauty was Victoria Falls in Zimbabwe. (Culwell Collection)

But the really unforgettable stops were in places with such colorful names as Coolangatta, Wagga Wag, Taree, Yeppoon, Brunette Downs, Jabiru, Mataranka, Coober Pedy, and Warnampool. Side trips were made by river boat and van to see the kangaroos, koalas, tattooed aborigines, an opal mine and, of course, to climb the steep Ayers Rock in the Uluru National Park, "the scariest thing I've ever done," as Marilyn wrote in her diary. Along the way they met many pilots and aviation enthusiasts and landed on the private grass strips at cattle stations.

When they packed for home, they concluded that Australia is truly a flying country. They had been in the air in *Yellow Bird* for 77 hours; the longest was a five-hour flight from West Sale, Tasmania, across the Bass Strait to Latrobe, and several trips were over four hours. They decided that they would visit New Zealand on their next adventure, and arranged for the Cub to be shipped there before leaving for the States June 1.

***

The New Zealand adventure began when the Culwells landed January 2, 1990, at Auckland's International Airport on Air New Zealand, where it was summer time in the southern hemisphere. They drove to Ardmore Airport, where the Cub was removed from the container, a repaired oil cooler was installed, and minor engine problems were solved. The first flight was a week-long air safari hosted by the AOPA of New Zealand that was touring North Island. They then flew to a number of private strips to visit people Cully had contacted previously. The names of their sites are as colorful as in Australia—Waipukurau, Makarika, Kerikeri, Rotorua, Paraparaumu, Hokitika, Kaikoura, Te Anau, and Wairoa. They visited a gold mine, a castle, and an albatross observatory, and took a four-day, 33-mile hike in a national park. They also visited sheep farms and took a scary jet boat ride. They departed for home on February 14, 1990. Cully's log book shows that they had flown just over 50 hours during the six weeks spent in "The Land of the Long White Cloud."

After Cully and Marilyn tucked the Cub into its container, they intended to have it shipped to Durban, South Africa, for another adventure on the Dark Continent the following year. However, they found that some countries, including New Zealand, had imposed trade embargoes on South Africa. The container had to be shipped to Bangkok, Thailand, and off-loaded. Arrangements then had to be made to ship it to Durban.

***

The Culwells departed the States by airliner on April 19, 1991, and flew to Johannesburg and Durban via Rio Janeiro and Capetown. The container had arrived at Durban's Virginia Airport, and *Yellow Bird* was liberated with everything intact, just as it had been loaded fourteen months before. After connecting everything and cleaning off the anti-corrosive preservatives, Cully made a test hop and was ready for whatever adventure was to come, as they visited with people Cully had contacted many weeks before.

Marilyn's daily diary carefully notes the social side of their peregrinations, which included side visits to many local eateries, beautiful homes, sugar and tobacco farms, native villages, game preserves, a casino, fishing spots, and attendance at an EAA fly-in, where *Yellow Bird* won a 2nd place trophy. They left South Africa for a brief visit to Swaziland, and then flew on to Namibia, Botswana, and Zimbabwe before returning to Durban. One of the highlights of the trip was the flight over Zimbabwe's famous Victoria Falls. Cully had attached a video camera to one of the wing's struts, and Marilyn noted in her diary:

"I hope the video and photographs can somewhat convey the magnitude of this indescribable place."

One of the highlights of this visit was a drive through the Chobe Game Preserve in Botswana, where they saw and photographed

Marilyn Culwell pens the address for the next destination for the *Yellow Bird* on its container door. Neither the container nor the plane suffered any damage during the overseas shipments. (Culwell Collection)

baboons, guinea fowls, puku, and other members of the antelope family, buffaloes, wildebeests, many species of birds and, of course, elephants, hippopotamus, and crocodiles.

Cully's log book shows the unusual names of places where the Cub landed: Mtubatuba, Nelspruit, Mala Mala, Uitenhage, Luderitz, Namutoni, Swakopmund, Xugana, and Phalaborwa. The total flight hours logged was 64:30; the longest flight was 4 hours, five minutes from Grootfontein, Namibia, to Maun, Botswana. They returned to Durban and prepared for the trip home to Texas in mid-June 1991. The Cub was carefully disassembled and packed in the container for shipment to Chile, where it would be waiting for them to start the next flying adventure with the *Yellow Bird* that they planned to begin just six months later, starting in Santiago. They had hoped to ship the Cub to Argentina instead of Chile to start their next trip but, although they at first had authorization to do so, some government bureaucrat, without explanation, had canceled the permission.

***

The 1992 trip actually started on December 27, 1991, with their arrival in Santiago on Lan Chile Airlines. The container was located at Valparaiso Airport, about 65 miles north of Santiago, and was cleared through customs. Cully met with his Chilean EAA contact, who helped assemble the Cub, and the first flight took place on New Year's Day 1992 up the coast to La Serena, where they were met by a family that Cully had contacted by mail. As usual, they traveled with no advance reservations. As Cully explained:

"On these trips we rarely knew where we were going to spend the night. For many reasons, the weather being one of them, we do not like to be on any schedule."

During their tour of southern Chile they met an American who convinced them that they should fly to the bottom of Chile and see Patagonia. They did this by way of Argentine airspace to avoid some of the harshest, unforgiving country they had ever seen. If they had a problem they would not have stood a chance for survival, and they could not count on anyone ever looking for them.

They continued south to Balmaceda in strong winds, so strong that Cully was able to take off after refueling there from the adjacent ramp in only a few feet. What followed for the next six hours to Puerto Natales was the roughest turbulence they had ever experienced. They agreed that they did not like Patagonia because of the harsh climate, winds, and rugged landscape. Marilyn commented in her diary:

"Why anyone would recommend visiting southern Chile and Argentina is beyond me!"

The itinerary was changed to avoid Rio Gallegos because of reported surface winds of 50 knots, so they flew via Punta Arenas to Comodoro Rivadavia, a 450-mile flight through instrument flight conditions consisting of snow, rain, sleet, and volcanic ash. When they landed, they were charged $70 for customs clearance and a $200 airport user fee.

The IFR flight plan out of Comodoro Rivadavia was to the regional airport near downtown Buenos Aires. Before their arrival, the air traffic controller asked if Cully could speak Spanish. When he answered that he spoke some, the controller said he could not land at the small airport because no one spoke English there; they would have to go to Ezeiza, the large international airport which, as it turned out, had no facilities for private planes. When they arrived they were directed to the American Airlines gate, where they were treated very cordially and were given a ride to the city by the airport manager.

They had a welcome respite of five days before departing for Rosario, where they flew briefly through Uruguayan airspace. The trip continued to Carlos Paz, a lake resort west of Cordoba, Santa Rosa (where the world glider championships would be held in 1997), Lake Lumine (where they landed on a road), Bariloche, and Lake Tchuquen, with the trip ending back at Vina del Mar, Chile.

One difference between this trip and previous adventures was that they had a GPS (Global Positioning System) that had been loaned to them by Bill Signs, a pilot who had flown a Cessna 210 around the world and established a new international record-setting category by landing on all seven continents. Until this adventure Cully had navigated over uncharted land areas using only dead reckoning.

Cully and Marilyn cleaned out the container and packed two large boxes of souvenirs they had stashed inside from their previous flights to take home with them. The Cub was stored in a hangar at the Vina del Mar Airport until the following May, when they planned to return and fly it home to Dallas. The container was given to the local aero club.

Cully tallied the Cub's flight time for this trip at 67 hours and estimated they had flown 6,000 miles; the longest flight was 5 hours, 15 minutes between Comodoro Rivadavia and Bahia Blanca, Argentina.

***

It was May 17, 1992, when the Culwells returned to Santiago and drove to Vina del Mar to check on the Cub. It was in excellent shape and did not have to be assembled this time. Cully installed new spark plugs, and their first flight took place on May 21 to Antofagasta, nearly six hours up the coast. From there they flew in almost constant haze to Arica to clear out of Chile for Peru, then on to Tacna, Ariquipa, and a small Peruvian Coast Guard base at San Juan before landing at Lima, the capital city.

A round-trip flight on a local airline was made across the Andes to Cuzco to visit the Incan ruins at Machu Picchu. Their flight in the Cub then continued from Lima to Guayaquil and Quito, Ecua-

dor, then on to Cali, Colombia, and Panama City, Panama, the latter a five-hour flight. They were advised by local pilots not to land in Honduras and Guatemala to avoid clearance and customs hassles, but to continue their flight north to San Jose, Costa Rica, then to Managua, Nicaragua, and San Salvador. They arrived in Tapachula, Mexico, then flew to Vera Cruz before flying to Matamoros, Mexico, where they cleared to Brownsville, Texas, and home to Dallas.

"All of a sudden," Marilyn wrote in a final entry, "the fantastic five-year odyssey is finished. I feel let down and sad, even though I am so happy to be home.... Home—what a wonderful word, what a wonderful place. I think that's what makes travel such a fantastic experience."

They had flown about 7,000 miles in the previous three weeks and the Cub had performed magnificently. The only problem was a small split in the fabric on the left side of the fuselage, which Cully

The inside of the Cub's shipping container is prepared by placing the wings on padded cradles on the side and attaching the cowled engine and prop in a firm position on the floor. The fuselage, minus tail feathers and tail wheel, then slides into the center. All other parts are stored so that a minimum of work is required to remove and reassemble the Cub. (Culwell Collection)

Marilyn Culwell writes in her diary while her husband works on the Cub before the wings are attached. (Culwell Collection)

repaired with duct tape. Cully logged 64 hours, 40 minutes for the Chile-U.S. flight.

***

The Cub needed some tender loving care by this time; its engine was rejuvenated with a top overhaul, and the fuselage with some fabric repair and paint. Cully and Marilyn decided that they would see more of western America from the special low altitude vantage point of the Super Cub. Beginning in September 1993, leaving from their summer home in Aspen, Colorado, they made a camping trip in the wilderness of Idaho using the airstrips built by the U.S. Forest Service and returned to Aspen. In the following month they flew to New Mexico and Arizona, then into Baja, Mexico, with stops there at small, somewhat primitive lodges and resorts along the east coast and the Sea of Cortez. They returned to Aspen via San Diego and three stops in Arizona. Then, in July and August 1993, still with Aspen as their base, they traveled to Iowa, Wisconsin, and Nebraska.

The following year they made another tour of the western states with stops at small fields they had not visited before. This was continued in July and September 1994. It was back to Mexico in February 1995, but with the deHavilland Beaver this time, followed by trips to Baja, Mexico, and Panama in January 1998.

***

The Cub was not flown much during these three years, and the Culwells did not plan any more flights overseas in *Yellow Bird* until July 22, 1998, when they met the Cub in Esbjerg, Denmark, in a new container that Cully had fashioned internally as before. Over the next two months they flew from there to Sweden, Norway, and Finland before returning to Esbjerg. They visited all four capital

cities and, as usual, made side trips by rented car to see the sights and visit Marilyn's Norwegian relatives. The weather was not friendly along the coastal areas, with frequent rain and low clouds, but the weather was much better when they flew inland. They visited museums, castles, cathedrals, fishing villages, farms, marinas, and an EAA fly-in of 130 planes at Siljansnas, Sweden, where *Yellow Bird* was put on display. Throughout their Scandinavian visit they experienced the high cost of everything, from taxi rides and hotel rooms to meals and clothing.

Despite the cold and overcast they were able to make short flights, and one of them was to Kiruma, Lapland, north of the Arctic Circle. The longest flights made were on instruments from Helsinki, Finland, to Stockholm, Sweden, and Stockholm to Almholt, both more than three hours. After returning to Esbjerg and storing the Cub in a hangar, they entrained for Germany and flew home from Frankfurt. They had already planned that their next adventure would be to Eastern Europe the following summer.

***

The Culwells returned to Esbjerg in mid-June 1999, and their first flight was to Sweden, where they met a couple whom they had known since touring New Zealand. They then flew the Cub across the Baltic Sea to Helsinki. They would have liked to fly to Russia, but it could only be arranged if a Russian pilot were taken along to handle the navigation and communications.

"In the case of our little Cub," Cully explained, "I would have had to put Marilyn on the train and take the pilot with me. It was not worth the effort and expense just to be able to say we had flown the Cub to Russia."

Instead, they took a train from Helsinki to St. Petersburg, where they hired a driver and guide for a city tour, attended a ballet, and visited the cathedrals, palaces, and art museums. Marilyn's diary notes say:

"St. Peterburg is at once shoddy, dirty, worn out, run down, and unkempt, and at the same time filled with dazzling splendor."

She was especially referring to the palace of Peter the First, which she found:

"...hard to describe – so much gold, lapis-lazuli, and marble! No wonder the masses finally revolted."

They returned to Finland, pre-flighted the *Yellow Bird*, and flew across the Gulf of Finland to Tallinn, Estonia, and on to Riga, Latvia, and Kaunas, Lithuania, where they were disappointed at the lack of general aviation activity in these small countries.

"These people have not had the freedom, the means, and the spirit to develop much of anything," Marilyn noted.

The next flights were to Gdansk, Grudziadz, Warsaw, Rybnik, and Bielsko-Biala in Poland, where Cully's previous contacts by mail eased their way through customs, gained assistance in hotel accommodations, and resulted in invitations to meals at various homes. One of the side trips was to Auschwitz, the infamous concentration camp with its shocking photographs and displays, after which Marilyn wrote, "I'll try to put it out of my mind."

When they were ready to return home, arrangements were made for the Cub to be hangared by a friend at Bielsko-Biala, Poland, until they returned in 2000. Only 25 hours had been flown in *Yellow Bird* on this adventure, the longest being the three-hour flight from Esbjerg, Denmark, to Jonkopping, Sweden.

***

Cully and Marilyn arrived in Krakow, Poland, on June 2, 2000, and traveled to Bielsko-Biala, where Cully tested the Cub. They could not clear out of Poland from there and had to fly to the airline airport at Krakow to go through customs for departure. They found the Cub had a slight gas leak at the top of the tank which, fortunately, leaked only when the tank was full. Cully decided it was flyable, so they took off for Ostrava, in the Czech Republic. They departed from there for Prague, but had to land on a grass strip outside the city to avoid a thunderstorm. Just after touch-down heavy rains and high winds pelted the Cub. As Cully was looking for a place to taxi, a hangar door opened and some men motioned for them to head there. The men grabbed the Cub's struts and pulled it inside.

The Culwells' baggage is unloaded from *Yellow Bird*. Its normal load includes two rolling suit cases, a hang bag, soft carry-on bag, large camera and tripod, survival gear, dehydrated food, blankets, flares, medical kit, water purification system, mosquito nets, folding umbrella, tools, tie-down kit, plastic chocks, hatchet, extra oil, tire repair kit, cleaning supplies, and flight materials. (Culwell Collection)

"The next thing I knew, one of the men handed me a cold beer," Cully said. "Pilots the world over are indeed a great bunch!"

The Cub was flown next to Slovakia, which they found gloomy and depressing, as they took short side trips, including a ride up a mountain on a railway cog train. They were anxious to leave Slovakia for Austria, but had to fly to Poprad first to clear, and then made a two-and-a-half hour flight to Vaslau, south of Vienna, and on to Graz. The visit there was short, and they flew on to Hungary and the island of Brac, Croatia, on the Adriatic Sea. To get there, they had been ordered to fly around a NATO "no-fly zone" in Bosnia-Hertzegovina because of the unsettled political situation in that area. They next flew to Slovenia and then to Klagenfurt, Austria, for a landing at that country's highest airport (3,600 feet), a grass strip used for glider operations.

Since Venice was only 90 miles away, the Culwells decided to see the historic Italian city and flew south over the rugged mountains and along the coast of the Adriatic Sea to a landing on Lido Island. A day later they returned to Austria, where they made trips to Wals and Salzburg in less-than-favorable weather. They rented a car and took a trip to Berchesgaden and Hitler's Eagle's Nest retreat.

The final flights on this adventure were to Switzerland, with landings at Innsbruck, St. Gallen, Loomis, and Ecuvillens Aerodrome, near Fribourg, the French-speaking part of Switzerland. By this time Cully and Marilyn had agreed that they would return the following year to continue their European tour in the Super Cub, so Cully made arrangements for it to be stored in a hangar at the Ecuvillens airport. The only unpleasant experience took place on boarding the train to Zurich, where Cully almost lost his billfold to a pick-pocket. They returned to Dallas on July 10, 2001.

Cully totaled up the Cub's flying time for this adventure as nearly 37 hours. The longest leg had been a flight of 3 hours, 20 minutes between Brac, Croatia, and Klagenfurt, Austria.

***

The energetic Culwells took a trip to Antarctica in January 2001 before they decided to continue their Cub tour from Switzerland the following March. Meanwhile, at Ecuvillens, the Cub had an annual inspection, a new turn-and-bank indicator installed, and the fuel tank leak repaired. After they arrived Cully made a short test hop, then the pair flew to Chambery and Aix-eu-Provence, France, for a shopping tour. They then proceeded to Perpignan to clear out of the country for Barcelona, Spain. Over the next five days they made short hops to Alicante, Granada, Cordoba, Seville, and Cadiz, often contacting new friends Cully had made through previous correspondence. Each stop was followed by local sightseeing and side trips by rented car. One of the highlights was the drive to British-owned Gibraltar and Tarifa, Spain, the southernmost town in Europe.

Cully next piloted the Cub across the Strait of Gibraltar to Tangier, Morocco, to clear into Africa, and then to Fez, where they stayed in the Palais Jamal Hotel, "one of the most luxurious places we've ever stayed," Marilyn noted. Marrakesh was next after a flight of nearly three hours.

After four days in Africa the Cub was flown to Faro, Portugal, where for the first time in all their years of foreign flying, Cully had to show the Cub's Certificate of Airworthiness. The weather was unfavorable, so the two rented a car and drove to Lisbon, after which they made a two-hour Cub flight to Cordoba and a four-and-a half hour flight to Reus. They cleared into France, visited an EAA contact in Toulouse, then flew on to Bordeaux. They intended to return to Ecuvillens near Fribourg, but the weather forced Cully to land at Besancon. The weather did not relent, and time was running out to make their airline flight home, so they took the train to Zurich. Cully made arrangements to have the Cub flown by a Swiss friend to Ecuvillens, where it was stored in a hangar until they returned the following year.

"It's always a little sad to leave the Cub," Marilyn wrote. "It's such a trusty little plane that has taken us safely to so many places. So many adventures!"

***

After these interesting years of flying, the Culwells decided they would take only one more foreign trip in the Cub, and returned to Fribourg in July 2002. The first flight was to Normandy, where they spent three days visiting the D-Day invasion sites. They flew to Dijon, Caen, and Calais for several days of sightseeing, then crossed the English Channel and made a quick trip over England, stopping briefly for one night at Sywell. Their itinerary then took them to Carlisle, on the west coast of Scotland, before crossing the Irish Sea to Northern Ireland.

These ultimate Cub adventurers spent the next two and a half weeks touring Ireland, sometimes by rental car, and attended two fly-ins, where they met people with whom Cully had corresponded. Cully's flight log shows short flights to eight towns in the Republic of Ireland; Marilyn's diary shows many side trips by rented car to visit local sights and enjoy the landscape. When weather permitted they flew to the Aran Islands off the west coast, and then returned to Scotland and England, with stops at Nottingham and Duxford, home of the impressive American Air Museum.

They returned to the continent for more visits to places they had not seen before. Marilyn's diary for August 25, 2002, notes they had "breakfast in France, lunch in Belgium, and dinner in Germany." They returned August 31 to Esbjerg, Denmark, after 37 flight hours in the faithful Cub, where it was disassembled and placed in the container that had been left there since 1998. Marilyn writes that they both felt:

"...sad and strange that this fantastic part of our life is over. The people we've met and all the wonderful experiences we've had have combined to make us realize how truly blessed and fortunate we are."

The container arrived safely at Addison Airport, near Dallas, in late September 2002.

***

The flying odyssey of the Culwells in the Super Cub had spanned 16 years and 804 hours in the air, and they decided to end their world tour for several reasons. They believe the world has changed drastically since the 2001 terrorist catastrophes in New York City, Pennsylvania, and Washington.

"Besides," Cully said, "We had already been to nearly all the countries and continents where you can safely fly a private plane. During these years we have flown *Yellow Bird* in every imaginable kind of weather, including zero visibility in volcanic ash, extremely high winds (sixty knots), snow and ice, high altitudes (crossed the Andes four times), and at times very low altitudes. We have landed on large international airports where they had no facilities for light aircraft, farmers' fields, beaches, and roads. Navigation was very challenging in the days before GPS, especially so in Africa, where there are few roads and rivers, and everything looks the same to a newcomer. Not being able to find your destination dirt strip next to a tented camp can get interesting when you have a thunderstorm overhead and it's getting dark. Landing over a pride of lions, then taxiing to the other end of the short grass runway makes for an exciting arrival when there is no one else around and no buildings.

Cully and Marilyn Culwell pose beside their faithful Super Cub with native onlookers in Africa after one of their flights. They visited 50 foreign countries and flew 82,516 statute miles during their multi-year odyssey. (Culwell Collection)

Cully Culwell's Super Cub finds a shady spot under the wing of an out-of-service Boeing 747. (Culwell Collection)

"One thing is certain. The world has no shortage of nice, friendly people, especially those involved in aviation. Prior to our trips we would correspond with members of the EAA and AOPA in those faraway places. In our letters we would tell them what we were doing, but ask for nothing other than advice and suggestions. Back would come maps, books, and invitations. Although we chose not to, we could have stayed in sixty homes in Australia and New Zealand. Over the years, many of our new friends have come to visit us in the States.

"By choice, Marilyn and I have kept a fairly low profile in regards to our Cub tours. It has never been our intent to seek any publicity, but we thought it would be appropriate to leave some sort of record of what two crazy people did with their Super Cub. I'm sure there has never been a plane of any type that has been to all the places *Yellow Bird* has. The bureaucrats in many countries hardly knew how to deal with us, as our visit was a 'first' for most of them."

The Culwells admit that age has gradually crept up on them, and they feel that there are very few places left to explore now that are somewhat safe and can reasonably accommodate small private aircraft. Instead, they plan to continue flying their restored 1956 De Havilland DHC-2 Beaver, a former U.S. Army L-20 used by the CIA in Southeast Asia. Cully helped rebuild it and included the latest in avionics and structural enhancements. They will fly wherever they choose in the U.S. and Canada, but will not make any more flights overseas as they did in *Yellow Bird*. Would they do it again?

"You bet," Cully says. "Would we recommend a flying tour like ours to other couples? Yes, provided they have the flying experience, the right plane, and both of them love adventure."

***

Cully Culwell reviewed their years of adventuring in the Super Cub exclusively for this book. His comments include wise air safety advice and tell of the unusual capabilities of the airplane:

"Looking back on our flights, there are few aircraft types that would have been up to the task. The Super Cub, when modified, has the capability to carry heavy loads and surprisingly enough space to pack it all on board. When we would land and start unloading, we always attracted attention from the local pilots.

"We carried two normal size rolling suit cases, one hang bag, one soft carry-on bag, a good size camera case and Marilyn's travel purse. In the back of our extended luggage compartment we packed survival gear consisting of dehydrated food, space blankets, flares, flashlight, medical kit, water purification system, mosquito nets, folding umbrella, camera tripod and giveaway caps.

"In the compartment under the back seat we carried extra oil, tools, tie-down kit, plastic chocks, hatchet, emergency tire repair kit and aircraft cleaning supplies. Improved seats were obtained from Cub Crafters with the rear one being modified to accommodate a complete tent system and air mattress. In addition to all this we had our maps, Jeppesen charts and approach plates, travel books, and a folder with the information about people we had corresponded with, plus necessary plane documents. The plane itself had extra equipment, including an IFR panel, single side-band radio, an ADF, Loran C, plus hand-held VHF radio, and a GPS when it became available.

"As to the dismantling and assembly of the Cub, its design makes it fairly easy to take apart and put together. We did it seven times. I think Marilyn could have done it almost by herself.

"Two things seem to get pilots into trouble flying light aircraft—weather and running out of fuel. We would not have been able to make this flying adventure with the standard 36 gallons that a stock Super Cub carries. In some instances, fuel was not available within the range of a standard PA-18. The two 32.5-gallon tanks gave us up to ten hours duration if we reduced our power setting. It gives a pilot great peace of mind to know fuel and range are not going to be a concern when he heads out. Sometimes we would go for days, making short hops without refueling. An example of how necessary this range capability was came into play when we flew from Tacna, Peru to Lima, stopping along the way at San Juan where no fuel was available and we flew for a total of 7 hours, 45 minutes on that run.

"There is no way that flights like ours could be made safely without the plane and pilot having IFR capabilities. We tried to avoid flying in instrument weather but it was not always possible. In some parts of the world, mostly Africa, weather reporting and forecasts were not available. We were able to get weather information occasionally from other pilots. Only once did we file an IFR flight plan on purpose and that was when we were stuck in Sydney, Australia because of low ceilings and rain. On that flight, as we were climbing to our assigned altitude, a surprised Qantas 747 pilot inquired of the radar controller, 'Is that a Piper Cub up here with me flying instruments?' There was no response when he was assured it was. As it turned out, we had to make only four instrument approaches during our 16 years of touring: One each into Quito, Ecuador; Helsinki, Finland; Stockholm, Sweden, and Riga, Latvia. The Super Cub is not difficult to fly on instruments.

"Since we were flying a very heavy Super Cub, it required an understanding about how the aircraft had to be flown. Speed for takeoff and landing had to be somewhat faster, rate of climb was less, and the service ceiling was lower. It took a little longer to get to altitude and we were slower when full of fuel. The large tundra tires also created additional drag. However, the two of us are not heavy people (280 pounds total) which was a plus. The aircraft had been modified structurally to accommodate the additional weight. The Cub did everything I asked of it.

"We flew out of some very unusual airfields during our many flights. Some were very short—the shortest was 300 feet up a steep hill. In New Zealand, almost no private airfields are on flat ground and many are not straight. On one occasion, a down-hill strip had a 90-degree turn at the half way point but this was compensated by a suitably banked surface as on a race track to make the turn. This was no problem for our Cub.

"As to accidents, I put only one minor scratch on the plane during our 16-years of adventures. That was when I ran through a single-strand electric wire fence in a farmer's field.

"We must not forget the power plant in the Super Cub. I have flown behind several types of aircraft engines – Continentals, Lycomings, Franklins, Limbachs and Pratt & Whitneys—all great engines, but from my standpoint the 150-hp Lycoming, in its size class, is at the top for reliability and performance. When Piper chose this engine for the Super Cub, it was a big factor in the plane's success and popularity."

The Culwells' faithful Super Cub PA-18 will not be seen flying again in foreign skies. Still in outstanding flying condition, it has been placed on loan for display at the Frontiers of Flight Museum at Love Field in Dallas as a tribute to an outstanding airplane.

Appendix I:
Evolution of the Cubs

This history of the legendary Piper Cubs portrays the improvements over the years for the planes that used the USA 35B airfoil and preserved the general contour of the original metal-tubed, fabric-covered, high-winged, single-engine light plane, except for a few experimental models, as shown below. Although Cub owners and aircraft service companies have modified them in many ways, the following listing is intended to define and clarify the various Cub models from the beginning, first produced by the Taylor brothers and then the Piper company:

Arrowwing Chummy, Model A-2: This was the first high-wing monoplane built by the Taylor Brothers [C. Gilbert and Gordon Taylor] Aircraft Manufacturing Co. in 1928. It was a side-by-side, two-seat model powered by a radial Anzani 90-hp engine. A follow-on model, labeled the Taylor A-2, was powered with an 84-hp Ryan Siemens-Halske radial engine. While being demonstrated at an air show in Detroit in 1928, it crashed and Gordon Taylor was killed.

Taylor Model B-2 and C-2 Chummy: The B-2 was powered by a 90-hp air-cooled Kinner radial engine and had minor improvements over the A-2. A variable incidence wing was installed to improve the B-2's capability in order to qualify for the 1929 Guggenheim Safe Airplane Competition. A re-designation was required and it became the C-2 Chummy.

Taylor D-1 Glider: This was a single-seat glider with a welded-steel framework, very light-weight wings and elementary controls. Only one was built and was never flown but may have been used to test the lifting ability of the wing design.

Taylor Model E-2 Cub: Designed by Clarence Gilbert Taylor, it was a tandem-seat, open-sided model originally powered by the Brownbach "Tiger Kitten" two-cylinder inverted 30-hp engine which inspired one of Taylor's employees to name the plane a "Cub." The Brownbach was replaced by a nine-cylinder French Salmson

AD-9, a 40-hp engine, then a 37-hp Continental A-40, four-cylinder, single-ignition engine. A total of 353 E-2 Cubs were built; production ceased in February 1936.

Taylor Model F-2 Cub: The Continental A-40 engine was troublesome at first and Taylor searched for a replacement. He chose the 40-hp Aeromarine AR 3-40. a three cylinder air-cooled type which required a new type designation for the aircraft. It was not much better than the first Continental A-40; only 33 F-2s were built. Originally open-sided, it could be equipped with a flimsy detachable enclosure, called a "storm shelter," for cold weather flying. To promote sales, William T. Piper, Jr. made a demonstration flight from Lock Haven to the west coast in the winter of 1934-35.

Taylor Model G-2: Unable to find a suitable engine, Taylor designed and built his own 35-hp engine. Only one G-2 was built and little is known about it. The plane may never have flown with the Taylor engine installed. It was rebuilt as an H-2 in 1935.

Taylor Model H-2: This model actually was a G-2 with a Szekely SR-3-35 three-cylinder, 35-hp engine installed. It was not satisfactory and only four H-2s were built. However, in June 1937, Beverly Dodge, carrying a woman passenger, reportedly flew a Szekely-powered Cub to an altitude of 16,800 feet over Honolulu for a new altitude record for women pilots.

Taylor J-2 Cub: This model incorporated improvements over the E-2 by streamlining changes in the tail surfaces and wingtips, and including cabin improvements that were originated by Piper engineer Walter C. Jamouneau. A J-2S seaplane prototype was equipped with EDO pontoons. While many believe the J-2 designation was to honor the young engineer, it was actually a progression of model numbering from the H-2 but it was decided that if it were to be labeled an I-2, the public might be confused. Although the J-2, advertised as "The New Cub" was still powered by the Continental

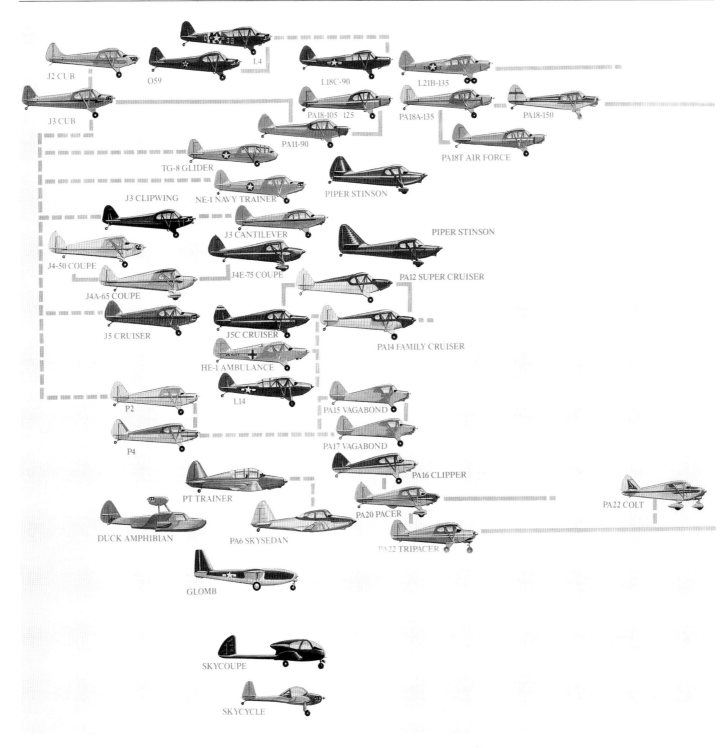

Evolution of the Piper Cub and derivatives from the J-2 to the PA-22 Colt. (Piper Aviation Museum)

A-40, the engine had been improved with twin-ignition. One brief experimental addition that did not catch on was the installation of a one-bladed Everel propeller that purported to provide increased efficiency.

One off-shoot model designation for the J-2 was the J-2S for those fitted with floats. However, there was no separate designation for those fitted with skis. There was a J-2X unofficial designa-

tion in the Piper records for an experimental J-2 powered by a 60-hp test engine manufactured by Glenn D. Angle but it was never produced. A so-called "Western Cub" was fabricated from major parts provided by Taylor and produced under license by Aircraft Associates in Long Beach, California. Only minor structural parts and wing spars were made at Long Beach. Taylor established the Cub Aircraft Corporation in 1936 to assemble J-2s in foreign locations. One company was located at Hamilton, Ontario, Canada and another at Copenhagen, Denmark. A total of 1,207 J-2s were built until production ended in May 1938.

Piper J-3 Cub Trainer: This is the tandem-seat Piper model that is the most well-known of all light planes ever built. Although a few of the final J-2s were painted "Cub Yellow," all subsequent J-3s bore this distinctive color that became its trademark as well as the bear cub logo on the vertical stabilizer. Improvements over the J-2 included brakes, a steerable tail wheel, and more comfortable seats. The Continental engine was gradually improved with more power, twin ignition, carburetor heat and smoother cowling. Eventually, new ailerons replaced older, less efficient ones. A pilot-initiated engine starter was devised but later abandoned. Other engines were tried such as the Menasco, Aeromarine and Lycoming, all air-cooled flat models rated at 50-hp. Optional items included

EDO twin floats and skis. A total of 6,143 Piper J-3 Cubs was manufactured from 1937 until civil production of J-3s ceased in 1942 in favor of war contracts for the L-4. When sales for the public were resumed after the war and ended in 1947, a total of 19,888 J-3s had been turned out.

Various designations were given to the J-3s as the federal government required when different engines were installed. The models were labeled as J-3s with a suffix that indicated the rated horsepower of the engine. For example, there was the J-3C-40, J-3C-50, J-3C-65, J-3C-65, J-3C-75, J-3C-85 and J-3C-90. Lycoming engines meant designations of J-4L-50 and -65. Later, when Franklin engines were installed, the designations of J-3F-50, J-3F-60 and J-3F-65 were given. In 1942, the J-3F-65 was adopted by the U.S. Army as the L-4D.

The J-3P-50 label indicated a Lenape Papoose three-cylinder radial engine and was the rarest of all the Cubs, as only 30 were produced. However, in the Miami Air Races of 1938, Cub pilot Ellis Eno won over all other entries by a wide margin with his J-3P-50.

The J-3L-50, -55 and -65 identification was for the installation of Lycoming engines. Almost all of these various engine models had some minor changes in the exhaust stacks and cowling that were usually identifiable on sight.

Piper J-3 Sport: For reasons never explained, this model did not carry the dash number that indicated it had a Continental 40-hp engine when it was certified in November 1937. It looked similar to the J-2 and represented the lowest-priced Cub ever produced. Originally advertised at $1,270, the price was lowered several times and bottomed out at $995 in 1940.

Piper J-4 Cub Coupe: The J-4 was the first Piper monoplane with side-by-side seating and represented competition with the basic Taylorcraft B. Formally introduced at the National Air Races in

September 1938, the type certificate was granted in March 1939. It represented a new conception of luxury in light planes. It was equipped with hydraulic brakes, lights, compass and large gas tanks. Cub Coupes were available with Continental, Franklin and Lycoming 50- and 65-hp engines. A slight change in the center of gravity required a wider landing gear which was supplemented with spring shock absorbers. The cabin featured a door on each side and the fuselage was slightly wider. The prototype was powered by an experimental 60-hp Skymotor built by a Milwaukee company. It was not acceptable and the Continental 50-hp engine was chosen so the plane was designated as simply the J-4, while the attachment of a 65-hp Continental engine changed it to J-4A, indicating a change from the previous identifications of engine manufacturers and horsepower. The J-4A was followed by the J-4B, J-4C, J-4D, J-4E and J-4F models with many improvements and different Continental, Lycoming and Franklin engines. There was one experimental Cub shown in the Piper records as a J-4RX which was actually a J-4E with a slotted wing. The last of the Cub Coupes was built in 1942.

Piper J-5 Cub Cruiser: This three-seat Cub model, introduced in December 1939, was designed to interest private owners and commercial air taxi operators by providing side-by-side seating for two passengers, while the pilot sat alone in front. This necessitated a slightly wider fuselage. There was increased fuel capacity and a large hinge-forward door on the right side that eased entry. It was introduced from December 1939 to the middle of 1942. Two prototype Cruisers were flown as J-5s, then subsequent J-5As were given suffixes to indicate the various horsepower engines initially, such as J-5A-80, J-5A-85, and J-5A-90 for the Continental or Lycoming engines. The J-5B reflected a new certification policy as it was powered by a geared Lycoming 65-hp engine.

In early 1942, the Cub Cruiser, a deluxe version of the J-5C, was introduced for sale on the civil market with a Lycoming 100-hp engine, improved landing gear with internal shock absorbers, plus additional fuel capacity that could hold as much as 48 gallons. The number of Piper J-5C Cruisers actually produced is variously reported as only 35 to 40, since production was halted in September 1942 because of war orders. The U. S. Navy wanted a small ambulance plane and the J-5C was the answer. Known first as the HE-1 when about 100 were ordered, the designation was changed to AE-1. At war's end, Piper put the Cub Cruiser back into production and it was marketed as such until the PA-12 Super Cruiser was introduced in 1947.

Piper P-1 Amphibian or Cub Clipper: This was a home-built, high-wing, two-seat amphibian with an all-metal hull and retractable gear introduced to Piper by Ray Applegate in 1939. Different engines were tried on two prototypes and J-3 wings were fitted and landing gear changed but it was abandoned in 1941 because of a shortage of aluminum.

Piper P-2: This was an experimental model that was actually a J-3 Cub with tandem-seating and some J-4 Cub Coupe changes such as a hinge-forward door and closed engine cowling. Franklin and Continental engines were tried. Only one was built and was not certificated.

Piper P-3: It is not clear from the records but this may have been the original designation for the J-4RX experimental Cub Coupe with slatted wings, flaps and ailerons invented by William Rose.

Piper P-4: An off-shoot of the P-2, it had four seats and had a 120-hp Lycoming engine installed. Only one was built and the model was never certificated. Reportedly, some of the internal structure was used as a guide for the HE-1 ambulance plane ordered by the Navy.

Piper PT-1: This was intended to fulfill a military specification for a low-cost primary/basic trainer. Powered with a Franklin 130-hp engine, it was a two-place tandem, low-wing model with full cantilever wings, conventional steel tubular construction, fabric-covered, retractable landing gear, flaps, and plywood turtleback. It had a 40-gallon fuel capacity and over 600-mile cruising range. Designed by Dave Long and Walter Jamouneau, it used the 35B basic airfoil and first flew in March 1943. Only two were produced and one has been restored for display in the Piper Aviation Museum at Lock Haven.

YO-59, O-59, O-59A and L-4A: The YO designations indicated the aircraft were designated for Army Air Forces service testing. The first YO-59s delivered were stock models of the J-3s. As testing progressed, various modifications were required by the Army for the O-59As, such as radio and electrical systems, reversible rear seat, increased window areas for an observer and minor structural changes. After 649 O-59As were produced from the original order for 948 O-59s, the designation was changed to L-4A.

L-4B through L-4K: A number of structural and engine changes based on experience in the combat areas. A total of 118 L-4C through L-4Gs were actually J-3, J-4, and J-5s purchased from private owners on a war emergency basis and used for pre-flight training of glider pilots. One of the J-5A Cub Cruisers was designated UC-83 under a supposition that it might be used as a small transport plane. Model L-4Hs were improved versions of the L-4B with a one-piece windshield. The L-4K was a designation for about 15 modified L-4As that were used by the U. S. Army in Korea.

TL-4: A few L-4s were modified to tow light gliders and given the unofficial designation with the pre-fix T (for Tug).

YL-14 and L-14: The L-14 was the U. S. Army designation for a plane that was a redesigned, over-powered, highly-modified Super Cruiser of the J-5C series. Piper received an order for 850 of them late in World War II but the order was canceled except for all but about five of them on VJ Day. It was the first Piper aircraft to have wing flaps and slots, reinforced landing gear and many features that were later used in Piper post-World War II models. One notable change was a convertible interior and a hinged rear section that could carry a large patient, similar to the Navy's HE-1/AE-1.

TG-8 Glider: Aeronca, Piper and Taylorcraft answered the call by the U. S. Army for a training glider and each received orders for 250. The Piper model was a J-3C airframe with spoilers and a new nose structure that was attached to the original engine mount. It had three seats in tandem, each with flight controls. The front cockpit had a hinge-up canopy and the landing gear was considerably shortened. After the war, with no public demand for three-seat gliders, those made available as surplus were easily modified to two-seat tandems.

XLNP-1 Navy Gliders: The Navy ordered three TG-8 gliders from Piper and gave them this designation. There is no record that they were used for training Navy or Marine pilots. However, the Navy bought 25 similar models from Taylorcraft.

NE-1, NE-2, HE-1/AE-1 Navy Cubs: The U. S. Navy issued orders for 230 stock J-3C Cubs in "Cub Yellow" that were designated NE-1s for use as utility transports by units in the coastal areas. Some were camouflaged and equipped with electrical systems to control radios and lights for short patrol missions. About 40 NE-2s were camouflaged L-4Js transferred from the Army and a few were modified with floats. Later, the Navy ordered 100 ambulance planes designated HE-1s (H for Hospital) at first, then in 1943 changed the designation to AE-1s (A for Ambulance). These were J-5C Cub Cruisers and although these could carry three persons, they were modified to carry a reclining patient on a stretcher that could be placed in the rear fuselage area through a hinged turtle deck canopy. Some were originally painted yellow but later ones were all silver.

Glimpy: This was a Navy experiment with an NE-1 that was suspended from the bottom of a Navy blimp with a depth bomb in the rear seat area. The plane, without a pilot aboard, was controlled by radio and the blimp pilot or Glimpy operator was to release it and steer it into an enemy submarine or ship. Several test flights were made with a pilot but the project was abandoned when the war's end seemed near.

LBP-1 Glomb: The Glomb LBP-1, a high-wing pilot-less glider, was made of plywood covered with fabric. Its intended purpose was similar in concept to the Glimpy. It would be towed by a fighter or transport plane and released to be steered to ground or water targets by radio and television. It was test flown in January 1945 and only three were built. This was also abandoned near the end of hostilities.

PWA-1: Skycoupe: The designation PWA was for Post War Aircraft, This was a side-by-side, two–seat, low-wing, twin boom type with a pusher engine and tri-cycle gear. It flew several times but had a poor rate of climb and was abandoned.

PA-5: Piper dropped the "J" designation after World War II began and adopted the "PA" prefix for Piper Aircraft. This was a J-3X that was proposed with a cantilever wing but was not produced.

PA-6 Sky Sedan: In 1944, Piper planned to introduce a four-place, fabric-covered, low-wing plane with metal-framed fuselage and wings after the war. It was to be a spin-off from the PT-1 Trainer that had been proposed for the armed forces in 1942.

PA-7 Skycoupe: This pusher design was similar to the PWA-1 but had a high tail to determine if it would be more efficient than the PWA-1. It was never flown.

PA-8 Skycycle: This was a mid-wing, fabric-covered, single-seat, single-engine aircraft. The fuselage was reportedly adopted from a droppable fuel tank from a Vought F4U Corsair fighter plane. A test flight was made but the aircraft was destroyed by fire and never produced.

PA-9: This was a low-wing, tri-gear observation plane designed in response to a 1946 Request for Proposal (RFP) from the U.S. Army to replace the Stinson L-5. No prototype was ever produced.

PA-10 Sky Skooter: This was to be a side-by-side, low-wing, all-metal design. By coincidence, John Thorp designed the T-11 Skyscooter which Piper was interested in adopting to save engineering costs. While Thorp's prototype flew in August 1946, Piper did not purchase the rights due to a downturn in business conditions and the cost of producing an all-metal aircraft. Thorp later developed his Sky Skooter to be sold in kit form.

PA-11 Cub Special: After World War II, Piper introduced the Cub Special which was a major up-grade of the J-3C with a noticeable change in the cowling that completely covered the 65-hp engine. An 18-gallon tank was installed in the left wing to replace the 12-gallon nose tank of the J-3. This welcome change caused the center of gravity enough rearward so that the pilot could solo it from the front seat. When more powerful engines of 90- and 100-hp were

installed, federal regulations required solo flight from the rear seat only. Nearly 8,000 Cub Specials were sold over a three-year period until 1950. It was also marketed as the PA-11 Trainer. Several were made with tricycle landing gear.

PA-12 Super Cruiser: To satisfy an impatient public as World War II ended, Piper produced the three-place Super Cruiser which was actually an improved three-seat PA-11 with increased fuel capacity, engine power increases, and different propeller options, including two-position props. It was introduced in November 1946 and became famous the following year when two of them were flown around the world. More than 3,500 were built at Lock Haven and 200 at the Ponca City, Oklahoma plant. The PA-12S seaplane version first flew in April 1947. As a three-place plane, the PA-12, powered by a 104-hp Lycoming engine, received some public interest when Piper introduced it as a "Taxi-Cub" to provide service at a cost of six cents a mile for passenger pickups at places not served by the airlines. The last Super Cruiser was rolled out in May 1948.

PA-13: Piper never used this designation, probably because of its "bad luck" connotation.

PA-14 Family Cruiser: Piper decided to skip the number 13 for its next post-war model and produced what was a four-seat upgrade of the Super Cruiser. A widened fuselage allowed side-by-side seating with dual controls in front and two seats behind. It was powered by a Lycoming 115-hp engine and had wing flaps. Although it was the first four-seat Piper plane, it did not sell well and only 238 were built.

PA-15 Vagabond: This was a side-by-side, no-frills, two-seater with a "short wing" design that first flew in October 1947 but was not introduced until June 1948. Equipped with a 65-hp Lycoming engine, it followed the tradition of high-wing, fabric-covered Pipers offered at a low cost with high fuel efficiency. Only 387 were produced during the period 1948-50. The Vagabond was the first of the five Piper short wing planes produced between 1947 and 1963. The others were the Clipper, Pacer, Tri-Pacer and Colt. The Piper Aviation Museum now has a special short wing plane display.

PA-16 Clipper: A follow-on to the two-seat PA-15 Vagabond, the Clipper was a four-seater that first flew in January 1948 and was produced in 1949 and 1950. A seaplane version was first made available in April 1949. A total of 726 Clippers were turned out at Lock Haven in 1949.

PA-17 Vagabond Trainer: This was also called a Vagabond Deluxe. It was a modestly-priced, light, short-coupled, high-winged cabin monoplane, with side-by-side seating for two and many extras. An optional door on each side was offered. All 214 manufactured were from the fuselages and wings of the PA-15 and powered by a Continental A-65 engine. The PA-17 prototype first flew in May 1948. Several were converted to tri-cycle landing gear.

PA-18 Super Cub: This became the ultimate Piper two-seat tandem aircraft. Introduced in November 1949, the first models seemed similar in profile to the PA-11. Gross weights gradually increased as more powerful engines were certificated and the Super Cub became known for its unusual versatility and short-field takeoff capability. Many were used as agricultural aircraft. It was also available on amphibious floats. The Civil Air Patrol was assigned U. S. Air Force aircraft labeled as PA-18Ts. A total of 10,326 PA-18s were built between 1950 and 1994.

PA-19 Super Cub: While the PA-18s were being built, the U. S. Army ordered a short-range variant for observation purposes which was a PA-11 with a rectangular wing section, a PA-14 rudder and powered by a 90-hp engine. Later, Piper proposed the PA-19 as a reconnaissance aircraft with slotted flaps and competed unsuccessfully for a contract against Cessna. Only three PA-19s were built.

PA-20 Pacer: The four-seat PA-16 Clipper was redesigned to become the Pacer by installing a slightly larger tail, larger fuel tank, wheel controls, upgraded cabin interior and flaps. The seaplane version seated three. It was available with different engines ranging from 115-hp to 135-hp. The cabin was accessible by means of a front and rear door with rear seat quickly removable for hauling cargo. Production began in January 1950. It was promoted as an air ambulance and later, the fuselage was widened to accommodate a larger baggage compartment. 874 Pacers were built between 1950 and 1954.

PA-21: Piper acquired a four-seat Baumann Brigadier B-250 aircraft with twin pusher engines in July 1949 to determine if it should buy the rights to put it into production. Piper engineers re-designed the wings to accommodate twin tractor engines and it was given the PA-21 designation. One prototype was built. However, production costs were predicted to be too high and the project was cancelled.

PA-22 Tri-Pacer, Caribbean and Colt: An updated version of the PA-20 Pacer, the PA-22 Tri-Pacer had a tri-cycle gear and was the first Piper aircraft to have the rudder and ailerons interconnected.

First flown in May 1950, the Tri-Pacer underwent various changes during the production period 1951-1964, such as a bubble windshield, sound-proofing, improved cabin flow, widened fuselage and increased baggage space. Tri-Pacers could carry four people nearly 600 miles between gas stops. In late 1958, a less expensive version of the Tri-Pacer was introduced to appeal to the airport operator. Although still a PA-22, it was labeled the Caribbean. Production of Tri-Pacers and Caribbeans was completed in August 1960 and replaced by the Colt, a two-seat "compact" or baby version of the Tri-Pacer for use as a trainer with less powerful engines and was obtainable in three options: Standard, Custom or Super Custom. In addition, a seaplane version was available. A total of 9,490 of the Tri-Pacers, Caribbeans and Colts were produced. The successor to the Tri-Pacer was the four-place low-wing, fixed gear Piper Cherokee.

L-14 Army Cruiser: This was a re-designed, over-powered J-5C Super Cruiser. It had a highly-modified interior to serve various military purposes, including flying patients. It was the first Piper aircraft to have wing flaps. The U. S. Army ordered 850 toward the end of World War II but the order was canceled on VJ-Day for all but five.

L-18C: The U.S. Air Force placed orders for 839 Super Cubs under this designation over a three-year period (1950 through 1953) and many were sent to other nations under the post-WW II Military Defense Assistance Program.

YL-21: Two PA-18s with tri-gear were purchased by the Air Force for testing and evaluation of rough-terrain landing gear and research on wing boundary layer design and as a glider.

L-21A, TL-21A, L-21B: The successful tests of the YL-21 led to an order by the Air Force and Army for 150 L-21s with 125-hp engines. The TL designation was used on a number of these L-21s that were modified for use as trainers and designated TL-21As. A total of 584 L-21Bs was delivered with 135-hp engines and many were sent to foreign nations under the MDAP authorization. The U.S. Army used the L-21B extensively overseas, especially in the Far East.

U-7A: This designation was the result of a 1962 change in Department of Defense regulations that assigned the U prefix to Utility aircraft. Thus, the L-21s still in the U.S. military inventories at that time became U-7As.

Appendix II:
General Specifications
Cubs and Their Derivations

Taylor E-2/Piper J-2 Cub

Wing Span	35 ft, 3 in.
Length	22 ft, 3 in.
Empty Weight	532 lbs.
Useful Load	400 lbs.
Fuel Capacity	9 gals.
Cruising Speed	65 mph.
Service Ceiling	11,000 ft.
Range	175 mi.

Piper J-3 Cub

Wing Span	35 ft. 2 1/2 in.
Length	22 ft., 5 in.
Wing Area	183 sq. ft.
Empty Weight	680 lbs.
Useful Load	480 lbs.
Fuel Capacity	12 gals.
Cruising Speed	65-70 mph.
Service Ceiling	12, 000 ft.
Range	200 mi.

Piper PA-11 Cub Special

Wing Span	35 ft., 2.5 in.
Length	22 ft., 4.5 in.
Empty weight	730 lbs.
Useful Load	490 lbs.
Fuel Capacity	18 gals.
Cruising Speed	87 mph.
Service Ceiling	14,000 ft.

Piper PA-12 Super Cruiser

Wing Span	35 ft., 5 in.
Length	22 ft., 6 in.
Empty Weight	855 lbs.

Useful Load	695 lbs.
Fuel Capacity	19 gal.
Cruising Speed	100 mph.
Service Ceiling	12,000 ft.
Range	420 mi.

Piper PA-14 Family Cruiser

Wing Span	35 ft., 6 in.
Length	23 ft., 2 in.
Empty Weight	1,020 lbs.
Useful Load	830 lbs.
Fuel Capacity	35 gals.
Cruising Speed	110 mph.
Service Ceiling	12,000 ft.
Range	500 mi.

Piper PA-15 Vagabond

Wing Span	29 ft., 3 in.
Length	18 ft., 8 in.
Empty weight	620 lbs.
Useful Load	480 lbs.
Fuel Capacity	12 gals.
Cruising Speed	90 mph.
Service Ceiling	12,500 ft.
Range	255 mi.

Piper PA-16 Clipper

Wing Span	29 ft., 3 in.
Length	20 ft, 8 in.
Empty Weight	850 lbs.
Useful Load	800 lbs.
Fuel Capacity	36 gals.
Cruising Speed	112 mph.
Service Ceiling	11,000 ft.
Range	480 mi.

Piper PA-17 Vagabond

Wing Span	29 ft., 4 in.
Length	18 ft., 8 in.
Empty Weight	650 lbs.
Useful Load	500 lbs.
Fuel Capacity	12 gals.
Cruising Speed	90 mph
Service Ceiling	10,500 ft.
Range	250 mi.

Piper PA-18 Super Cub

(with Lycoming 108-hp engine)

Wing Span	35 ft., 4 in.
Length	22 ft., 5 in.
Empty Weight	825 lbs.
Useful Load	675 lbs.
Fuel Capacity	18 gals
Cruising Speed	105 mph.
Service Ceiling	15,750 ft.
Range	270 mi.

Piper PA-18 Super Cub

(with Lycoming 150-hp engine)

Wing Span	35 ft., 3 in.
Length	22 ft., 5 in.
Empty Weight	946 lbs.
Useful Load	1,750 lbs.
Fuel Capacity	35.8 gals.
Cruising Speed	115 mph.
Service Ceiling	19,000 ft.
Absolute Ceiling	21,300 ft.
Range	460 mi.

Piper PA-20 Pacer

Wing Span	29 ft., 4 in.
Length	20 ft., 5 in.
Empty Weight	970 lbs.
Useful Load	830 lbs.
Fuel Capacity	36 gals.
Cruising Speed	125 mph.
Service Ceiling	14, 250 ft.
Range	580 mi.

Piper PA-22 Tri-Pacer

Wing Span	29 ft., 4 in.
Length	20 ft., 7 in.
Empty Weight	1,110 lbs.
Useful Load	910 lbs.
Fuel Capacity	36 gals.
Cruising Speed	123 mph.
Service Ceiling	16,500 ft.
Range	550 mi.

Piper PA-22 Caribbean

Wing Span	29 ft., 4 in.
Length	20 ft., 6 in.
Empty Weight	1,100 lbs.
Useful Load	900 lbs.
Fuel Capacity	36 gals.
Cruising Speed	125 mph.
Service Ceiling	15,000 ft.
Range	500 mi.

Piper PA-22 Colt

Wing Span	29 ft.,3 in.
Length	20 ft.,1 in.
Empty Weight	985 lbs.
Useful Load	665 lbs.
Fuel Capacity	36 gals.
Cruising Speed	108 mph.
Service Ceiling	12,000 ft.
Range	690 mi.

Appendix III:
FAI, NAA, and Piper Cub Records

When the dirigible, and then the airplane, came into being and long distance flight became possible, fliers wanted to establish speed, distance, endurance and altitude records. Shortly after the Wright brothers flew at Kitty Hawk, it became obvious that some organization was needed to make rules and keep records to ensure fairness and accuracy among record claimants.

On June 10, 1905, the Olympic Congress, meeting in Belgium, passed a resolution calling for the creation of a universal aeronautical body to regulate aviation and the sport of flying. The result was the founding of the Federation Aeronautique Internationale (FAI) in October 1905. Each nation was encouraged to form its own association and participate in the development of standards for record-keeping and record-setting.

Today, the FAI includes the aviation associations of 70 nations and acts as the governing body for all official aircraft and space records. The sole representative organization for the United States is the National Aeronautic Association (NAA).

The rules of the FAI and NAA are administered to ensure equal opportunity for all competitors; competent, unbiased judging, and scientific, accurate records. Certified observers and timers are required; only the latest electronic time and altitude measuring equipment is used. Distances flown are confirmed by precise techniques of measurement. National records are sanctioned and certified by the NAA. Only the FAI may certify world records; the NAA forwards potential entries for the world record listing to FAI for consideration.

It is the FAI, then, that spells out the regulations for evaluation and comparing performances of aviation vehicles. Throughout its history, FAI has defined, controlled and approved world aeronautical and astronomical records, set sporting codes and regulations that permit fair and scientific comparison of performance, that aid education in aviation, promote world air travel by noncommercial aircraft, encourage proficiency and safety of flight, and confer medals and diplomas on individuals who have contributed significantly to achievement of these goals.

Information concerning classes of records, as well as applications for official sanction of attempts to make record flights, can be obtained from NAA or the FAI. The NAA's main office is located at 815 N. Ft. Myer Drive, Suite 500, Arlington, VA 22209. Telephone: (703) 527-0226.

The headquarters of FAI is located at Avenue Mon Repos 24, CH-1005, Lausanne, Switzerland. Telephone: 011 41 21 345 1070.

As of this printing, the pilots of the following Cubs have established official records that have been approved by the NAA and FAI:

Class C-1.a
OSHKOSH/SANTA PAULA (USA)
C. Michael Bowers   50.04 kmh
Piper J-3 Cub   31.09 mph
Continental 85 bhp
5/25/87

SAN FRANCISCO/LOS ANGELES (USA)
C. Michael Bowers   104/33 kmh
Piper J-3 Cub   64.83 mph
Lycoming C-85, 85 bhp
5/25/87

HOUSTON/DALLAS (USA)
Gerry Griffin, Pilot   202.95 kmh
Larry Griffin, Co-Pilot   126.11 mph
Piper Super Cub
Lycoming O-360, 180 bhp
5/17/91

HOUSTON/DENVER (USA)
Larry Griffin, Pilot   182.88 kmh
Gerry Griffin   113.64 mph
Piper Super Cub
Lycoming O-360, 180 bhp
5/30/87

TYLER, TX/OSHKOSH (USA)
Harry Bergman   146.57 kmh
Piper Super Cub   91.07 mph
Lycoming O-320, 150 bhp
7/25/90

Class C-1.c
SEATTLE/OSHKOSH (USA)
Robert I. Dempster, Pilot   180.12 kmh
Diane W. Dempster   99.49 mph
Piper Super Cub
Lycoming O-320, 150 bhp
8/23/00

Class C-2.a
ALTITUDE (USA)
Charles L. Davis   7,467 m
Piper Super Cub   24,498 ft
Lycoming O-290, 125 bhp
Detroit, MI
6/18/52

SPEED OVER A 3 KM STRAIGHT COURSE (USA)
Verne Jobst   151.11 kmh
Piper J-3S   93.88 mph
Continental C-90-8F, 90 hp
McHenry, IL
5/21/88

SPEED OVER A 15/25 KM A STRAIGHT COURSE (USA)
Verne Jobst   154.17 kmh
Piper J-3S   85.80 mph
Continental C-90-8F ,90 hp
McHenry, IL
5/21/88

SPEED OVER A 100KM CLOSED CIRCUIT WITHOUT PAYLOAD (USA)
Charles L. Davis   175.1 kmh
Piper Super Cub   108.8 mph
Lycoming O-290. 125 hp
8/29/52

SPEED OVER A 500 KM CLOSED CIRCUIT WITHOUT PAYLOAD (USA)
Charles L. Davis   169.56 kmh
Piper Super Cub   105.35 mph
Lycoming O-290, 125 hp
8/29/52

Acknowledgments

The bibliography will show the daunting number of books published about the Piper Cub, its derivative high-wing, single-engine follow-on models, and the history of the Taylor and Piper companies; I am grateful for the insights they provided. I am also indebted to the many Cub pilots who led me to stories and donated photographs that documented their own experiences, and showed what this gentle little light plane and their progeny have done and still can do. During my research at the History of Aviation Collection at the University of Texas, Dallas, I found literally hundreds of aviation magazine articles documenting the progress of the company that produced such memorable aircraft.

There were many pilots and resource persons who generously provided photographs and personal information about the original Cubs and their progeny, and how they gave them a start in aviation. They include William D. Strohmeirer, former Piper pilot, salesman, and publicity manager; Roger W. Peperell, a recognized expert on the development of the various Piper designs; the late Peter M. Bowers, noted aviation historian; retired Air Force Colonel William R. Fuchs and his wife, Alice, former Piper test and ferry pilots; Tom Haines, editor-in-chief of *AOPA Pilot* magazine and Michael E. Kline, art director; Susan A. Lurvey, EAA librarian and archives manager; Beverly E. Howard, Jr., son of the famous aerobatic pilot "Bevo" Howard; F. Clifton Berry, aviation publisher and author; Drew Stecketee, Executive Director, Civil Air Patrol Foundation; Bob Kovalchik, National Air & Space Museum docent; Robert Kopitzke, William K. Jones, Don Lane, John Luckadoo, Lothar Maier, G. C. "Cam" McGill, George Smith and Ken Rice, my aviation-savvy colleagues at the History of Aviation Collection, University of Texas, Dallas; Donald P. Taylor, round-the-world pilot; Bill Stratton, president of the International Liaison Pilot and Aircraft Association; David W. Lucabaugh, aviation historian; retired Air Force Col. Joel C. Gaydos, loyal fan; Jay Miller, aviation writer/publisher; Matthew Simek, television producer; Harmon "Bud" Helmericks, Alaskan photographer; the volunteers at the Piper Aviation Museum in Lock Haven; and Bill Cooper, Jan Collmer, Ken Cordier, Ken Larson, Jim Marshall, Richard Mulberry, Jim Sara, and other members of the Dallas Hangar of the Quiet Birdmen.

I also appreciate the editing advice of my wife, Mary Ellen, and the extensive assistance that Kevin K. Hudson, one of our grandsons, gave in digitizing photographs and illustrations, as well as his companionship during several research trips. Rod Eyer, multi-talented computer illustrator for *Newsday* and aviation enthusiast noted for his meticulous aircraft artworks, contributed the detailed Piper Cub drawings. And I am especially indebted to William T. Piper, Jr, for the Foreword and his cheerful encouragement.

I want to thank herewith Cub Adventurers Rinker Buck, George Erickson, and Lyle Wheeler for permission to quote from their respective books and copy their photographs. Special appreciation is extended to Charles "Cully" Culwell and his wife, Marilyn, for allowing me to select photographs from their extensive albums and quote from Marilyn's colorful diary about their foreign flying adventures. A cross-country flight with Cully in his Super Cub was a special treat that brought back fond memories of my earlier flying life.

Bibliography

There have been a large number of excellent books written about the Piper Cub or that have featured it in memoirs. I recommend the following to all who truly want to increase their knowledge about the Piper Cub series of high-wing, single-engine, fabric-covered monoplanes, or the age in which they began and flourished. All were consulted during the writing of this book.

Abel, Alan; Drina Welch Abel and Paul Matt, *Piper's Golden Age*. Brawley, CA: Wind Canyon Books, 94 pp., 2001.

Bowers, Peter M., *Piper Cubs*. Blue Ridge Summit, PA: TAB Books, 212 pp., 1993.

Buck, Rinker, *Flight of Passage*. New York: Hyperion, 351 pp., 1997.

Buegeleisen, Sally, *Into the Wind*. New York: Random House, 260 pp., 1973.

Churchill, Jan, *On Wings to War*. Manhattan, Kansas: Sunflower University Press, 184 pp., 1992.

Clarke, Bill, *The Piper Indians*. Blue Ridge Summit, PA: TAB Books, 280 pp., 1988.

Cleveland, Reginald M., *The Coming Air Age*. New York: Whittlesey House, 359 pp., 1944.

Duncan, John, *The Single-Engine Pipers*. New York: Sports Car Press, 111 pp., 1975.

Erickson, George, *True North: Exploring the Great Wilderness by Bush Plane*. Guildford, CN: The Lyons Press, 306 pp., 2002.

Francis, Devon, *Mr. Piper and His Cubs*. Ames, Iowa: The Iowa State University Press, 256 pp., 1973.

Gordon, Joseph Furbee, *Flying Low*. Middletown, CN: Southfarm Press, 216 pp., 2001.

Johnston, S. Paul, *Wings after War*. New York: Duell, Sloan and Pearce, 129 pp., 1944.

Love, Terry M., *L-Birds: American Combat Liaison Aircraft of World War II*. New Brighton, MN: Flying Books International, 84 pp., 2001.

Mason, Mort, *Flying the Alaska Wild*. Stillwater, MN: Voyageur Press, 335 pp., 2002.

Merryman, Molly, *Clipped Wings: The Rise and Fall of the Women Airforce Service Pilots (WASPs) of World War II*. New York: New York University Press, 237 pp., 1998.

Moore, Don, *Low and Slow: A Personal History of a Liaison Pilot in World War II*. Upland, CA: San Antonio Heights Publishing Co., 234 pp., 1999.

Peek, Chet, *The Taylorcraft Story*. Terre Haute, IN: Sunshine House, 221 pp., 1992.

Peperell, Roger W., *Piper Aircraft: The Development and History of Piper Designs*. Tunbridge Wells, Kent, England: Air-Britain (Historian) Ltd., 464 pp., 1996.

Phillips, Edward H., *Piper: A Legend Aloft*. Eagan, MN: Flying Books International, 172 pp., 1993.

Piper, William T., *Private Flying: Today and Tomorrow*. New York: Pitman Publishing Company, 295 pp., 1949.

Pisano, Dominick A., *To Fill the Skies with Pilots*. Washington, DC: Smithsonian Institution Press, 197 pp., 2001.

Politella, Dario, *Operation Grasshopper*. Wichita, Kansas: Robert E. Longo Co., 215 pp., 1958.

Schultz, Alfred W. with Kirk Neff, *Janey: A Little Plane in a Big War*. Middletown, CN: Southfarm Press, 288 pp., 1998.

Simbeck, Rob, *Daughter of the Air: The Brief Soaring Life of Cornelia Fort*. New York: Grove Press, 263 pp., 1999.

Simpson, Rod, *Piper Aircraft*. Stroud, Gloucestershire, England: Tempus Publishing, Ltd. 128 pp., 2000.

Sparks, Bill, *Close Encounters of a Vagabond Ferry Pilot*. Privately published, Fort Myers, Fla., 323 pp., 2001.

Stratton, Bill, *Box Seat Over Hell*, Volume II, San Antonio, TX: Internationaol Liaison Pilots and Aircraft Association, 138 pp. 2003.

Strickland, Patricia, *The Putt-Putt Air Force*. Washington, D.C.: Federal Aviation Administration, Government Printing Office, 116 pp., undated.

Ten Eyek, Andrew, *Jeeps in the Sky*. New York: Commonwealth Books, 151 pp., 1946.

Triggs, James M., *The Piper Cub Story*. Blue Ridge Summit, PA: TAB Books, 108 pp., 1978.

Wakefield, Ken, *Light Planes at War: U.S. Liaison Aircraft in Europe, 1942-1947*. Charleston, SC: Tempus Publishing, Inc., 271 pp., 1999.

Weick, Fred E. and James R. Hansen, *From the Ground Up: The Autobiography of an Aeronautical Engineer*. Washington, DC: Smithsonian Institution Press, 447 pp., 1988.

Wheeler, Lyle, *Cubs on the Loose: Old Airplanes—New Adventures*. Sarasota, FL: AMEA Cottage, 280 pp., 2001.

Index